CW00832825

Composers of the **Twentieth** Century

The Music of Ser

YALE UNIVERSITY PRESS · New Haven and London

gei Prokofiev

NEIL MINTURN

"Sun filled the room . . ." by Anna Akhmatova is translated by Judith Hemschemeyer and reprinted from *The Complete Poems of Anna Akhmatova* (expanded edition, 1992) with the permission of Zephyr Press. Translation copyright 1990, 1992 by Judith Hemschemeyer.

Designed by Richard Hendel
Set in Monotype Garamond type by The Marathon Group, Durham, North Carolina.
Printed in the United States of America by Edwards Brothers, Inc., Ann Arbor, Michigan.

Library of Congress Cataloging-in-Publication Data
Minturn, Neil.
    The music of Sergei Prokofiev / Neil Minturn.
        p.   cm. — (Composers of the twentieth century)
    Includes bibliographical references and index.
    ISBN 0-300-06366-0 (cloth : alk. paper)
        1. Prokofiev, Sergey, 1891–1953—Criticism and interpretation.
I. Title.   II. Series.
ML410.P865M56   1997
780.92—dc20   96-27064
                                                    CIP

A catalogue record for this book is available from the British Library.

The paper in this book meets the guidelines for permanence and durability of the Committee on Production Guidelines for Book Longevity of the Council on Library Resources.

10 9 8 7 6 5 4 3 2 1

For Barbara, Eric, and Hannah

Contents

Acknowledgments

any people have helped with the writing of this book. Steve Laitz and Anne-Marie Reynolds read parts of early drafts and made helpful comments. Jan Pejovic read the entire manuscript several times; her editorial comments were invaluable. Allen Forte is responsible for starting me on this project; he also read the manuscript and offered suggestions and wisdom born of experience.

I would like to thank the Eastman School of Music and the University of Rochester for a leave in the fall of 1993. During that time considerable work on the manuscript was completed.

At Yale University Press, Harry Haskell guided me through the book's early stages. Mary Pasti read the entire manuscript very closely; I greatly appreciate her expertise and her patience with me in the final stages of preparation.

David Lewin advised the dissertation from which this book grew. His work continues to be an inspiration.

Finally, Barbara, Eric, and Hannah have put up with me and the book for a long time now. I thank them for their understanding and support.

Introduction

This book about Prokofiev's music emphasizes the analyses of particular pieces, but within a theoretical framework. The framework is developed in the first part of the book, Chapters 1–3; the second part of the book, Chapters 4–8, contains the analyses.

Chapter 1 situates Prokofiev historically: he trained as a composer in Russia; following his time in the West he returned to his homeland and became, nominally, a Soviet composer; and always he was an early twentieth-century composer who was influenced by Romanticism. In Chapter 1 I also survey Prokofiev scholarship and, from that, develop some key points about the perception of Prokofiev's music. Most notable in this regard is the concept of the wrong note as a characteristic feature of his music. I go on to develop the notion of a distinctive interplay in Prokofiev's music between wrong note and traditional background. Analogues to this interplay are then shown in the broader spheres of Russian nationalism and nineteenth-century Russian musical culture. Finally, as a means of exploring the traditional nature of Prokofiev's music, chapter 1 studies an analysis of the opening of the Piano Sonata no. 8 which regards the work as traditionally tonal and amenable to a Schenkerian approach.

In Chapter 2 I turn to a self-analysis by Prokofiev in which he discusses five lines in his music. An analysis of this analysis helps us understand both the music and the composer. One example of each of the five lines that Prokofiev applies to his music is studied. Through ad hoc analysis, I also seek to rehabilitate the notion of the wrong note and to situate it in a positive light.

Chapter 2 concludes with an outline of the constant features in Prokofiev's music and the changing ones. The constant features mainly concern pitch structure. The changing features engage both pitch and rhythm. As Prokofiev's compositional skills evolved, his phrase structures and forms exhibited a marked increase in flexibility. A chronological sweep through his music also reveals his changing concentration on harmonic and contrapuntal surfaces.

In Chapter 3 I develop the findings in Chapters 1 and 2 into more precise concepts and analytical categories, making more formal the ad hoc analytical approaches used in Chapter 2.

The second part of the book consists of a collection of analyses. As a means of fairly representing Prokofiev's extensive musical production, I organize the music by genre and, within each chapter, present material chronologically. For the most part, the analyses center on selected aspects and passages of a work rather than complete works or movements.

Chapters 4–8 are designed so that the reader may move directly to the works that are of the most interest to her or him. There are some necessary qualifications to this, however. More than any other genre, piano music, discussed in Chapter 4, gives the best overview of Prokofiev's evolution as a composer because he was continually composing piano music, and he composed a large quantity of it. A reader interested in the relation of chronology to style might turn to Chapter 4.

In Chapter 5 I discuss the orchestral works. These works, and in particular the symphonic works, do not provide such a representative tour through the composer's various stages because the forces that motivated Prokofiev to compose the individual symphonies varied greatly. For instance, he composed the First Symphony in a lighthearted vein, while in the Second he sought self-consciously to display to the world his depth and technique. The Third salvaged an opera that did not come to production, and the Seventh was written with the Soviet government looking over his shoulder. Though orchestral music does not yield such a clear picture of the composer's evolution as piano music does, it highlights issues of design. These issues of design, along with aspects of Prokofiev's developmental techniques, are discussed in the first movements of three of his symphonies (the First, Fifth, and Sixth).

Prokofiev's output of chamber music is relatively small, but it is of such high quality that one chapter, Chapter 6, is devoted to its study. In Chapter 7 I study movements from three concertos, a genre in which Prokofiev showed remarkable maturity from the outset.

In contrast to his production of chamber music, Prokofiev's production of operas is sufficiently large to merit a specialized study. Consequently, the operatic music is underrepresented in this book. Most of Chapter 8 concentrates on art-song, but it does conclude with a discussion of the *Gambler,* act III. In most of the analyses in Chapters 4–8 I eschew complete works, primarily because of their size. However, Prokofiev's art-songs are small enough so that the reader interested in comprehensive structure might turn there.

1 Approaching the Music

The 135 completed works in Prokofiev's catalogue constitute a large and varied output in many different genres, including symphony, sonata, ballet, opera, art-song, string quartet, and film music.[1] The works are stylistically diverse, ranging from the traditional "Classical" Symphony, op. 25, to the experimental Quintet, op. 39, and including music more moderately situated, such as the Piano Concerto no. 3, op. 26, and the Symphony no. 5, op. 100. Yet the vast majority of the pieces are recognizable as Prokofiev's.

The music of Prokofiev is as high in quality as it is popular. The children's piece *Peter and the Wolf,* the "Classical" Symphony, the Symphony no. 5, the ballet *Romeo and Juliet,* the opera *Love for Three Oranges,* and the nine piano sonatas all attest to the quality and diversity of the music and to the fertility of the composer's mind.

Prokofiev was born in 1891 into a middle-class family and attended the St. Petersburg Conservatory. He lived in Russia for four more years after graduating from the Conservatory. Among the works composed before he left are the *Sarcasmes, Visions Fugitives,* Piano Concertos nos. 1 and 2, the "Classical" Symphony, and the Violin Concerto no. 1.

He left the Soviet Union in 1918; the Revolution of 1917 was a harbinger of change not only for the country but for Prokofiev himself. He remained in the West for nearly twenty years, from 1918 until 1935. During this period he completed three more piano concertos; the Quintet, op. 39; the String Quartet no. 1, op. 50; the *Mélodies*, op. 35; the Symphonies nos. 2, 3, and 4; and *Love for Three Oranges*.

At the end of 1935 he returned permanently to the Soviet Union, a country radically transformed. His first years back were fruitful, and among the well-known works composed during this period are *Romeo and Juliet*, *Peter and the Wolf*, the Violin Sonatas nos. 1 and 2, the Symphony no. 5, and the Piano Sonatas nos. 6, 7, and 8. Initially, Prokofiev's return to the Soviet Union appeared not to have brought on any problems due to political interference in his artistic affairs. But his life was not to continue so smoothly. In 1936 *Pravda*'s attack on Shostakovich's opera *Lady Macbeth of Mtsensk* revealed a government eager to control music produced by native composers.

In 1945 Prokofiev suffered a concussion in a fall, an accident from which he never fully recovered. The fall, initiating a deterioration in Prokofiev's health, was a portent, for three years later Prokofiev was severely criticized in the Decree of 1948 and placed in official disfavor. The final, ironic parallel between Prokofiev's life and that of the government occurred when death claimed Prokofiev and Stalin on the same day, March 5, 1953.

We may divide Prokofiev's life into three broad periods. The first period extends up to his departure for the West; his return to the Soviet Union in 1935 separates the second and third periods. Each of these periods differently realizes the interplay of the two most important forces shaping Prokofiev's musical and artistic life: tradition and innovation. By tradition I mean the tendency to preserve received practice. By an innovative force I mean one that encourages novelty and experimentation.

I regard the interaction of tradition and innovation as a key feature of much of Prokofiev's music. This interaction has been recognized since the first Prokofiev biography, although its author, Israel Nestyev, interprets it negatively. But the interaction between tradition and innovation is not peculiar to Prokofiev's music. In fact, it is a feature of Russian history, generally and plainly evident in nineteenth-century Russian musical culture, where it is best exemplified in the musical life of St. Petersburg.[2] The St. Petersburg Conservatory, a bastion of Western musical tradition, vied with the Balakirev Circle, a group committed to cultivating individual talent and innovation.

Let us begin by reviewing Prokofiev biography, perhaps the most active area of Prokofiev scholarship, and then inquire into the nature of Prokofiev's music, where we encounter so-called wrong note music. Having established the nature of tradition and innovation in Prokofiev's music, we can consider these themes in the development of Russian nationalism and in the Balakirev Circle, which we see mostly through the eyes of Rimsky-Korsakov.

Biography

Attempts at building a comprehensive picture of Prokofiev's music begin with Israel Nestyev's informal accounts, set forth in his two biographies.[3] Biographical and political issues absorbed most of the intellectual attention to Prokofiev for about twelve years following his death in 1953. Sophisticated and detailed analytical work on Prokofiev's music is scarce, however, in large part owing to the central position held by biography in Prokofiev scholarship.[4]

Prokofiev's biographers have been occupied with interpreting the nature of Western and Soviet influences on Prokofiev. For an illustration we have only to turn to Nestyev, whose two biographies of Prokofiev differ in how they assess Western and Soviet influences on the quality of his music. Nestyev, in his first biography, published seven years before Prokofiev's death, avoids focusing on the salutary or deleterious effects of Western or Soviet influence on Prokofiev. The book was deemed unfit by Soviet censors precisely because of its political neutrality. In Nestyev's second biography the extent to which political pressures motivate the "revised" judgments is painfully transparent.

For instance, in discussing *Pensées,* op. 62, Nestyev comments in the first biography that "certain compositions of the Paris period [1923–1935] gave evidence of new and vital style features: . . . the *Third Symphony, . . . L'Enfant prodigue, . . .* the quartet, *Le Pas d'acier,* and some of the piano pieces (*Pensées,* Op. 62)."[5] But within the corrected ideology of the second biography, "new and vital style features" could not have been conferred upon Prokofiev's music by Western influence, and Nestyev dramatically revises his opinion of op. 62: "It was difficult to recognize the old Prokofiev in any of these pieces [including op. 62]. Rhythmic resilience and clarity of thought had vanished. Intense emotion and impulsive youthful vigor had given way to dull, rational speculation, and rich tone color had faded into colorless outlines."[6] Nestyev's description of op. 62's "dull, rational speculation" could well have supported the charge of Formalism, though Nestyev does not explicitly make it. "The old Prokofiev" refers to music composed before Prokofiev left the Soviet Union, music which at least passes ideological tests, if not musical ones as well.

Nestyev's plan in the second biography is clear: he is able generally to support music written or conceived either before Prokofiev left the Soviet Union in 1918 or after he returned in 1935. Music written in the West but conceived in the Soviet Union may sometimes pass the ideological test. And a work written in the Soviet Union after 1935 may be judged harshly if it shows too much Western influence.

The extent to which politics and ideology drive the second biography renders its judgments and conclusions highly suspect. But Nestyev's descriptions, while not detailed, can be very useful to us in interpreting Prokofiev's music if we can identify the ideologically affected component.

Aiming to counterbalance Nestyev's ideologically tainted account, Victor Seroff published his response, *Sergei Prokofiev: A Soviet Tragedy*, in 1969. Seroff's book essentially reverses the conclusions drawn in Nestyev's, especially in its account of Prokofiev's return to the Soviet Union. Where Nestyev finds the return to be an artistic rescue, Seroff sees disaster. For example, Seroff bitterly and confidently ascribes the reason for Prokofiev's fall in 1945 to stress brought on by living in the Soviet Union: "Nor can the reason, given by the Soviet sources as 'overwork,' be accepted as satisfactory. It is much more likely that the constant 'disappointment,' to put it mildly, in the 'existing conditions under the Soviet regime,' the struggle to survive through the years of the purges, the tragedy of his family life, and his failure to 'please' the critics and those in power, had taken a heavy toll on his nervous system."[7]

The biography by Lawrence and Elisabeth Hanson, published in 1964, is more neutral politically than either Nestyev's or Seroff's.[8] Nevertheless, a considerable passage of time was required to sweep away politics as the motivating force in Prokofiev biography. Not until the publication of the biographies by Harlow Robinson and David Gutman was our picture of Prokofiev's life clearly and insightfully drawn.[9]

As we have seen, Nestyev bemoans Prokofiev's loss of "intense emotion and impulsive youthful vigor" in op. 62 and other pieces, as though exposure to Western influence had somehow drained an innate Russian musical potency. In addition to finding fault with a cerebral compositional turn, he also objects to the apparently unmotivated pairing of familiar Russian diatonic themes with modern harmonies. Discussing *Le Pas d'acier*, Nestyev remarks: "In keeping with the idea of a Soviet ballet, Prokofiev made an honest effort to compose distinctly Russian melodies. Thus, the diatonic theme with which the introduction opens even recalls the well-known refrain of an old factory song. But unfortunately, these Russian themes lost their national character when subjected to artificially coarsened harmony (such as ostinato figures in the form of harsh chords), which was not in keeping with their simplified melodic patterns."[10] According to Nestyev these themes lose their national character because of an incongruity between diatonic melody (so-called white-key melody) and modern chromatic harmony. Nestyev identifies, but puts a pejorative spin on, two important aspects of Prokofiev's compositional style.

If we detach the nationalistic component of Nestyev's remarks from the musical component, then we find that he perceives a lacuna between familiar white-key diatonicism on the one hand and modern dissonant and chromatic harmony on the other. In fact, Nestyev points out a characteristic way in which tradition and innovation interact in Prokofiev's music.

Jonathan D. Kramer and Suzanne Moisson-Franckhauser expand upon Nestyev's observation that there are surprising juxtapositions of traditional features with innovative ones. Let us turn first to Jonathan Kramer. Although Kramer does not purport to engage in any sort of sophisticated analysis, he articulates a reaction to the music shared by many. In discussing the "Classical" Symphony, op. 25, Kramer seizes on the metaphor of the "wrong note":

> We can "hear" a hypothetical original version of the music lurking beneath the surface. In other words, it is as if we could remove the witticisms and discover a truly classical symphony. Prokofiev's son once remarked that his father first writes music and then "Prokofievizes" it. It is certainly possible to imagine such a compositional process producing the "Classical" Symphony.
>
> This is "wrong-note" music. . . . We smile more than laugh at the quirky turns of phrase and unexpected harmonies, because they are not so very wrong. Out of place in a symphony of Mozart or Haydn, these "wrong" notes gain in Prokofiev's hands an integrity and a rightness appropriate to 1917. They give the symphony its charm and grace.[11]

Along the lines suggested by Kramer, one might imagine Prokofiev creating a two-layered composition. The first layer is a traditional composition, cast in the mold of the common practice of the eighteenth and nineteenth centuries. It is this first layer that Kramer calls a "hypothetical" version of the music, one that proceeds according to one's expectations of traditional musical structure. Pasted onto this first layer is a second, in which Prokofiev has innovated by adding "wrong notes," notes that in the most drastic and least charitable view might be arbitrary and that in a more favorable view are surface features which conceal the underlying hypothetical version. In the "Classical" Symphony (among other works) some context is sufficiently clear and well defined to present some notes or gestures as "wrong."

While this two-layered picture of the "Classical" Symphony may capture part of one's unmediated impression of much of Prokofiev's music, it does raise some questions: Does an unbridgeable musical chasm separate a traditional base from a modern, embellishing superstructure? Are the two layers of the music competing? Are they not coequals? Is this music's central organizing feature its traditional underpinning, which is apparent once we strip away the "wrong note" witticisms?

For Suzanne Moisson-Franckhauser, Prokofiev's music is fundamentally tonal and its underlying structure is traditional. "Prokofiev's music is always very tonal, with a certain predilection for simple tonalities, often C major. This is not surprising if one thinks of the attraction of modal music in Russia. By a subtle game of chromatic alterations, he develops a sort of broadened diatonic scale which is not absolutely allied with the traditional chromatic scale, since it conserves its tonal function. All the pitches of diatonic scale can be altered without otherwise causing modulation; the basic tonality remains."[12] In Moisson-Franckhauser's view, then, Prokofiev's wrong notes are chromatic alterations of a more basic diatonic tonality.[13] "Wrong notes" are surface, accessory elements and do not represent fundamental innovation.

Implicit in Moisson-Franckhauser's point of view is that a theory of traditionally tonal music can adequately address Prokofiev's music. Her attitude finds precedent in nineteenth-century music theory, which was confronted with developments in chromatic harmony. Specifically, Moisson-Franckhauser's point of view echoes the harmonic theories of Simon Sechter (1788–1867), who insisted "on the complete reduction of all chromatic phenomena to a diatonic basis."[14] (Her invocation of modality in this connection is not felicitous. She speculates about the influence of modality but does not explain in what sense Prokofiev's "very tonal" music is simultaneously modal.)[15]

One presumes that the apparent immiscibility of traditional and innovative elements communicates to the listener the quality that Kramer refers to as wit. M. 3 of the Piano Sonata no. 4/III gives such an instance (see example 3.1). The C-major context is traditional and clear, and the intrusive A♭ presents itself as a wrong note. Defined only by this brief passage, the relation between tonal context and wrong note may be obscure at best, but that fact need not be interpreted as evidence of the composer's lack of craft. One activity in the analyses in this book will be exploring how the wrong notes shape the music, an impact often belied by their first appearance.

Prokofiev was convinced that innovation was a significant criterion in aesthetic judgment. Suggestive in this connection is his essay "Can There Be an End to Melody," in which he fretted over the question of whether and when original note successions might be exhausted.[16] Prokofiev begins his essay by recalling a friend's attempt at writing a book which would provide the answer to any given chess situation. Prokofiev, himself a devoted chess player, gets only up to White's fourth move before he calculates about sixty million variants and concludes that his friend's book is impractical.

Prokofiev reasons analogously about the succession of notes in an eight-note tune. He calculates about six billion possibilities, without considering the variety that would be introduced by rhythm, harmony, or counterpoint. Prokofiev thereby satisfies himself from a statistical point of view that there is virtually no danger of exhausting all the possibilities of musical expression. His mathematical approach presumably aims to put the matter on an objective footing. Appealing to mathematics rather than to aesthetics may seem wrongheaded for investigating an artistic question, but Prokofiev's personality had a strong rational component. What could be more apt than for him to demonstrate rationally the inexhaustibility of musical invention? Though an apparently frivolous endeavor, the essay provides interesting insight into Prokofiev's preoccupation with originality and the need to preserve its possibility.

Not surprisingly, simplicity and epigonism are labels that Prokofiev wished to avoid and are criticisms to which he was always sensitive. In a well-known passage in his autobiography, he recalls composing an exercise for Reinhold Gliere, his composition teacher during the summer. Prokofiev then shows the work to Sergei Taneev, his composition teacher in Moscow, who rates it acceptable but harmonically tame and unadventurous.

> In the summer of the same year [1902, when Prokofiev was eleven], R. M. Gliere came to Sontsovka on the recommendation of Taneev. . . . I insisted on writing a symphony. After some hesitation Gliere agreed, and by the time he left me in August a four-movement symphony in G major was written and half of it orchestrated. In November I showed the symphony to Taneev. . . . He praised the counterpoint (which Gliere had inserted in the development), but remarked that the harmony was a little too crude. "Mostly I, IV, and V," he said, and laughed. I was deeply offended. Not that I cried or lost any sleep over it, but somewhere the thought that my harmony was crude rankled. The seed had been planted and a long period of germination began. It was not until four years later that my harmonic experiments began to be noticed, and when some eight years later I played Taneev my *Etudes,* op. 2, and he grumbled, "Far too many wrong notes," I reminded him of what he had said that time. Clutching his head in mock horror, he exclaimed, "So it was I who launched you on that slippery path!"[17]

Without overestimating the effect of this incident, we ought still to note it, if for no other reason than that Prokofiev himself remembered it so vividly. The encounter implanted the idea that a composer should take risks and attempt to break new ground. What were wrong notes for Taneev were for Prokofiev marks of individuality and innovation.

Prokofiev also maintained an interest in other composers' innovations. Early in the second decade of the century, his involvement in the Evenings of Contemporary Music, a St. Petersburg group founded in 1901, provided him contact with much modern music, music to which the Conservatory would not expose him.[18] At these gatherings, Prokofiev performed his opp. 2 and 3 and, at the request of the group, gave the Russian premiere of Arnold Schoenberg's op. 11. The positive reception with which his own piano pieces met could only have reinforced Prokofiev's desire to continue the harmonic experiments he mentions in the Taneev anecdote.

Prokofiev's concern with innovation could not, unfortunately, guarantee the quality of some of his own compositional endeavors. One occasionally senses Prokofiev's traditional musical rhetoric uncomfortably cohabiting with a deliberately injected modernism. When Prokofiev's distance from traditional musical rhetoric is the greatest, in pieces such as the cantata *Seven, They Are Seven,* the Quintet, op. 39, or the Symphony no. 2, we sense a corresponding discomfort on the composer's part; he is not thoroughly at home. Prokofiev shows complete awareness of this discomfort when he writes about the Symphony no. 2 in his *Autobiography*: "It [the Symphony no. 2] was too densely woven in texture, too heavily laden with contrapuntal lines changing to figuration to be successful, and although one critic did comment admiringly on the septuple counterpoint, my friends preserved an embarrassed silence. This was perhaps the first time it occurred to me that I might perhaps be destined to be a second-rate composer."[19] Because he overzealously pursued originality and effect, permitting craft to overwhelm content, Prokofiev was forced to confront the possibility that he had produced the bane of the iconoclast, art without soul.[20]

Still, Prokofiev hoped that the Symphony no. 2 might enjoy a beneficial effect from the passage of time and that future critics (as well as Prokofiev himself) might revise their estimation of the work. Prokofiev writes to his friend Nikolai Miaskovsky that "somewhere in the depths of my soul is the hope that in a few years it will suddenly become obvious that the symphony is respectable after all, and even a graceful thing."[21] However Prokofiev may have ultimately assessed the Symphony no. 2, its dense polyphony and orchestration and unyieldingly dissonant style are not characteristic of the compositional lines that he subsequently pursued.

When composing for a master other than himself, Prokofiev's compositional powers could be sapped; at those times he composed music which was not always his best. (On the other hand, that Prokofiev could succeed in composing for another master testifies to his natural and tremendous ability.) Below I explore some of the forces which were able to dominate Prokofiev.

Prokofiev was, by many accounts, a self-assured man, tending toward acerbity and even arrogance. Yet his openness to criticism and respect for authority was somewhat at odds with his self-confidence. In his youth, authority and tradition were merged in the Conservatory. In spite of his rebelliousness, his attitude toward academics and regimentation may indicate a need for the validation which authority can provide. Harlow Robinson writes:

> Pedagogues and Prokofiev rarely got along very well. He refused to become a "nice student" who behaved, performed, and composed in a docile way that pleased the teacher. He was too idiosyncratic, definite and artistically self-confident to be a teacher's pet. Neither was he willing to conceal his knowledge and talent for the sake of ingratiating himself with the instructor—as his generally undistinguished grades throughout his Conservatory career seem to prove. And yet he was never so much a rebel as to reject the value and necessity of Conservatory training. Prokofiev might criticize, resist and try to outsmart his professors, but he still wanted the institutional stamp of approval and respectability. Later on, his attitude toward the Soviet government was similarly motivated: although uncomfortable with certain aspects of the system, he still wanted its official approval.[22]

Prokofiev graduated from the Conservatory at the age of twenty-three and entered the international musical world, where he met another force of authority, Sergei Diaghilev, the impresario of the Ballets Russes, to whom he showed unexpected deference in musical matters. Diaghilev rejected Prokofiev's first commission, the ballet *Ala and Lolly*, a judgment which Prokofiev, somewhat surprisingly, accepted rather calmly.[23] But Diaghilev was a figure of authority, and Prokofiev chose not to argue with him. He adopted the same attitude toward the Soviet government.

Of all the sources of authority in his life, perhaps the most fateful was the Soviet government, to whose desires and artistic policies he earnestly tried to conform after his return to the Soviet Union in 1935.[24] In the first years after his return, Prokofiev was spared the sort of governmental pressure that plagued Shostakovich, for example.[25] But by 1948 Prokofiev, too, was under direct attack from the party bureaucrats, and in particular from A. A. Zhdanov, a seasoned and brutal party leader in charge of Soviet musical policy.[26]

Governmental pressure on the musical community peaked in 1948 but began before Prokofiev's return to the Soviet Union in 1935. The Resolution of 1932 had begun to shape the aesthetic climate in Soviet music to which Prokofiev returned. Its main purpose was to impress the concept of Socialist Realism upon Soviet music. To explain what Socialist Realism means for composers, Boris Schwarz quotes an excerpt from Victor Gorodinsky's article "On the Problem of Socialist Realism in Music": "The main attention of the Soviet composer must be directed towards the victorious progressive principles of reality, towards all that is heroic, bright, and beautiful. This distinguishes the spiritual world of Soviet man and must be embodied in musical images full of beauty and strength. Socialist Realism demands an implacable struggle against folk-negating modernistic directions that are typical of the decay of contemporary bourgeois art, against subservience and servility toward modern bourgeois culture."[27] Schwarz points out the emphasis on "folk-negating modernistic directions" and how such directions were eventually translated into the concept of Formalism.[28] Socialist Realism is an aesthetic response to Formalism, that aesthetic category which elevates formal considerations above a work's content.[29] Within the context of Soviet ideology, a work's content is roughly equivalent to its ability to communicate to the people. Formalist work sins by being overly complex; it is, ipso facto, inaccessible and therefore anti-Soviet.

For the party, and especially for Zhdanov, Formalism was to become a damning label which could be attached to any music considered to be anti-folk. Viewed dispassionately, Formalism was often synonymous with music that was challenging or that demanded careful and thoughtful listening.

In trying to comply with the ideas outlined in the Resolution of 1932, Prokofiev strove for something he called the new simplicity. "It [Soviet music] should be clear and simple, but should not fall into the routine. The simplicity should not be the old simplicity, it must be a new simplicity."[30] New Simplicity, Prokofiev's musical version of Socialist Realism, would guarantee music's greatness and originality without sacrificing an ability to communicate to the people. Prokofiev had set himself no small task. In 1948 the mentality driving Stalin's purges swept into the musical community, guided by Zhdanov. Prokofiev's new simplicity offered him no protection.

Formalism offered Zhdanov a weapon for attacking modern music, and epigonism provided a label for work that was too derivative and hence traditional. By differently drawing the boundaries of Formalism and epigonism, Zhdanov created a vise that could crush any work to which he objected. In 1948, at the Conference of Musicians, Zhdanov blasted Prokofiev and others. In his second speech, given on the third day of the conference, Zhdanov rounds up and labels the offending composers: "Let us consider these comrades [Dmitri Shostakovich, Prokofiev, Nikolai Miaskovsky, Aram Khachaturian, Gavril Popov, Dmitri Kabalevsky, Vissarion Shebalin] as the principal figures of the formalist school. This school is radically wrong."[31] Zhdanov goes on to castigate the formalists for "[renouncing] classical traditions . . . [and catering to] the individual experiences of a clique of aesthetes."[32]

Zhdanov's charge supports the notion that Formalism produces unacceptable works which cannot be comprehended by the public. But might Formalism be too hasty in its condemnations? One might argue that some works are only apparently formalist, and are not irredeemable but simply extremely progressive. This argument could be used to defend Prokofiev et al.; with sufficient time and opportunity, education might draw the public closer to the progressive work so that even progressive pieces might be understood and appreciated eventually. Zhdanov counters this argument without elegance, merely restating his position and declaring that art not immediately understood is art insensitive to the people. "Some Soviet composers also have a theory that they will be appreciated in fifty or a hundred years. That is a terrible attitude. It means a complete divorce from the People."[33]

As a final defense, might one argue that formalist art, in its revolutionary aspects, is ideologically true to the principles of communism? But this argument, which rests on the glorification of innovation, Zhdanov disposes of in a most contradictory manner. After accusing formalist art of aesthetic parochialism and insisting that it is too distant from the Soviet people, Zhdanov goes on to tighten the vise's other jaw; he accuses formalist art of epigonism: "We also often hear the word 'innovation.' Is not this word used as propaganda of bad music? Stunts and contortions are not innovation. Innovation does not always mean progress, yet young composers are taught that if they don't 'innovate' they will not be original. Moreover, the 'innovation' of our formalists isn't particularly new in any case; for it smells of the decadent, bourgeois music of Europe and America. Now here's a case when one can talk of epigones!"[34] Zhdanov's charges touch on Prokofiev's perennial aesthetic dilemma: how to innovate without losing touch with tradition. That Zhdanov simultaneously charges Prokofiev with the crime of innovation and the crime of epigonism must have caused Prokofiev considerable distress. There seemed to be nowhere to turn.

The Symphony no. 6 and the Piano Sonata no. 9 were the last large works that Prokofiev composed before Zhdanov's attack. In fact, the premiere of the symphony appears to have been partly responsible for bringing on that attack. Works composed after the Symphony no. 6 are, in fact, in a simpler, more reserved style, but they are of uneven quality. For example, the *Sinfonia Concertante,* op. 125 (a revision of the Cello Concerto, op. 57, that was undertaken in collaboration with Msitslav Rostropovich), is highly regarded by Schwarz and by Robinson.[35] On the other hand, Prokofiev himself had misgivings about having oversimplified in the Symphony no. 7.[36]

The Influence of Romanticism, Nationalism, and Tradition

Prokofiev's traditional side is manifest in his music's tonal signs, such as triads, diatonic scale fragments, and stepwise motion. Prokofiev also often composes in tonally generated forms like the sonata. Yet despite the influence of a traditional force such as tonality, Prokofiev's concern with novelty and innovation never abated.[37] At the root of his desire to compose new and novel works is the influence of Romanticism.[38]

Romanticism arose in large part as a response to the Enlightenment's veneration of reason and logic. Goethe articulates the romantic case against the reason of the Enlightenment: "If we [romantics] heard the encyclopedists mentioned, or opened a volume of their colossal work, we felt as if we were moving amidst the innumerable whirling spools and looms of a great factory, where, what with the mere creaking and rattling—what with all the mechanism, bewildering both to eyes and brain—what with the mere impossibility of understanding how the various parts fit in and work with one another—what with the contemplation of all that is necessary to prepare a single piece of cloth, we felt disgusted with the very coat we wore upon our backs."[39] Goethe's factory metaphor is a powerful one, capturing two of Romanticism's key objections to Enlightenment thinking: the subordination of the individual to a larger system and reason's inability to comprehend the panoramic sweep of true human experience.

To rescue the artist as well as humanity from the Enlightenment's mechanically rattling reason, Romanticism offers genius. Genius elevates the individual's natural talent to a position superior to reason's. Voltaire tells us: "It seems that the term *genius* ought not to be applied in a very general way to all highly talented people, but only to those who are gifted with invention. In ancient times invention was particularly regarded as a gift of the Gods, a sort of divine inspiration or 'ingenium qua si ingenitum.' However perfect an artist may be, he will never be thought a *genius* if he lacks originality, if he is wanting in invention. He will only be looked upon as a man who has been inspired by his artistic predecessors, even though he may surpass them."[40] From medieval through baroque times, the artist was viewed largely as a craftworker whose duty was to God or to the state. A picture of Bach humbly piecing together the *Musical Offering* for the King of Prussia comes to mind. Composers of an earlier era, particularly composers of church music—composers like Bach—might have viewed their task as the production of well-constructed music worthy of either a patron or a noble or worthy of use in the church.

Voltaire dramatically transforms this historically prior image of the artist. By comparing the artist and God, Voltaire points out their shared ability to create that which has not been before. It is the ability to bring into existence something new which now confers upon the artist the status of a deity. Art crafted well may be derivative, but art created by genius lies apart from any derivative chain. Romanticism transforms "derivative" into a negative label. Beginning at least by the nineteenth century, musical artists aspired to the divine in their pursuit of originality; crafting well was no longer the most important measure of an artist. True invention—creating something which has not been before—is possible only through genius.

Judith Shklar points out that the divine nature of the creative faculty—imagination—was clear to the romantics as well as to "the pious."

> For the romantic, however, imagination was not only "fancy"; it was the nucleus of all man's powers, rational and emotional, from which creative action grew. It was by definition that force in man which could make him whole again [following the fragmenting influence of Enlightenment's reason], and even recreated him in a higher form. Imagination, its creations, its originality—these were the divine element in man, the primary quality of Prometheus. One could not miss the religious origin of these ideas. The pious were quite properly shocked by these pretensions. It was the human aspiration to be God. "(Imagination), wrote Coleridge, "I hold to be the living Power and prime Agent of all human Perception, and as a repetition in the finite mind of the eternal act of creation in the infinite I AM."[41]

Immanuel Kant laid the basis for Romanticism's inward turn by showing that we cannot know a "thing-in-itself"; instead we can only know a "thing-as-perceived." Kant thereby undermines the Enlightenment's concerns with the external, material world, a world which, according to Kant, is ultimately unknowable.[42] In place of curiosity about the material world, Romanticism offers concerns about human perception. The path to which Kant points naturally turns inward, to the individual. Romantic genius replaces Enlightenment logic as the way to truth.

In his analysis of Kant's *Critique of Judgment,* Hans-Georg Gadamer expresses the idea of genius: "Wherever one must 'come upon something' that cannot be found through learning and methodical work alone, i.e. wherever there is inventio, where something is due to inspiration and not to methodical calculation, the important thing is ingenium, genius."[43] Method assures that each step in a process links to the next so that the necessarily derivative product, or conclusion, is clearly connected to the beginning, or premise. Therefore, methodical calculation and competence can yield nothing truly original. The price exacted by strictly logical methodology is unacceptably high in a romantic view. Gadamer is here stressing the incompatibility of logic with the product of genius. Inspiration—sudden and unaccountable insight—leads to products of genius, just as logic leads to products of methodical calculation. Ultimately, however, inspiration and logic do not communicate.

Carl Dahlhaus affirms Gadamer's analysis in a more specifically musical context. Genius's ascendancy in the nineteenth century carves out the new aesthetic categories of originality and novelty, categories which dominate all others. "The pre-eminent aesthetic principle of the nineteenth century was the dogma of originality, an ideal which gave rise to a constant search for novelty. The seal of aesthetic authenticity was placed only on what was unfamiliar; imitation was no longer, as in the past, applauded as a pious honoring of tradition, or what was 'old and true,' but condemned as epigonism, the products of which were intellectually disreputable, however faultless they might be technically."[44] As Dahlhaus points out, the rise of the "cult of genius" forced a reevaluation of the meaning of imitation: before the nineteenth century, imitation was an accepted and recognized sort of flattery; during the nineteenth century, it was aesthetically demoted and became evidence of inferior art. The other victim of the cult of genius was craft, now occupying an aesthetic category subordinate to originality.

Prokofiev's preoccupation with novelty is surely a sign of Romanticism's influence. But in virtually all of his music, his pursuit of innovation never completely dominates a strong traditional element. The coexistence of such divergent impulses has, in fact, a peculiarly Russian complexion and is generalizable to both the development of Russian nationalism and nineteenth-century Russian musical life.

In the early eighteenth century, when Peter the Great came to power, Russia began to emerge as a major player in international politics. In the course of Russia's developing nationalism, two forces interacted in the political-cultural sphere much the way tradition and innovation interacted in Prokofiev's music: Slavophilism represents tradition, Westernism represents innovation. Slavophilism extols and develops distinctive national characteristics and conserves the established order. Westernism seeks to advance Russia by imitating the West, whose nations are perceived by westernists as more advanced than Russia and as worthy models for change and progress. Westernism challenges the established order.

In an analysis of nationalism, Liah Greenfeld traces the beginning of Russian nationalism back to Peter the Great's reign (1694–1725) and locates the impetus toward nationalism in a phenomenon she terms *ressentiment*. "*Ressentiment* refers to a psychological state resulting from suppressed feelings of envy and hatred (existential envy) and the impossibility of satisfying these feelings."[45] *Ressentiment* is the political reflection of the circumstances which create the wrong note in Prokofiev's music. Greenfeld finds *ressentiment* to be a peculiarly Russian phenomenon. "In certain cases—notably in Russia— . . . *ressentiment* was the single most important factor determining the specific terms in which national identity was defined."[46] In Russia's case, *ressentiment* directly opposed conservative Slavophilism with progressive Westernism. The two forces did not mingle congenially. "Both Westernism and Slavophilism were steeped in *ressentiment*. Both arose out of the realization of Russia's inferiority [to the West] and a revulsion against its humiliating reality. In Slavophilism, this revulsion was transformed into excessive self-admiration. In Westernism, the very same sentiment led to the generalized revulsion against the existing world and to the desire to destroy it. Yet the difference was that of emphasis."[47]

An essential trait of *ressentiment*, then, is the difficulty of reconciling envy and hatred. Greenfeld quotes an eighteenth-century Russian writer, Denis Fonvisin (1744?–1792), who articulates the bind. "How can we remedy the two contradictory and most harmful prejudices: the first, that everything with us is awful, while in foreign lands everything is good; the second, that in foreign lands everything is awful, and with us everything is good?"[48]

Just as conservative Slavophilism and progressive Westernism converge in *ressentiment*, tradition and innovation converge in the wrong note. To strengthen the analogy between politics and music one may recall the ideological battle fought about Prokofiev's music. Zhdanov and the Nestyev of the second biography held an essentially Slavophilic position, finding fault in Prokofiev's music when there was detectable Western influence and further identifying that influence as unacceptably progressive. In political terms, Prokofiev in his music seeks to reconcile his Slavophilism—a deep-seated and virtually genetic belief with nationalistic origins—with his Westernism, a romantic belief with Western intellectual roots. The music which results can appear not fully to integrate traditional tonal features with innovative ones.

The dual and sometimes paradoxical aspects of Prokofiev's character—his striving for innovation while simultaneously accepting tradition and authority—can also be found in nineteenth-century Russian musical history. The musical tradition which produced Glinka, Tchaikovsky, and the Balkirev Circle (or Mighty Handful) grew up almost entirely in the nineteenth century. Such a young, proximate, and circumscribed tradition could not but influence Prokofiev.[49] Let us now consider aspects of one of its particularly active forces, the Balakirev Circle.[50]

The Balakirev Circle encouraged a Russian musical tradition and strove against the creation of Russian music that blindly imitated Western models. Its members attempted to accomplish this by nurturing the individual and eschewing both foreign influences and institutional training that was insensitive to individuality. They adopted the romantic idea of genius and used romantic aesthetic tenets as a basis for rejecting foreign (Western) influences. Undoubtedly reflecting Balakirev's thinking, they also preached the danger of obliterating innate artistic sensibility and genius with conservatory training. In place of conservatory training they advocated developing in the musician a sort of musical libido unchecked by the superego of the Western musical tradition.[51]

Without denying the importance of nationalism in the Balakirev Circle's aesthetic platform, I find that Balakirev placed innovation in virtually the loftiest aesthetic category. Robert Ridenour comments: "Dedication to the cause of 'nationalism' in Russian music cannot alone explain Balakirev's tastes and aesthetic judgments about the music of Russian and Western composers. If his views have consistency, it must lie in some principle other than nationalism. The single thread that runs through all these opinions appears to be an admiration for what he judged to be innovative, original, free of hidebound tradition, and 'expressive' in a truly contemporary way that rejected the canons of musical orthodoxy, especially as embodied in academic composition."[52] Though his music occasionally sounds very "Russian" (as, for example, in the slow movement of the Symphony no. 5), Prokofiev, too, could not be accused of being obsessed with nationalism.

The Conservatory must have represented to the Balakirev Circle a two-headed monster: the import of foreign influence into Russia and a systematic and institutionalized approach to teaching music that was wholly unable to cultivate genius in general and Russian genius in particular. Suspicious of westernized conservatory training to the point of outright antagonism, the Balakirev Circle protected and nurtured the individual through self-education and one-on-one exchange. (Still, to ignore Balakirev's dominating and authoritarian personality would be to miss an important dynamic of the Circle.)

Rimsky-Korsakov, a member and diarist of the Circle, embodies in a virtual caricature the antagonism between the Balakirev Circle and the Conservatory.[53] Upon being asked to join the St. Petersburg Conservatory in 1871, Rimsky-Korsakov admitted his considerable compositional talents but also confronted his lack of formal musical training and confessed: "I not only could not decently harmonize a chorale, had not written a single counterpoint in my life, but I had hardly any notion of the structure of a fugue."[54] As is well known, Rimsky-Korsakov compensated for his educational shortcomings, assiduously studying counterpoint in Cherubini, Bellerman, and Bach.[55] He accepted the Conservatory position, and Balakirev, eager to infiltrate the Conservatory with an "agent" from his Circle, supported him.[56]

Members of the Balakirev Circle looked disdainfully upon precisely the traditional skills that Rimsky-Korsakov sought to acquire, skills the Circle considered pedantic. They regarded traditional instruction as a very real threat to musical creativity. In rejecting traditional, Western training, they show their debt to Romanticism at the same time that they create an interesting paradox: the philosophical source for rejecting and opposing Western influence turns out to be precisely a Western one.

In music, largely as a result of Beethoven, the image of the artist as craftworker was replaced by the image of the artist as independent and original creator. Rimsky-Korsakov confirms the Balakirev Circle's judgment of Beethoven along with some other composers: "The tastes of the circle leaned towards Glinka, Schumann and Beethoven's last quartets. Eight symphonies of Beethoven found comparatively little favour with the circle. . . . Mozart and Haydn were considered out of date and naive; J. S. Bach was held to be petrified, yes, even a mere musico-mathematical, feelingless and deadly nature, composing like a very machine. Handel was considered a strong nature. . . . Chopin was likened by Balakireff to a nervous society lady. . . . Berlioz . . . was highly esteemed. Liszt was comparatively unknown and was adjudged crippled and perverted from a musical point of view, and often even a caricature. Little was said of Wagner."[57]

Most of us today find it difficult to concur with the Balakirev Circle's judgment of Bach, Mozart, and Haydn. Members attack Bach from a romantic point of view, seeing him as purely a craftworker, guided only by logic in the form of "musico-mathematics" and altogether lacking in ingenuity, invention, and inspiration; Goethe's factory metaphor resonates here with considerable power. They appear not to be interested in composers such as Mozart and Haydn because their work crystallized a style and came toward the end of a style rather than at its inception. They found more suitable and attractive models in composers whose music was more overtly progressive and pioneering. That Glinka's name heads the list of those who were favored is no surprise; Circle members must have regarded him as the progenitor of distinctly Russian music. The high regard for Berlioz is also predictable; he represents their spiritual kin, a thoroughly romantic spirit, truly creative while also lonely and isolated.

Innovation became a pressing concern for the Balakirev Circle when, at the end of the nineteenth century, there were the first hints of a conception of common-practice tonality as a finite and nonrenewable resource. Certainly Schoenberg felt this to be true. In this view, common-practice tonality's gradual depletion over time amplified the urgency with which composers had to innovate, and forced composers both to confront their own nature—helping to foster the twentieth century's peculiar brand of self-consciousness—and to seek originality in unorthodox compositional strategies, sometimes lying well outside the sphere of common practice. The Balakirev Circle faced a more acute problem than its predecessors did.

But the so-called neo-romantic movement of recent years shows that it is too simple to interpret the turn away from common-practice tonality as evidence that the source had run dry, yielding up its last, hard-won, dominant-tonic cadence by the end of the nineteenth century.[58] The idea that the resource of tonality over time resembles Saint-Exupéry's snake swallowing an elephant, thin at the ends and fat and rich in the middle, is a facile one.[59] Yet composers in the early part of this century were consciously experimenting with new schemes for organizing musical material. For these composers the quest for originality became a significant compositional force, one which often made them strive against common-practice tonality while worshiping novelty.

Precisely how the aesthetics of the Balakirev Circle influenced Prokofiev is difficult to ascertain. Rimsky-Korsakov is a likely conduit, though Prokofiev, unlike Stravinsky, did not hold him in high regard as a mentor.[60] There is, nevertheless, a clear parallelism between the aesthetic positions of the Balakirev Circle and Prokofiev. The Balakirev Circle was suspicious of the West while simultaneously holding to Western romantic ideals, and in particular to the Western idea of genius. Similarly, Prokofiev self-consciously strove for originality while simultaneously clinging to a musical rhetoric deeply indebted to common-practice tonality.

Prokofiev's Music

TWENTIETH-CENTURY MUSIC AND THEORY

Until recently, the radical strains of early twentieth-century music have drawn most of the theoretical attention. We need only think of the insights provided by twelve-tone theory and pitch-class set theory. However, no such well-developed body of theory exists for music which, though it seems to share some features with music that is traditionally tonal, is nevertheless new and different in many respects. Music such as Prokofiev's has been regarded as sufficiently traditional for tonal music theory to explain it.

But traditional tonality has at least two important components: signs or elements of tonality, such as triads, diatonic scale fragments, and familiar bass progressions; and tonal function, such as the tendency of a dominant chord to progress to a tonic. One thrust of research into early twentieth-century music has been investigating precisely how tonal signs interact with tonal functions.[61] It seems only natural that the more signs of tonality one perceives on the surface of the music, the more one is likely to conclude that the music is governed by principles of functional tonality.

Under the rubric of tonal function also belong explanations of tonal coherence, ones which explain large-scale tonal structure either in a specific piece or in the body of music from some composer, for example. If one accepts that the first and easiest test of functional tonality is that it contains signs of tonality, then much early twentieth-century music is invitingly tonal. But a piece is not functionally tonal until it is shown how tonal elements are bound together by tonal processes.

One theoretical approach to invitingly tonal music is to strip away nontraditional features in order to demonstrate that "underneath" lie supportive structures which are generically identical with those of the common-practice period of the eighteenth and nineteenth centuries. Prokofiev, in this view, decorates traditional tonal structures in new ways, and his music is therefore part of a continuum reaching back to the eighteenth century.

I will have many opportunities to refer to this traditional conception of Prokofiev's music—traditional both because it is longstanding and well entrenched and because it places Prokofiev's music within the common-practice tradition. In most of the theoretical work that has been done on Prokofiev Prokofiev is viewed as traditional.[62]

Virtually all of Prokofiev's music clings to triadic harmony. That this is true of music from the Soviet period is not surprising, but even in compositions written before 1935 reliance on triadic harmony is evident. In what is certainly one of Prokofiev's greatest achievements, the nine piano sonatas, all but two movements end with a triad, usually a complete one.[63]

Prokofiev's forms are for the most part traditional—sonatas, concertos, and types like marches, gavottes, and waltzes.[64] His harmonic-contrapuntal style, too, has a strong traditional resonance. Stepwise voice leading, triadically based harmony, and tonal focus all betray an ever-present traditional orientation.

Categories of embellishing notes, such as neighbor note, passing note, and embellishing skip, are recognized in traditional tonal theory, and the underlying structure of a piece is shown by first clearing away surface ornament. Prokofiev's music magnifies the dichotomy between surface ornament and underlying structure because the "wrong notes" are apparently more radical representatives of traditional embellishing categories. Since wrong notes are surface ornaments, the traditional conception of Prokofiev's music limits their potential impact on underlying structure. But does the immiscibility of tradition and innovation in Prokofiev's music also necessarily imply that the innovative, wrong notes are accessory? Are such notes charming but ultimately superfluous?

The analytical approach in this book reflects the fact that wrong notes are characteristic of much of Prokofiev's music. In developing this analytical approach, I shall demonstrate that the wrong notes are not haphazardly added embellishments but integral structural components. We shall find in the wrong notes clues, not obstacles, to underlying structure. Necessarily, the approach is not based on the assumption that underlying structure is traditionally tonal. Though I want to show how surface and underlying structure communicate, I also want to recognize that a distinction between wrong note and context is useful and forms part of our immediate perception of much of Prokofiev's music.

Any theory of extended tonality would have to clarify how and where to invoke traditional tonal principles. If the new theory makes too-extensive modifications, it may end up vitiating precisely the principles which make it a tonal theory in the first place. Though there are problems with a theory of extended tonality, there are also attractions, and theorists such as Salzer and Austin have followed that course.[65]

SALZER'S ANALYSIS: AN EXCERPT FROM PIANO SONATA NO. 8

Felix Salzer accepts the challenge of applying traditional tonal theory to Prokofiev's music when he analyzes the opening the Piano Sonata no. 8, first movement (mm. 1–8), according to his modified Schenkerian principles. Salzer's analytical graphs appear in volume 2 of *Structural Hearing* (pp. 208–9). His explanatory remarks are reproduced below.

> A harmonic progression constitutes the main harmonic prolongation of the tonic. . . .
>
> The mediant, since it does not proceed to the V, becomes a . . . contra-puntal-structural chord. Here the main melodic and chordal parallelisms are of outstanding interest. The first measure with its motion to E-natural appears enlarged within the first phrase (meas. 1–5). This tone E turns out to be a neighbor note of the neighbor E-flat of higher order. A parallelism occurs in meas. 6–9, only here the motion does not go beyond the main neighbor note E-flat.
>
> The whole section shows a row of expressive transfers of register and great contrapuntal activity of the middle voices, both of which make the structural understanding of this music rather difficult at first. In addition we mention the bass, which shows equally interesting parallelisms; in both phrases it moves with a half-tone step to tones which become inner voice tones of chords (the dominant of meas. 4 and the mediant of meas. 8).[66]

Salzer regards the initial melodic D as a *Kopfton*. The opening bar contains the basic motive of this passage, D–C–E♭–E–♮, which Salzer brackets at *a* in m. 1; this motive is subsequently composed out—a process which can be observed in Salzer's analysis at *a*. The pitch D, the first note of m. 1's basic motive, is elaborated, on a higher level, through m. 1. C, the basic motive's second note, is elaborated in m. 2. E♭/D♯, the basic motive's third note, enters on a higher level at the end of m. 2. Finally, the basic motive's final note, E♮, enters during m. 4's excursion to A minor. Salzer reads E♮ as an embellishment of E♭, shown in Salzer's analyses at *b* by the two different sizes of the letter "N" (for *n*eighbor). Mm. 6–9 unfold the basic motive up to E♭ without continuing on to E♮. The high D in m. 7 is projected up from a lower register, passing from C to E♭. The melodic E♮ in mm. 6–9 is a high-level neighbor to the *Kopfton* D (as it was in mm. 1–5).

Both the structural melody and the structural bass are shown as stemmed open noteheads in Salzer's graph. The structural melody closes $\hat{3}$–$\hat{2}$–$\hat{1}$ in mm. 8–9, with each element of the structural melody receiving octave support in the structural bass. Salzer labels the structural chords on D and C "CS" for *c*ontrapuntal-*s*tructural chord. The contrapuntal-structural chord is not a member of one of Salzer's fundamental harmonic progressions (I–V–I, I–II–V–I, I–III–V–I, I–IV–V–I), but it nevertheless supports a structural tone in the melody.

Salzer calls the structural chord on D in m. 8 a mediant chord. The chord to which the mediant progresses, the chord built on C, has only contrapuntal and not harmonic significance; therefore it receives the label "CS" instead of a roman numeral.

Salzer analyzes G♯2 in m. 3 as a chromatic lower neighbor to A, to which it resolves by implication in m. 4. A♭2 in m. 8 is a chromatic lowering of an inner voice A. The inner voice A comes in via a register transfer (as A3) above D2 in m. 8, last half of beat 4. At the end of m. 8 Salzer's graph also shows an implied A2 in parentheses, presumably completing a neighbor motion.

There is much which makes good sense in Salzer's analysis. Most compelling perhaps is his isolation of the opening four-note motive and his identifying in that motive neighbors on two levels: E♭ is a neighbor to D, and E♮ decorates E♭. To the extent that Salzer recognizes the influence of a motive on several levels, I agree with his analysis.

Disconcerting in Salzer's analysis, however, is the reading of the close in mm. 8–9 as a series of three parallel octaves between the outer voices. Such a structure flatly contradicts the contrapuntal underpinning of Schenker's theory. Positing this structure within Salzer's modified Schenkerian framework would seem to merit and require explanation, an explanation which is not forthcoming.

Below I suggest some aspects of an alternate reading. The large-scale points of articulation and form are traditionally tonal. The eight measures together comprise a two-phrase parallel interrupted period. The first phrase moves from tonic to dominant; the second moves from tonic to tonic, closing with a perfect authentic cadence.

On a more local scale, however, some nontraditional features are apparent.

Example 1.1. Piano Sonata no. 8, op. 84/I, mm. 6–9, Tn-type [0234] in the bass

The tenor of m. 1 sets out the pitch classes F, C, Ab, and A♮. Mm. 3–4 retrograde these same pitches in the bass, where their registral placement and agogic accents mark them out for special emphasis. Enhancing the retrograde relation of these pitches in m. 1 and mm. 3–4 is the sense that F–C–Ab–A lead us away from the tonic and A–Ab–C–F return us to it. Taken as an unordered set, the tenor is a form of [0347], the major/minor tetrachord, at the dominant level.[67] If we hear the Db in m. 2 as an inflected chordal third of tonic harmony, then that Db hints at [0347] at the tonic level.

Example 1.1 shows an alternate reading for the bass of the second phrase. Salzer reads the basic bass motion for that phrase as Bb–D–C–Bb, relegating A, Ab, and F♯ to embellishing roles. In example 1.1 I virtually reverse that reading by assigning priority to a line descending stepwise from Bb through A and Ab to F♯. D and C in this reading embellish Ab and F♯, respectively, as shown by the slurs in the example.

The bass notes in the second phrase, Bb, A, Ab, and F♯, taken together are a form of Tn-type [0234], inversionally related to the opening motive, itself a form of Tn-type [0124].[68] The inversional balance, while not exact in pitch space, is not difficult to hear if one concentrates on following an ascending chromatic line in the melody, D–Eb–E at the beginning of the period, which is answered by a descending chromatic line in the bass, Bb–A–Ab at the end of the period.

One can also hear inversional balance in the melodic motive of m. 1. The step down from D to C is answered by a step up from Eb to E. This is a contour inversion and not a strict intervallic inversion. Yet when the same motive returns in the transition at m. 46, its potential for strict intervallic inversion is realized through its transformation to a form of 4-3 [0134]. The same kind of inversional balance — opposing half-step motions — controls the root succession of right-hand chords in mm. 48–49: C to B is answered by F♯ to G in m. 48; Db to C is answered by G to Ab in m. 49.

Let us return to Salzer's analysis of the Eb–E–Eb neighbor motion. If we view this as a process, we can represent it as $T_1(x)$ in its incomplete form, patterned on our foreground perception of it in m. 1.[69] M. 46 realizes the T_1 displacement in the right-hand succession Bb(7)–B♮(7). Mm. 48–49 realize the T_1 displacement on a slightly larger scale, whereby the right hand in m. 49 transposes the chordal roots of m. 48 up by T_1: $T_1(C, B, F♯, G) = (Db, C, G, Ab)$.

Having studied this excerpt from the Piano Sonata no. 8 from two different points of view, once using Salzer's Schenker-derived approach and once using an alternative, we are in a position to assess some of the problems accompanying Salzer's stance, one which accepts, a priori, a traditionally tonal basis for Prokofiev's music. To analyze Prokofiev's music, Salzer applies a theory developed from studying traditionally tonal music. But Salzer's strategy runs into trouble on two fronts. First, the Schenkerian model underlying Salzer's approach cannot engage Prokofiev's music in the same way it would engage traditionally tonal music. Instead, it must be radically modified: structural outer-voice octaves, which are absolutely foreign to traditional tonal syntax, appear in Salzer's model. The explanatory power of the theory becomes diluted when its readings, in straining to accommodate music which is not traditionally tonal, contradict the theory's underlying premises.

Second, proceeding from the theory to the music, rather than vice versa, automatically limits the sorts of insights one can obtain. As we have seen, inversional balance and the influence of certain collections, relations, and processes which, in fact, saturate the music may go entirely unnoticed in Schenkerian theory.

The aim of the present study is to elucidate how, in Kramer's words, the "'wrong' notes gain in Prokofiev's hands an integrity and a rightness," to understand what Moisson-Franckhauser terms "a subtle game," because the true character of Prokofiev's music is closely tied to its wittiness, its play on our expectations of traditional continuation. That character is lost when the analytically right notes absorb the characteristic wrong ones. The analytical approach developed in this book rescues the wrong notes from the maw of traditional consonance and dissonance and shows their large-scale impact as well as their local distinctiveness. We need an analytical approach that recognizes the characteristic and delicious tension between familiar structures, such as diatonic fragments and triads, and wrong-note challenges, but we need not demand at the same that the approach take sides.

2 Constancy and Change

I n his *Autobiography*, written at the age of fifty, Prokofiev enumerates five categories into which he could place the music composed up until his graduation from the Conservatory, or roughly the time identified in the previous
chapter as his first period. The five categories, or "lines," as he called them,
are the classical, the modern, the toccata, the lyrical, and the grotesque.

The first was the classical line, which could be traced back to my early
childhood and the Beethoven sonatas I heard my mother play. This line
takes sometimes a neo-classical form (sonatas, concertos), sometimes imitates the 18th century (gavottes, the "Classical" Symphony, partly the Sin-
fonietta). The second line, the modern trend, begins with that meeting
with Taneev when he reproached me for the "crudeness" of my harmonies. At first this took the form of a search for my own harmonic language, developing later into a search for a language in which to express
powerful emotions ("The Phantom" in the Piano Pieces op. 3, "Despair"
and "Suggestion Diabolique" in the op. 4 Piano Pieces, the *Sarcasmes*, the
Scythian Suite, a few of the songs op. 23, *The Gambler, Seven, They Are Seven*,
the Quintet and the Second Symphony). Although this line covers harmonic language mainly, it also includes new departures in melody, orches-

tration and drama. The third line is the toccata, or "motor" line, traceable perhaps to Schumann's Toccata which made a powerful impression on me when I first heard it (*Etudes* op. 2, Toccata op. 11, the "Scherzo" in the Piano Pieces op. 12, the Scherzo of the Second Concerto, the Toccata in the Fifth Concerto, and also the repetitive intensity of the melodic figures in the *Scythian Suite, Le pas d'acier* [*The Age of Steel*], and passages in the Third Concerto). This line is perhaps the least important. The fourth line is lyrical: it appears first as a thoughtful and meditative mood, not always associated with the melody, or at any rate, with the long melody ("Fairy Tale" in the Four Pieces for Piano op. 3, *Dreams, Autumnal,* the songs op. 9, the "Legend" op. 12), sometimes partly contained in long melody (the two Balmont choruses, the beginning of the First Violin Concerto, the songs to Akhmatova's poems, *Grandmother's Tales*). This line was not noticed until much later. For a long time I was given no credit for any lyrical gift whatever, and for want of encouragement it developed slowly. But as time went on I gave more and more attention to this aspect of my work.

I should like to limit myself to these four "lines," and to regard the fifth, "grotesque," line which some wish to ascribe to me as simply a deviation from the other lines. In any case I strenuously object to the very word "grotesque" which has become hackneyed to the point of nausea. As a matter of fact the use of the French word "grotesque" in this sense is a distortion of the meaning. I would prefer my music to be described as "scherzo-ish" in quality, or else by three words describing various degrees of the scherzo—whimsicality, laughter, mockery.[1]

Prokofiev, his world reputation established, wrote the *Autobiography* to document properly the events of his life. In describing stylistic aspects of his music, he is sensitive to the pigeonholing and oversimplification that necessarily accompanied his celebrity and is touchy about his identification with the toccata and grotesque lines. He was eager to right the record, making this self-analysis read as part apology and part self-promotion.

There are several reasons why the West, in particular, would seize on Prokofiev's toccata and grotesque lines more than his lyric and classical lines. Given his penchant for modernism and innovation, grotesque and modern lines naturally stand out. Prokofiev's lifelong interest in driving rhythms understandably accounts for a prominent toccata line. But America had its own way of interpreting Prokofiev's idiosyncrasies, and it greeted the composer as a living specimen of Soviet man. "Ironically, from the very beginning of his American career, which would sporadically flourish and decline for the next twenty years,

Prokofiev was known as 'that Bolshevik composer.' Forgotten in the journalists' mad quest for a label was the indifference to the politics that led Prokofiev to leave Russia in the first place."[2]

Particularly in the cultural centers of New York, Chicago, and Paris, Prokofiev appeared to be an exotic creature, an envoy from a distant country, one which had only recently undergone an astonishing revolution.[3] Prokofiev recalls the relish with which the critics searched out exoticism in the music of his New York recital of 20 November 1918. "In appraising my music the critics wrote a good deal of nonsense; for example, the best of them maintained that the finale of the Second Sonata made him think of a herd of mammoths charging across an Asiatic plateau."[4] Russia's history of relative isolation from European affairs fueled the West's impression of it as a strange and barbaric country, thereby enhancing Prokofiev's exotic aura. The performances of Diaghilev's Ballets Russes further fueled the West's fascination with Russia in the 1920s, Prokofiev's first years in the West.[5]

Thus, Western reaction to Prokofiev may have been initially shaped by a curiosity factor. Viewed in that light, Prokofiev's touchiness about which lines in his music are most valid is understandable. But lines such as the toccata or the grotesque are not thereby invalidated. Below I consider each of the five lines in turn, expanding upon the remarks and hints provided by Prokofiev.

Prokofiev's Five Lines

The rhythmic aggressiveness which marks so much of his music and is especially evident in early works, was the musical manifestation of the barbarism which fascinated the West. Prokofiev reports a review in the *New York Times* which said that he had "steel fingers, steel wrists, steel biceps and triceps."[6] The reviewer describes Prokofiev's piano playing, though the description could easily be adapted to his music as well: "His harmonies are steel, his rhythms are steel." The perception of steeliness in his playing and in his music seemed to sting Prokofiev. As we saw in the quotation from the *Autobiography,* he remarks that "this [toccata] line is perhaps the least important."

Prokofiev himself is not entirely blameless in fostering this impression. For example, while working on *Ala and Lolly* for Diaghilev, Prokofiev strove for precisely a barbaric, motor quality in the music. As early as the Toccata, op. 11, rhythmic aggressiveness was a prominent quality of Prokofiev's music, one he never discarded completely. But in the *Autobiography,* Prokofiev shows his awareness of the disproportionately strong role which rhythmic aggressiveness played in shaping his reputation, and he works to paint a picture of an artist with a diverse stylistic palette.

Though virtually forced to admit a toccata line and a grotesque line, he relegates them to positions of relatively low importance. He waits until the last paragraph of his self-analysis to mention the grotesque line, admitting to it grudgingly, almost as an afterthought. Though he is reluctant to recognize it, this line is characteristic of and well suited to Prokofiev because in it his wit is allowed its fullest play.

The effect of the grotesque depends upon one's knowledge of a model against which one can play grotesque distortion. Pieces such as the *March* from *Love for Three Oranges* play expertly on our knowledge of the traditional march type. Grotesque, in this critique, epitomizes the interaction of tradition and innovation, the same dynamic which produces the wrong note. Despite Prokofiev's eagerness to recast his identity for the West, the analysis in this book restores the grotesque line to a central position from the marginal one which Prokofiev had hoped to establish for it, because it presents essential style characteristics, especially the interaction of tradition and innovation.

As though compensating for unfairly overemphasized aspects of his style, Prokofiev is eager to tell of his lyric line. His lyric gift was, in fact, considerable and is clearly evident in pieces such as the Akhmatova songs, op. 27, the Violin Concerto no. 2, and the ballets *Romeo and Juliet* and *Cinderella*.[7] Ironically, it was openly acknowledged during the musicians' conference preceding the Decree of 1948. Even though Prokofiev was one of the composers whose formalist practices were mentioned, the lyrical quality in his music was also praised. Hinting at a lyric gift which developed most fully only in the Soviet Union, Dmitri Kabalevsky says: "Compare, for instance, Prokofiev's early works like the *Scythian Suite* with his *Romeo and Juliet* or *Alexander Nevsky*."[8] Victor Belyi, avoiding any remarks about the supposedly salutary effects of the Soviet climate, compliments Prokofiev's lyric gift explicitly: "He [Prokofiev] has a melodic gift which is in the best Russian traditions of Moussorgsky and Liadov."[9]

The classical line is strongly represented by Prokofiev's firm attachment to tradition even when he was striving to compose original and modern pieces. Under the heading "classical" belong, among other things, traditional vehicles and forms such as symphonies and sonatas and types such as gavottes, waltzes, and marches. In identifying a classical line Prokofiev shows himself fully aware of the traditional ties that his music enjoys in spite of—and coexisting with—any strains of iconoclasm which are also present.

While the Balakirev Circle viewed the quality "classical" as a sign of artistic stasis (and even stagnation) and epigonism, Prokofiev viewed it as a metaphorical mantle of protection, a sanctioning by tradition, rather than a symbol of aesthetic ossification.[10] Several times Prokofiev was inspired by Beethoven: he modeled the experimental Symphony no. 2 on the form of Beethoven's last piano sonata, op. 111, and he studied Beethoven's quartets prior to composing the String Quartet no. 1, op. 50.

It is natural to construe "modern" as denoting a nontraditional harmonic vocabulary, especially one which employs daring and unresolved dissonances. Leaving aside the highly experimental examples of Prokofiev's harmonic modernism, we can still point to the *Sarcasmes,* op. 17, some of the *Visions Fugitives,* op. 22, or the Balmont songs, op. 36, as pieces in which Prokofiev is carrying on harmonic experimentation.

Surely harmonic invention is part of what Prokofiev has in mind when he says modern, but he goes on to tell us that his notion of modern also covers "melody, orchestration, and drama." He likely had in mind *The Gambler* when he wrote these remarks. *The Gambler* was a piece of which Prokofiev was always fond and upon which he expended considerable energy. *The Gambler* has a relatively dissonant harmonic style. Prokofiev is modern to the extent that he rejects nineteenth-century operatic practice. Instead of pouring his libretto into the mold of traditional set pieces, he patterned the musical structure after the lead of the libretto and followed the natural declamation of speech. The epithet "modern," then, applies not only to harmonic experimentation but also to any challenge to tradition.

The modern line, more than any other, was the real proving ground for Prokofiev's ability to innovate and thus to exhibit romantic genius. Consequently, with the stakes so high, it is easy to understand how he might have occasionally strayed into uncomfortable styles and produced some of his less successful pieces. For Prokofiev, a strong lyric line shows a composer with considerable and diverse skills. But a strong modern line shows more than craft; it validates the music aesthetically.

The five lines are best understood as characteristics whose presence in most of Prokofiev's music is a matter of degree rather than presence or absence. In regarding a piece as an example of one of the five lines we are in a sense treating that piece as a caricature and thus each piece, in its own way, as grotesque.

Prokofiev claims, in his *Autobiography,* to describe works composed up until he graduated from the Conservatory in 1914. Even so, several works composed later than that find their way into the list, such as the Piano Concerto no. 5, op. 55, composed in 1932. Prokofiev's inclusion of post-Conservatory pieces invites us to apply his scheme to his entire corpus of work.

Below, I rely on Prokofiev's five lines as the basic scheme for sorting his works. I augment this approach with analysis of pitch and rhythm. To obtain more breadth in the sampling, works are drawn from several time periods.

Of the two songs in op. 9, the first best exemplifies the lyric line in Prokofiev's music. Prokofiev said of op. 9/1 that "poor as it is, I have a paternal affection [for it]."[11] The slow tempo, the dense and widely spaced sonorities, and the soft intervals of perfect fourths and fifths all accentuate its lyricism.

In m. 1, the first beat in the piano left hand plays B♭–E♭–A♭, introducing stacked perfect fourths in the music. Though the characteristic stacked fourths and fifths represent nontraditional harmonic practice, the tonal focus is consistent with the written key signature of two flats, and alternates, in the first four measures, between B♭ major and G minor. The piano introduction divides into two 2-bar subphrases: on the second beat of m. 2, mm. 1–2 cadence on B♭; on the second beat of m. 4, mm. 3–4 cadence on G minor.[12]

At m. 9, the left hand relinquishes its single-note motion and settles on a dense chord partly arrayed in fifths. A strict traditionalist might analyze this chord as a suspension formation comprising a G dominant seventh over a C pedal. In this reading, the upper voice C_5 delays and displaces B_5, which arrives on beat 2.[13]

However, two matters complicate this analysis. First, when C "resolves" to B on beat 2, the upper voice G begins to pass chromatically through G♯ up to A. This destabilizing chromatic passing motion in the upper voice obfuscates any perceived resolution of C_5. In fact, the goal of the piano right hand is A_6—a pitch belonging neither to a G dominant nor to a C tonic. Rather than reinforcing a C tonal focus, the arrival of A_6 extends the fifths cycle with which the measure began from F–C–G–D to F–C–G–D–A. The second problem with reading m. 9 as implying a G dominant is that there is no C-major chord hereabouts which could be the object of the G dominant. Thus, a traditionally tonal interpretation of this passage is awkward at best.

Mm. 9th ff. conceal a transpositional process which occurs explicitly later in the piece. In M. 10, beat 1, the right hand of m. 9, beat 1, is transposed down a major third while the bass is transposed up a minor third. The ascending bass motion is only apparent, however, as we discover by looking ahead to mm. 31–34. The stacked-fifths chord recurs in these measures. In m. 32, as in m. 10, the bass enters with A♭ rather than E♭ so that, like the right hand, it also descends a major third. M. 34 is a transposition of m. 33, just as m. 32 was a transposition of m. 31. M. 34, like m. 32, rises in the bass by a pitch interval of ip3 from downbeat to downbeat, but the right hand again descends by ip4.[14] We can most easily follow the transposition in the right-hand chords on downbeats, beginning with m. 31: T8(0257) = (8t13) and T8(8t13) = (469e).[15] Thus the passage sequences through the intervals of an augmented triad. In retrospect, the bass motion of

Example 2.1. Op. 9/1, complementation and chromatic pitch-class saturation

mm. 9 ff. is best understood as incomplete: in m. 10 the composer simply fails to transpose the bass C of m. 9; the remaining pitches of the set from m. 9, however, do get transposed down a major third.

The downward major-third transposition produces complete variance, making the harmonic move from m. 9 to m. 10 and analogous places sound fresh and forward-driving. Example 2.1 schematizes this process. Cycling through three successive pitch levels a major third apart brings in the complete chromatic pitch-class collection, shown by the bracket above the staff. Further, any contiguous pair of 4–23s forms 8–23, the complement, shown by the brackets below the staff. There is, then, ample reason for hearing these chords as self-standing rather than tonal suspension formations.

In this piece Prokofiev retains tonal focus and an emphasis on perfect fourths and fifths, which are characteristic tonal intervals. Thus he displays the influence of tradition. But he also explores untraditional organizational strategies, as when he transposes 4–23 at T8, achieving complete variance and harmonic freshness with each transposition, as well as systematic pitch-class saturation and pitch-class set complementation.[16]

THE GROTESQUE LINE: AN EXCERPT FROM
THE *MARCH* FROM *LOVE FOR THREE ORANGES*

In speaking of the grotesque line, Prokofiev cites no example, perhaps hoping to discourage those who imagine him possessing only a very limited, primarily grotesque style. We are left to find for ourselves the music belonging in this category.

"Grotesque" implies the distortion or caricature of a basic model. The *American Heritage Dictionary* defines it to mean "characterized by ludicrous or incongruous distortion."[17] Incongruity brings back yet again the unexpected juxtaposition of elements that arises from the way tradition and innovation blend in some of Prokofiev's music. Prokofiev's traditional types—the marches, gavottes, and waltzes which he so often composed—provide both the model (the type) and its grotesque interpretation.

The famous *March* from *Love for Three Oranges* is a clear instance of the grotesque. In the opera it is first heard by the Prince and Truffaldino as it wafts in through the Prince's window from outside. It signals the beginning of the festivities which are to cure the prince's hypochondria and melancholy. The *March*'s programmatic associations irrevocably color our perception of it, but its humor also derives from the tweaking and teasing of the composed military aspects of the type. Prokofiev regularly thwarts our expectations about how a march ought properly to behave but retains enough characteristics to preserve the identity of the piece as a march.

The following analysis uses the piano transcription, op. 33a, made by the composer in 1919. The piece is introduced by a drum roll, and by m. 3 the characteristic two-beat bass sets in. One might expect the D of the opening drum roll to be a dominant or a tonic scale degree. Neither expectation proves correct, and D slides up to E♭, as though realizing and correcting a mistake, and the first phrase begins. The bass in m. 3 has the opportunity to deliver the traditional î–ŝ pattern, but stubbornly refuses to get it right, hitting a "wrong note" a half step too high: instead of A♭–E♭, the bass opts for the diminished fourth A♭–E. E♭, the "correct" note to be paired with A♭, does arrive, in m. 8. But there it is paired with a different partner, G. We can hear E/A♭ in mm. 3–5 slipping down through a half step to E♭/G in m. 6, and so the *March* displays an inversional balance: the drum roll D sliding up to E♭ balances the bass E♮ sliding down to E♭.

E♮, apparently the wrong partner for A♭, proves not to be wrong; there are other reasons to consider than the inversional balance about E♭. The ip4 formed between A♭ and E♮ generates a characteristic transposition. Mm. 7–8 present T−4, which takes E♭ down to B, and T+4, which takes E♭ up to G. These transpositions are clues to the underlying structure.

As is common in Prokofiev's music, 4–19 [0148]—which is a superset of both 3–11 [037] (a major or minor triad) and 3–12 [048] (an augmented triad)—plays a prominent role. Example 2.2 displays the bass dyads separated by ip4 in mm. 3–8. Together they form 5–21 [01458], a characteristic pentachordal superset of 4–19. The melody approaches E♭5 in m. 8 by moving through two successive transpositions by T4, outlining the augmented triad, identical in pitch-class content to the last four pitches in the example.

The grotesque quality of the *March* arises from how our knowledge of marches is retooled by Prokofiev's distortions. And so, while Prokofiev experiences a certain amount of discomfort about the label "grotesque," it is in this

Example 2.2. Op. 33a, mm. 3–8, contiguous realizations of ip4

line that he exhibits one of his most natural and successful blendings of tradition and innovation. It is precisely the clear demarcation of tradition ("I know how a march ought to go") and innovation ("this isn't quite right") that animates the hybrid.

In terms of the grotesque, the five lines do not measure comparable musical attributes. The grotesque highlights the difference between expectation and reality. The space to which our expectations are rerouted is the space of the grotesque. The grotesque raises a kind of a partition in the music which separates the traditional from the innovative. It is across this partition that Prokofiev is able to play so wittily and so characteristically. The sharp division between traditional and innovative that exists in grotesque music may be absent in music of the other four lines, where the partition may be lowered so much that placing elements in either a traditional or an innovative category becomes a futile exercise. In the absence of the grotesque's clear partition, the music's context may be considerably more homogenous, as is the case in Prokofiev's modern and classical lines.

The lyric line and the toccata line do not depend upon the partition for their definition; "lyric" and "toccata" measure different musical attributes. The toccata line measures a rhythmic feature of the music which is independent of any grotesque elements. The lyric line, however, is the most difficult to define with precision. It often involves long melodies, slow to moderate tempos, carefully controlled chromaticism, and a reliance on quintessentially tonal harmonic structures, especially those that feature perfect fourths and fifths, such as [027] and its supersets—[0257] and [02457], for example.

As a final step in developing the idea of the grotesque, we need to eliminate its pejorative connotations, the ones which seemed to rankle with Prokofiev. "Grotesque" does not necessarily denote only humorous or somehow defective characteristics in the music.

THE CLASSICAL LINE: *ROMEO AND JULIET,*
NO. 11, "THE ARRIVAL OF THE GUESTS"

Prokofiev does virtually nothing in his self-analysis to compare the classical and the modern lines. He treats them simply as two of the five slices of his stylistic pie. However, the classical and the modern lines stand at stylistic extremes. Using proximity to common practice as a measure of traditional musical rhetoric, I could say that Prokofiev's classical line is very traditional and conservative, and the modern line is very innovative and progressive. The two lines delimit Prokofiev's stylistic breadth.

"The Arrival of the Guests" in *Romeo and Juliet* is a stately minuet in eighteenth-century style, one of the traditional types of which Prokofiev was so fond. It is a clear example of his classical line of composition. The minuet is not

Part 1

Section A

mm. 1–8	B♭	theme A
mm. 9–12	E♭	theme A
mm. 13–28	E♭	bridge
mm. 29–32	B♭	theme A

Section B

mm. 33–36		transition
mm. 37–46	A♭	theme B
mm. 47–55	B♭	theme B

Part 2

mm. 56–63	B	theme A
mm. 64–67	E	theme A
mm. 68–75	C	theme C
mm. 76–83	E	theme D
mm. 84–88	C	theme C
mm. 89–96	B♭	theme A
mm. 97–100	E	theme A
mm. 101–108	E	theme D
mm. 109–113	E	theme D
mm. 114–118	B	reference to theme C

Figure 2.1. *Romeo and Juliet,* op. 64/11, "The Arrival of the Guests," form outline

nearly as grotesque as the *March* from *Love for Three Oranges,* for two reasons. First, the context in which the minuet arises is devoid of the humor and farce surrounding the *March.* And second, in the minuet the demarcation between traditional features and distorted ones is not drawn with any particular harmonic sharpness. The minuet sounds more like a modern minuet than it does like a traditional minuet gone wrong.

Prokofiev's minuet is more complex than the binary form of the eighteenth-century minuet, but the general atmosphere and the voice leading in the piece are markedly conventional. Figure 2.1 gives the form, along with associated key areas. Overall, the piece is a large binary form, divided at m. 56 into a B♭-major section (part 1) and a B-major section (part 2), with the primary theme beginning each section.

Part 1 itself most closely resembles a binary form. Within part 1, mm. 1–32 are answered by mm. 37–55. Mm. 33–36 form a transition. Mm. 47–55 repeat mm. 37–46 in the home key of B♭ to close part 1 harmonically. Mm. 1–32 constitute a ternary form. Mm. 1–12 unfold theme A, and modulate from B♭ to the subdominant E♭. Mm. 13–28 introduce new, contrasting material which expands the E♭-key area. Finally, mm. 29–32 return to the tonic B♭ to recapitulate the primary theme in shortened form.

Part 2 (mm. 56–118) is in the new key of B major. Its tonal scheme through m. 67 resembles that of part 1, for mm. 56–67 state the primary theme first in the key of B, then in the subdominant E. The subdominant E is elaborated by a modulation to the key of C. The subdominant E returns in mm. 76–83 with a variation on the chromatic neighbor material from m. 5. C major intrudes once more in mm. 84–88 and leads in mm. 89–96 to a restatement of the primary theme in the key of B♭. The key of E returns at m. 97, and the piece draws to a conclusion in m. 118 in part 2's home key of B, with an interweaving of the primary theme and the chromatic neighbor material from m. 5.

As befits this "neo-minuet," the voice-leading techniques are traditional. Example 2.3a shows how voice exchange expands the tonic B♭ over mm. 1–4. The diagonal lines show the voice exchange; the parenthetical B♭5 is a cover tone representing a different voice-leading strand, which, at the end of m. 1, passes down to meet D5.[18] Example 2.3b, a distillation of 2.3a, shows the voice exchange more clearly.

Example 2.4 is a sketch of the voice leading of mm. 13–28. Characteristic through here is the projection of inner voices up, shown by straight lines, as in m. 21 and mm. 24–25. V–I progressions which occur above the pedal D♯/E♭ are shown parenthetically inside the grand staff. While the tonal focus is not unambiguous, there is a hint of mode change from E♭ major to its enharmonic

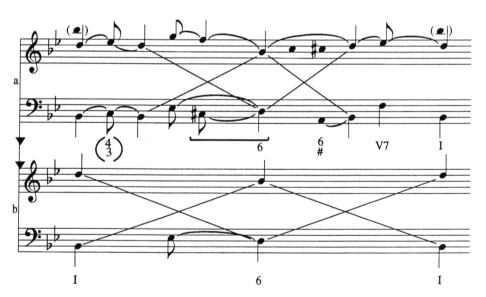

Example 2.3. *Romeo and Juliet,* no. 11, "The Arrival of the Guests," mm. 1–4

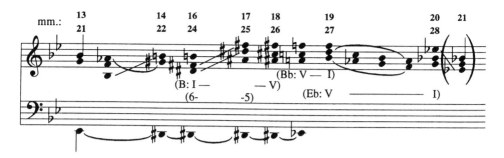

Example 2.4. *Romeo and Juliet,* no. 11, "The Arrival of the Guests," mm. 13–28

parallel minor, D♯ minor.[19] Overall, mm. 13–28 expand the E♭ cadence in m. 12, a procedure consistent with the structure of a traditional full-sectional ternary form. However, as was mentioned above, mm. 29–32's recapitulation of theme A in the tonic B♭ is somewhat shorter than might be expected normally.[20]

Mm. 68–75, in the key of C, introduce new, contrasting melodic material, and are tonally anchored by traditional and clear bass movement, either $\hat{5}$–$\hat{1}$ bass motion, $\hat{2}$–$\hat{5}$–$\hat{1}$ bass motion, $\hat{4}$–$\hat{5}$–$\hat{1}$ bass motion, or the plagal elaboration $\hat{1}$–$\hat{4}$–$\hat{1}$. This bass motion guides and clarifies the function of the complex harmonic structures in the upper voices, such as the dominant ninth chord with added raised fifth and raised seventh in m. 71, where the $\hat{5}$–$\hat{1}$ bass motion leaves no doubt as to tonal focus.

Several processes, occurring on different levels, unite large-scale and small-scale structures. Subdominant elaboration of the tonic is characteristic of this piece, as in mm. 1–32 or mm. 97–115. The large-scale plagal emphasis is fore-shadowed in mm. 1–2 by the root movement tonic–subdominant–tonic, expressed as I–IV–I6.

Within the otherwise purely diatonic context of mm. 1–4, the chromatic event C♯ stands out in m. 2 and again in the upper voice in m. 3. In example 2.3 the motive C♯–to–D is bracketed as an instance of chromatic elaboration. Chromatic elaboration occurs on two higher levels over mm. 5–6. As is demonstrated by its respelling at the end of m. 5, the D♭ augmented six-four triad is a neighboring chord of the B♭ tonic. The C♯–to–D motion from m. 5 to m. 6 also duplicates the original pitch-class motive bracketed in example 2.3. Within m. 5, however, chromatic elaboration expands the D♭ augmented chord itself on a lower level (A–F–D♭ to G♯–E–C to A–F–D♭). On the highest level, chromatic motion lifts all of part 1, in the key of B♭, into part 2, in the key of B.

In figure 2.1 we can follow the succession of tonal areas in part 1: B♭–E♭–B♭–A♭–B♭; the associated pitch-class transpositional scheme, beginning with B♭, is $T_2(T_{10}(T_7(T_5(B♭))))$. The same transpositional scheme applies to the harmonies of mm. 37–41, which occur above an A♭ pedal and begin with an A♭ chord: $T_2(T_{10}(T_7(T_5(A♭))))$. Thus, part 1's final theme encapsulates the large-scale key structure of all of part 1.

Before leaving this piece, let us turn our attention to the phrase structure of mm. 1–12. Prokofiev's admiration of Haydn is well known, particularly as expressed in the "Classical" Symphony.[21] One is reminded here of the type of sophisticated phrase and metrical structure which occurs in the music of Haydn: an apparently regular surface, such as one 8 measures long, actually conceals an irregular underlying phrase structure of, say, 4 + 5 bars, owing to overlap.[22]

In Prokofiev's minuet, the first phrase aims toward its conclusion in m. 4, concluding V^6_4–$^5_3$ to I in a typically "end-accented" cadential scheme.[23] But m. 4 begins the second phrase as well as concluding the first. Hence, the overlap in m. 4 creates an underlying 4 + 5 + 4 phrase structure. This sort of plasticity in phrase structure is typical of the mature Prokofiev, and at the end of this chapter I will explore two more examples of what I have termed Prokofiev's maturing design skill.

THE MODERN LINE: QUINTET, OP. 39/IV

At the stylistic extreme opposite to the classical is Prokofiev's modern line. The Quintet, op. 39, has already been mentioned several times as an exemplary piece in the modern line because of its experimental quality. I will now examine aspects of its fourth movement.

Op. 39/IV most closely resembles a rounded binary form ABA'. Section A is stated over mm. 1–6 and enjoys a varied and extended return over mm. 15–29. The B section, extending over mm. 7–14 unfolds first a canon (mm. 7–12) and then a retransition leading to section A'.

Section B, in the canonic treatment of its melody, contrasts with sections A and A'. However, in the unremitting eighth-note motion and dissonant, static harmonies carried over from section A, section B clearly derives from previous musical material, making the overall form a rounded binary. The movement's rhythmic proportions reinforce this binary reading. If we regard section A' as beginning exactly at the return of the melody from m. 1, that is, in the middle of m. 15, then the number of beats in sections A and B is exactly equal to the number of beats in section A': m. 1 to m. 15, beat 2 = 64 beats; m. 15, beat 2 to m. 29 = 64 beats. The following analysis will be concerned with aspects of sections A and B and not section A'.

The unyielding eighth-note rhythm in the melody is unusual in Prokofiev's music, where melodies are typically more rhythmically charged. All phrases begin on a weak beat and end on an upbeat. This rigid metrical scheme abets the rhythmic monotony of the melody, applying a strange brake to the forward

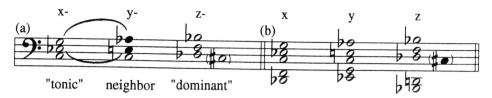

Example 2.5. Quintet, op. 39/IV, provisional chord functions

motion of the piece. The dearth of harmonic variety parallels the rhythmic monotony: Prokofiev uses only three different harmonies in the accompaniment throughout the entire movement.

I begin by testing a tonally oriented analysis. The viola line, while not traditionally tonal, is able nevertheless to suggest some tonal function. In example 2.5a I outline tentative harmonic functions, labeling and verticalizing the three viola figures, $x-$ (m. 1), $y-$ (m. 3), and $z-$ (m. 10). The figure $x-$ is a sort of C-minor tonic; $y-$ embellishes and displaces the tonic, as shown by the slurs connecting Eb/G to E/Ab; and $z-$ is a sort of dominant built on b$\hat{2}$ (Db), respelled in the example from C♯, Prokofiev's spelling.

Example 2.5b shows the complete harmonies x, y, and z. The bass Db/F, along with $x-$, creates a simultaneously sounding tonic-dominant chord. Complete harmony y sounds both minor and major thirds of the tonic. Complete harmony z is possibly understood as a Neapolitan dominant substitution in which b$\hat{2}$ and natural $\hat{2}$ simultaneously displace $\hat{1}$. Example 2.6a gives the oboe melody for the opening six measures. We can regard the oboe melody, beginning in m. 1, as a compound melody: B3/D4 moves to C4/Eb4, suggesting a dominant-to-tonic gesture consistent within a C-minor tonality.[24]

The problems with this outline are multitudinous. Most obviously, instrumental partitioning supersedes bass support as a criterion for tonal function. For instance, in example 2.5a I rely on theoretical thaumaturgy to explain away the actual Db bass of harmony x because the viola clearly arpeggiates a C-minor chord. Db and F presumably represent some sort of superimposed dominant harmony. But then one would have to justify why tonic and not dominant harmony prevails.

Example 2.6. Quintet, op. 39/IV, mm. 1–6

The melodic analysis runs into trouble in m. 2, where, by continuing the motivic structure of the compound melody, the oboe moves to Db/Fb (Fb = E?). Again one must face the possibility of simultaneous harmonic functions and consider that Db is a dominant element supported by the bass, while Fb (E) is possibly a tonic element.[25] But in m. 1, B/D represented dominant harmony and C/Eb represented tonic harmony; functions were not split within a single, motivically determined interval.

As I asked of Salzer's analysis in Chapter 1, here again I ask: When does the tonal theoretical structure collapse from the corrosive effect of overgeneralization? Rather than regarding this piece as comprehensively tonal, I shall adopt a different approach, one more attuned to the music's nontraditional aspects.

I will discuss melodic aspects of the music first, then harmonic aspects. Example 2.6 shows an analysis of the oboe melody over mm. 1–6. The staff marked "a" reproduces the oboe melody over mm. 1–6; also, brackets in m. 4 show the whole-tone dyads there. The staff marked "b" beams together (e14), a form of [025]. Over mm. 1–2 the first element of (e14), B3, ascends to the second element, Db4, through a passing note, C4, labeled "P" on the example. Db's arrival in m. 2 is marked by a repetition of the ascending "minor third" from m. 1, a form of 3–2 [013], as well as a threefold metrically accented reiteration on m. 2, beats 1, 3, and 4. Slurs on staff *b* show how the minor third is associated with B3, C4, and Db4. Over mm. 2–3 Db follows up on the stepwise passing motion which connects B3 from m. 1 to Db4 in m. 2: Db in m. 2 passes through D at the end of m. 2 to E/Fb, which completes (e14).

M. 4 leaps up to Gb, the highest pitch thus far, and, reversing the direction of the generally rising melody of mm. 1–4, Gb begins a chromatic descent to Eb; the notes are shown beamed together below staff *a*. The first and last pitches of the chromatic descent, Gb and Eb, along with Db from the end of m. 4, are (136), creating another form of [025] that overlaps with (e14). M. 5 brings back the ascending collection (e14), but in a shorter time than over mm. 1–2; (e14) is completed within two beats when E4 arrives at m. 5, beat 2½. The arrival on E4 is reiterated two more times over mm. 5–6. E4's last appearance in m. 6 is especially expressive when it is approached chromatically from the upper neighbor F4, a pitch which replaces the upper neighbor Gb from m. 5.

The melody shown in example 2.6 is structured around two forms of a single set class, [025]. The set class featured in the melody also occurs in the bass: [025] in the form (t13) makes up the bass pitches over the entire movement; (t13) is beamed together and labeled in example 2.7's middle staff. Contiguous pitches within the chromatic, predominantly stepwise melody naturally produce many forms of 3–2 [013], which saturate the music. While some forms are I- rather than T-related, they all span a minor third (ip3). These forms of 3–2 are

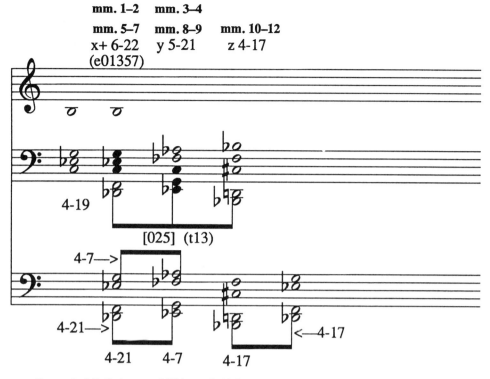

Example 2.7. Quintet, op. 39/IV, mm. 1–12, harmonic set-class relations

excerpted and beamed together in example 2.6c. Such economy of pitch-class sets is reflected in the harmony of this movement.

In example 2.7's upper two staves the three harmonies are extracted from mm. 1–9. A subset of the first harmony, (e037) (4–19), is shown to the left. The (e037) occurs explicitly at the movement's conclusion, where it is formed by the viola arpeggiation and G–E♭–B in the three upper voices. A subset of (e037), (037), is embedded in every sonority in the bass and viola over mm. 1–9. Example 2.7 shows (037) with filled-in noteheads.

Example 2.7's lowest bass staff is an analysis of the relation between horizontally and vertically formed tetrachords embedded in chords x, y, and z. Each vertically formed tetrachord contributes a dyad which pairs with a dyad from a neighboring tetrachord to form a series of intertwined and identical set classes. The set class 4–21 [0246] is formed within chord x and also by the two lowest dyads in chords x– and y–. Chord y contains a form of 4–7 [0145]; 4–7 is also made by the two upper dyads of chords x– and y– in the lowest staff of the example. Chord z contains a form of 4–17, which is also made by the two lower dyads of chords x– and z– on the lowest staff of the example.

Example 2.8 is a survey of the opening twelve measures of the quintet. It

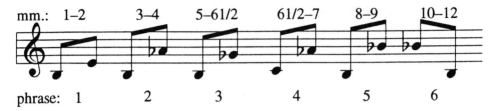

Example 2.8. Quintet, op. 39/IV, mm. 1–12, ambitus of phrases

charts the changing ambitus through its six phrases. The upward expansion of the ambitus is disturbed only once, when phrase 3 contracts phrase 2's ambitus by a whole step. Phrases 5 and 6 have the largest span, extending from B3 to B♭4. The gradually expanding phrase ambitus climaxes in m. 10 when the sixth and final phrase brings in B♭4, the melodic peak. Besides being registrally accented, B♭4 in m. 10 is stressed in several other ways. First, the dynamics have gradually increased from piano in m. 7, through crescendo in the middle of m. 9, to forte in m. 10, exactly coincident with B♭4 in the oboe; mm. 10–12 then fade into piano. B♭4 occurred earlier, in m. 9. There, however, though placed on the downbeat, B♭4 occurred in midphrase. In m. 10 B♭4 is highlighted: it begins both the phrase and the measure.

The upper strand in example 2.8—E, G♭, A♭, B♭—is a form of 4–21 [0246], a collection which derives from the whole-tone scale (02468t). All of the pitch classes in example 2.8 taken together make (468teo), a form of 6–22 [012468], the same pitch-class set as chord x+ in example 2.7, which comprises the harmonic chord x plus the melodic note B.[26] The overlapping of forms of identical set classes derives from the structures shown in the lowest staff in example 2.7.

In the foregoing analysis I seek to demonstrate that certain features of coherence in Prokofiev's music can be addressed by studying pitch-class structure. Many of these features are not detectable by traditional tonal analytical techniques.

THE TOCCATA LINE: AN EXAMPLE FROM
THE TOCCATA, OP. 11

Given both the association of the toccata with the keyboard and Prokofiev's pianistic career, one would naturally expect piano music to represent the toccata line. Indeed, most of the examples that Prokofiev cites are piano music, but he goes on to cite the *Scythian Suite* and *Le Pas d'acier* as illustrative pieces. The toccata might best be described, then, as a musical surface which consists of even, rapid, running figuration. To the piano music in the toccata line, we can add pieces such as the scherzo of the Violin Concerto no. 1, op. 19, and the scherzo from the Violin Sonata no. 2, op. 94a, a masterful instance of rhythmic drive, manipulation, and control.[27]

Of the three pieces which Prokofiev mentions as examples of his toccata line, two of them, the Toccata, op. 11, and the scherzo of the Piano Concerto no. 2, op. 16, exhibit absolutely unbroken sixteenth motion on the musical surface. For the pianist the relentless sixteenth motion challenges technique and stamina. The same motion differently challenges the composer, who must maintain rhythmic interest through means other than a varied attack-point rhythm.

Rhythmic aspects of the Toccata, op. 11, provide an example of Prokofiev's toccata line; I will concentrate on hypermetric structure.[28] The Toccata adheres to a four-bar hypermeasure comprising a total of eight written beats. A hypermeasure consists of four written measures; each written measure is one hypermetric beat, and each hypermetric beat consists of four written eighth notes. Measure numbers refer to written measures; hypermeasures are referenced separately.

Over mm. 1–12, the left-hand octaves syncopate but do not displace the written downbeat, thereby enhancing the piece's rhythmic force. A thickening of texture in m. 5, m. 9, m. 10, and m. 14 and the accented upbeat in m. 12 all help to mark the written downbeat.[29]

However, mm. 25–28 challenge the established metric scheme in two ways. First, as Prokofiev's beaming shows, the right hand attempts to shift the downbeat by placing it an eighth note earlier than it occurred in mm. 1–24. This challenge is rather weak in itself because once established, the four-bar hypermeter is not so easily abandoned. Although the arpeggios are beamed against the written barline, registral accent compensates. The right hand repeats a note on the last two sixteenths of every beamed-together four-sixteenths arpeggio. The repeated note is either the highest or lowest pitch of its arpeggio, and its onset (on the third sixteenth of each four-sixteenths arpeggio) coincides with each beat of the written measure, as is the case, for example, at the downbeat of m. 25. In the right hand alone, both written downbeats and hypermetric beats persist.

More effective at distorting the established metric scheme is a regrouping of the eighth notes in the left hand. The established pattern in mm. 1–24 is four eighth notes per hypermetric beat. But the left hand, beginning in m. 25, organizes the hypermetric beats differently, that is, into one group of four eighths, followed by two groups of three eighths, followed by three groups of two eighths $[4 + (2 \times 3) + (3 \times 2)]$. Mm. 25–28 thereby introduce a slightly quickened pulse, which intensifies and accelerates the drive toward m. 29 without, however, distorting the timespan of the original four-bar hypermeasure $[4 \times 4$ eighths $= 4$ eighths $+ (3 \times 2$ eighths$) + (2 \times 3$ eighths$)]$.

For the most part, Prokofiev refrains from tampering with the timespan of a hypermeasure in the Toccata, confining himself to syncopations and distortions of the hypermetrical beats within the hypermeasure.

Though one might expect harmonic structure and compositional process in works from the modern line to be uniquely constituted in comparison with more mainstream works, such is not the case. In fact, Prokofiev's harmonic vocabulary and compositional style are remarkably consistent throughout his entire oeuvre.

Two aspects of his compositional style do change, however. These are, first, Prokofiev's handling of rhythmic structure and, second, the relative balance of harmonic and contrapuntal surfaces. Though he always had a keen ear for surface rhythm—evidenced by the early inception of the toccata line—consistent control of large-scale rhythmic structure came only with experience and maturity. In his later works, Prokofiev's handling of transitions, pacing, and especially phrase structure show that his design skill eventually grew to encompass large-scale rhythmic design as well as surface rhythm. Strictly regular and square hypermetrical design, present in some earlier works, is absent in the later ones, where a remarkably plastic and flexible phrase structure animates the music.

As we have already seen, in the domain of pitch structure Prokofiev had predilections for certain set classes which cut across more than one line. For example, either 4–19 [0148] or one of its subsets, 3–12 [048], has appeared in op. 9/1, a lyrical piece; the *March* from *Love for Three Oranges,* a grotesque piece; and op. 39/IV, a modern piece.

While stylistic consistency is apparent in the small number of set classes that continue to appear in music of widely differing character that was composed during different periods, the relative predominance of harmony and counterpoint on the musical surface changes over time. A harmonically slanted surface in his earlier music yields to a contrapuntal emphasis in music written in the late 1920s and early 1930s. Beginning around the time of his return to the Soviet Union (that is, beginning around 1936), Prokofiev's music strikes a balance in which the textures favor conspicuous counterpoint no more than they favor harmonic density and complexity.

In the following discussion I examine the difference between "harmonic" and "contrapuntal" music. Prokofiev's early experiments in harmony are wholly understandable and consistent with his quest for novelty. Innovation in late nineteenth-century music is easily perceived in terms of harmonic evolution. Chordal structures become thicker; added notes reach past chordal sevenths; dissonance treatment is bolder and less strict. It was in harmonic terms, after all, that Schoenberg characterized the historical development of music when he discussed the "emancipation of the dissonance."[30] In the earlier experimental works, we find Prokofiev concentrating on rich and dissonant chords (as in *Sar-*

casmes, op. 17, or the Quintet, op. 39) that feature considerably embellished triads. The title *Sarcasmes* barely conceals his intent to mock tradition. Prokofiev also gave titles from philosophical texts to two pieces with overtly contrapuntal surfaces. One can only surmise that counterpoint was the musical manifestation of a scholarly seriousness which occupied Prokofiev after 1930 or so.

HARMONIC EMPHASIS: *VISIONS FUGITIVES,* OP. 22/10

The *Visions Fugitives,* op. 22/10, are an example of Prokofiev's harmonic emphasis. The *Visions Fugitives* were composed in 1912–1914, while Prokofiev was at the Conservatory. In the *Autobiography,* Prokofiev compares the *Visions Fugitives* with a group of other pieces, including the *Sarcasmes.* He speaks of "the search for a new musical language" in the *Sarcasmes.*[31] By contrast, he describes "a certain 'softening of temper' " which is evident in the *Visions Fugitives.*[32] Despite being rated by Prokofiev as less questing and modern than the *Sarcasmes,* however, the *Visions Fugitives* do provide a chronicle of his early harmonic experimentation.

The *Visions Fugitives* belong to the same tradition as Schumann's character pieces, Beethoven's *Bagatelles,* and Musorgsky's *Pictures at an Exhibition.* But where Schubert's waltzes and Chopin's mazurkas are studies of a single type, the *Visions Fugitives* are not affiliated with any single type. Unlike the *March* from *Love for Three Oranges,* op. 22/10 has a grotesque nature more broadly derived from playing with our expectations of traditional tonal function.

Op. 22/10, marked *Ridicolosamente,* owes its ridiculous character to large melodic leaps, sudden and exaggerated dynamic changes in mm. 3–6, abrupt changes of direction in mm. 16–21, and short, insistently repeating motives, as over mm. 7–10 and mm. 15–16. The relentlessly staccato accompaniment enhances its ridiculous character, as though Prokofiev intentionally eschews lyric grace.

Prokofiev gives enough clues and tonal signs that, with very little strain, tonal focus can be heard in B♭: the piece bears the five-flat signature; the left hand's registral extremes are marked by the B♭ octave; the repeated minor third B♭/D♭ in the left hand and the reiterated F and D♭ in the right hand together project a B♭-minor triad. However, several gestures challenge the B♭ tonality. For example, the left hand's upper third over mm. 1–18 is G♭/B♭, which, along with the left hand's lower third B♭/D♭, forms a G♭-major triad in six-three position. Over mm. 1–18 the left hand never states F, whose combination with B♭/D♭ would produce a B♭-minor chord, so the G♭ chord, even if generated by an implied 5–6 motion, never allows B♭ minor to settle in solidly.

Another challenge to a traditional B♭ tonality is posed by the D♭ augmented triad, which first clearly arrives in m. 11. Though an augmented triad built on 3̂

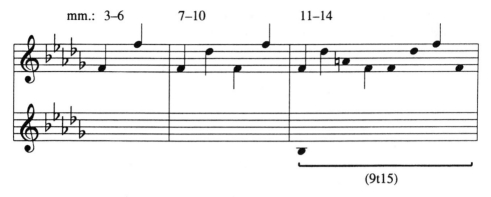

Example 2.9. Op. 22/10, mm. 3–14, emergence of (9t15)

in minor is common enough, it invariably arises within some dominant harmony: $\hat{3}$ displaces the dominant's $\hat{2}$ to produce an augmented mediant. Prokofiev does nothing unusual by devoting a great deal of attention to the D♭ augmented triad; however, he treats it in an unorthodox manner.

How the D♭ augmented triad gradually emerges is traced in example 2.9. In mm. 3–6, whose melody is compressed into a single gesture in the example, Prokofiev begins composing the D♭ triad by repeating the octave ascent F4–F5. A barline in the example separates the activity of mm. 7–10, which diminute the octave leap and create two upswinging intervals in place of one: now the music moves from F4–D♭5 to F4–F5. The notes stemmed upward in mm. 7–10 come from mm. 3–6; the notes stemmed downward are the new embellishing notes. Mm. 11–14 embellish F4–D♭5–F4–F5 from mm. 7–10 by increasing the rhythmic activity to continuous eighth-note motion (with sixteenths appearing in m. 14). Notes stemmed upward in mm. 11–14 come from mm. 3–6; notes stemmed downward come from mm. 7–10; and filled-in noteheads are the new embellishing notes.

In m. 11 and in m. 13 the melody brings in A♮, completing the augmented triad. Along with B♭ from the left-hand ostinato, the D♭ augmented triad shown on example 2.9 forms the larger set (9t15), a form of 4–19 [0148]. Other forms of set class 4–19 occur in m. 16 ((6912)) and in m. 24 ((te26), (67t2), and (t126)).

Witty and characteristic is Prokofiev's treatment of the note A as a stable tone in certain passages. The note A is, after all, the leading tone of B♭, and Prokofiev does, in fact, treat it as such at the piece's conclusion, where A3 resolves, by octave transfer, to B♭2. A4–to–B♭4 also occurs in the cadence over mm. 20–21. But in mm. 15–17 the pitch A does not resolve. Instead, D♭/F slides up to D/F♯, while B♭ and A remain invariant. Two forms of 4–19 are created in the process, (9715) and (69t2); these two forms are pitch inversions about A5/B♭4, the two invariant pitches between the two chords.

Registral and metric accent in mm. 17–20 project Db5 and A5 in m. 17, F4 in m. 18, Db4 in m. 19, and Db5 in m. 20, another form of the Db augmented triad. If we regard Db4 as an embellishment of Db5, then we can hear the high A5 balance with F4 about Db5, the pitch on which this excerpt begins and ends.

In figuration and metric design, m. 19 and similar passages clearly derive from mm. 1–16. The derived passages also feature augmented triads. For example, the D augmented triad first heard embedded in the last half of m. 16 reappears unadorned on the downbeat at m. 22 and at m. 30. The augmented triad, often expressed within a form of 4–19 [0148], thus saturates the music.

Dominant-to-tonic motions are first adumbrated in m. 16 when Db–F–A moves as a kind of leading tone to D–F♯–A. A more traditional dominant-to-tonic progression can be heard in the melody in example 2.10, taken from mm. 24–26.[33] Major triads move from a G root to a C root in mm. 24–25 and then from an Ab root to a Db root in mm. 25–26. On a larger scale, the leading-tone motion of C in m. 25 to Db in m. 26 expresses a slightly less traditional dominant-tonic relation. The cadence on Db, the relative major of Bb, is a traditional key relation.

But Prokofiev was not content simply to provide traditional tonal signs; instead, he twisted and distorted these signs. The G dominant chord, isolated by register, is embedded within a form of 5–21 (267te), a set containing two forms of 4–19 [0148].[34] As we have seen, the musical surface is littered with forms of 4–19 [0148] and 3–12 [048]. The C-major chord to which the G resolves is a major seventh chord, a form of 4–20 [0158], reproducing at T6 the opening "Gb major seventh chord" (also a form of 4–20 [0158]). More immediately perceptible is the tritone relation binding the roots of m. 24's left-hand chord, a Gb (six-three) chord to the C (major seventh) chord in the left hand in m. 25. Still, the G-to-C dominant-to-tonic progression is sufficiently strong to coexist with the tritone relation without losing its identity.[35]

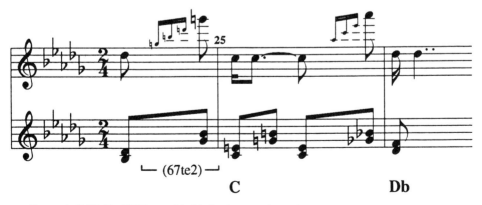

Example 2.10. Op. 22/10, mm. 24–26, dominant–tonic motion

Around 1928–1935 Prokofiev shifted his musical emphasis from harmony to counterpoint. During these years he seems to have been of a particularly serious turn of mind. In 1928 he composed the piano piece *Choses en soi* (Things in Themselves), op. 45, the work's sober style and its academic title being perhaps a delayed reaction to studying Kant, whose work he mentions reading in 1917.[36] The overtly contrapuntal textures of *Choses en soi* (1928); String Quartet no. 1 (1930), op. 50; *Sonatinas* (1932), op. 54; and *Pensées* (Thoughts) (1934), op. 62, are hallmarks of a new approach to composition. As though compensating for the extroversion of earlier music, the conspicuous counterpoint appears as a metaphor for seriousness and contemplation and is reflected in the two philosophically titled works which enclose this period, *Choses en soi* and *Pensées*. Despite the change in demeanor and style observed in works which were composed in 1928–1935, the pitch-structural substance is remarkably consistent with the earlier and more harmonically focused works.

It was quite natural for Prokofiev to carry on his early harmonic experimentation in music written for the instrument with which he was so naturally comfortable, as is the case in the *Sarcasmes* and in the *Visions Fugitives*. Similarly, the string quartet medium seems ideally suited for exploring contrapuntal surfaces.

Example 2.11 is an excerpt from the String Quartet no. 1, op. 50, part of the closing of the first movement's first theme group. The grand staff labeled "a"

Example 2.11. String Quartet no. 1, op. 50/I, mm. 21–23

shows the melody in the treble clef, and chords taken from the second violin and viola are verticalized in the bass clef. On the staff labeled "b" the harmonies from staff *a* are grouped and labeled. As is apparent already in the bass clef of staff *a*, there exists an archlike symmetry in the chord progression: a G♯-minor chord leads to a C (minor) chord, followed by a C (major) chord returning to a G♯-minor chord. The harmonies grouped together on staff *b* make staff *a*'s symmetry explicit: a single form of 6–20 [014589], (3478e0), which is segmented in two different ways, frames a form of 4–17 [0347]. First, 6–20 is expressed as an E major seventh chord in first inversion plus a C-minor six-three chord. Second, 6–20 is expressed as a C-major six-three chord plus a G♯-minor chord.[37] The two triads in the middle of the progression, C minor and C major, together form 4–17 [0347], another sonority of which Prokofiev was particularly fond.

As one might well expect, there is a tonal component embedded within staff *b*'s chord progression. The staff labeled "c" extracts this tonal component. By respelling E♭ as D♯ and G as F𝄪, I show a two-voice outline, shown by the opposed stems, which takes a G♯ tonic to a D♯ dominant, with leading tone, and back. As in op. 22/10, tonal function here successfully survives rather liberal obfuscation.

MATURITY IN DESIGN SKILL: THE SCYTHIAN
SUITE AND THE PIANO SONATA NO. 8

Counterpoint did not again dominate Prokofiev's musical textures as plainly as it did in the String Quartet no. 1 and the piano music of 1928–1935. In Prokofiev's later music, counterpoint and harmony were subtly balanced and elegantly integrated. One particularly clear and successful example of the fully mature Prokofiev is the Piano Sonata no. 8, op. 84, composed in 1939–1944. In addition to balancing harmony and counterpoint, the Piano Sonata no. 8 illustrates Prokofiev's mastery of large-scale rhythmic structure. Before reencountering the Piano Sonata no. 8 let us look at aspects of the *Scythian Suite* (1914–1915) to better gauge Prokofiev's maturing design skill. The *Scythian Suite* is structured along familiar harmonic lines, but it does occasionally suffer from a rhythmic squareness, a problem which the older Prokofiev was able to solve.

In the *Scythian Suite,* part I, the music of R0–R1 is introductory and prepares the arrival of the first main theme at R2 by establishing and incrementally embellishing an ostinato. The ostinato creates a regular four-bar hypermeter. Over R0–R7 there are two instances of this regular hypermeter being distorted. Mm. 1–7 constitute two hypermeasures. Mm. 1–4 are a regular four-bar hypermeasure, but in mm. 5–7 four hypermetric beats are compressed into three by deleting the last hypermetric beat (that is, the last written measure), thereby distorting the four-beat hypermetric scheme. Further, the third hypermetric beat of

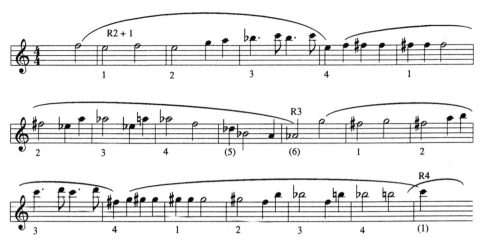

Example 2.12. *Scythian Suite,* op. 20, part I, R2+1 through R4

the distorted hypermeasure is itself compressed by deleting one written beat so that a written bar of $\frac{3}{4}$ (=1 hypermetric beat) replaces a written bar of $\frac{4}{4}$ (=1 hypermetric beat).[38] The deletion propels the music into R1.

Example 2.12 gives the melody over R2+1 – R4. Arabic numbers mark the constituents of hypermeasures. In the excerpt the established phrase / hypermetric scheme is distorted twice. The first instance occurs leading into R3, where a four-bar hypermeasure is extended by two written bars, shown by the parenthetical measure numbers. This distortion helps mark the varied restatement of melodic material. The crossed slurs in the last line of the example show the second distortion, an overlap, created where the fourth phrase of R3 concludes simultaneously with the beginning of R4's material. Both irregularities mark a formal boundary.

R4 – R7 adhere to a rigid design. Four-bar hypermeasures set in conspicuously—in fact, the four-bar hypermeter is undistorted from R3 to the end of R7, a total of forty-four written bars. The phrases are five bars long, with a constant overlapping of first and last bars.

The rhythmic design, while monotonous in some respects, is not without its sophistication, particularly in the hypermetric compression in m. 7 and at the distortion within R2. Overlap also helps to make the music more flowing. However, the strongest feeling imparted by the rhythm comes from repetition and inflexibility, so that the overlapping scheme of R4 – R7 quickly stymies the music's rhythmic fluency. As a means of dissipating the energy of the opening through R3, the music of R4 – R7 seems justified. But as a source of rhythmic development in the movement, the passage is less successful; its repetitiveness only enhances an already pronounced mechanical feel.

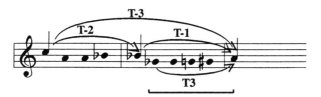

Example 2.13. *Scythian Suite*, op. 20, part I, inversional balance in melody of R4

The new melody which enters at R4 is simple and rhythmically uncomplicated, and it moves in small intervals. The rhythmic material is a four-bar pattern. The first and third bars both move in even quarter notes, while the fourth bar differs from the second by having the two eighth notes on beat 3 rather than on beat 2. The pitch material moves in two-bar blocks, with each successive block transposed down a minor third. There are only two harmonic chord types, 4–18 and 4–19, formed out of the dense chromatic texture. A fourfold transposition of the initial two bars returns their pitch classes.

The downward transpositional process, shown by the $T-3$ arrow above the staff in example 2.13, is diminuted in two increments: from the first downbeat to the second, the melody is transposed downward at $T-2$; from the second downbeat to the beginning of the next pattern it is transposed downward at $T-1$. In example 2.13 this descent is marked with upward stems. Driving to the downbeat of the example's third measure is an ascending, compensatory gesture, bracketed in the example, which sweeps upward through ip3 from below. The arrows labeled "$T-3$" and "$T3$" in the example show the inversional balance.

In example 2.14 I extract the bracketed gesture from example 2.13 and add the chords which harmonize it. A measured inversional process moves the music from one chord to the next, labeled in two ways below the staff. As "(a)" shows, consecutive chromatic increments raise the axes of inversion, as well as the beat-to-beat melody. As "(b)" shows, the index numbers increase in increments of two.

The rhythmic design of this passage, sophisticated in some respects, never-

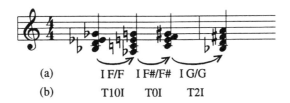

(a)	I F/F	I F#/F#	I G/G
(b)	T10I	T0I	T2I

Example 2.14. *Scythian Suite*, op. 20, part I, harmonic structure of the melody in example 2.13

theless stamps the piece as an early one because the piece has a relatively inflexible hypermetric structure and because Prokofiev allows motivic repetition to veer from sequential emphasis toward monotony. But the rich interaction of melodic pitch structure and harmonic progression over R4–R7 is not untypical of Prokofiev's compositional style generally.

The Piano Sonata no. 8 is invested with a phrase rhythm more closely approximating an easy, proselike flow than strict poetic regularity.[39] The first movement's first theme is notable also because of its moderately elaborate period structure, which is somewhat unusual for Prokofiev, who often preferred a single phrase to a period structure for sonata-form first themes.

The first theme group, mm. 1–34, comprises four two-phrase periods. The first and last of these are virtually identical, so that the four periods are arranged in the order ABCA. Strong cadences in m. 9, m. 17, m. 25, and m. 34 articulate each period. Period A is a two-phrase interrupted period in B♭ (I—V, I—I). Both phrases in period B cadence in B♭. Like period B, period C is a two-phrase repeated period (I—I, I—I), but in the subdominant key of E♭. Period C is the only non-tonic period.

The phrase and contrapuntal structures impart to the passage a rhythmic flexibility missing from the *Scythian Suite* excerpt. The bass in the opening nine measures contributes significantly to the rhythmic suppleness. Mm. 1–2 state a pedal B♭ while the upper voices mark off a clear $\frac{4}{4}$ meter. M. 2's downbeat is marked by the relatively large melodic leap from E4 to C5, contrasting with the confined melodic movement of m. 1. The rate of harmonic change quickens in m. 3 when the bass begins moving in half notes. The return to the original register, the increased rhythmic activity in the inner voice, and the faster harmonic rhythm leading to the dominant seventh chord in the last half of m. 4 all prepare a tonic arrival on the downbeat of m. 5. If the established half-note motion continues, then the dominant seventh chord will resolve on the downbeat of m. 5. But instead, the dominant root F is tied over through m. 5, no bass note at all is attacked on the downbeat of m. 5, and a half cadence closes out the first, five-measure phrase. Already the phrase rhythm is breathing unmechanically.

Mm. 6–9 begin parallel to mm. 1–5 but accelerate in m. 7 when the half-note bass motion arrives two beats earlier than in the first phrase. Then m. 8 directs the music toward E♭, especially through the bass tritone A♭/D and what would be a kind of leading-tone harmony in E♭ on the last eighth of the measure. The apparent double neighbor motion about E♭/G which begins in m. 9 continues to steer toward E♭. But on beat 2 of m. 9 the melody sidesteps the expected E♭ and jumps down to apply double neighbor motion to the B♭ tonic. In the bass at that same point C-to-F♯ comes in place of E♭/G (which would resolve m. 8's bass tritone) and also deflects the E♭ arrival. The upward leap in the bass from

C to the held half-note F# strongly syncopates the passage by placing registral and agogic accent on beat 2; B♭'s arrival at the end of the measure reinforces the syncopation by placing the first period's structural accent on m. 9, beat 4, another weak beat.[40]

If one can hear m. 5 distorting an underlying four-bar hypermeasure, then the first phrase extends the underlying structure from four to five measures. Similarly, and more locally, one could reinterpret the downbeat of m. 9, not as part of a syncopation figure, but as a wrongly notated extra fifth beat which should have appeared at the end of m. 8. In this new interpretation, m. 9, beat 2, is a strong downbeat, and beat 4 is a relatively strong third beat.[41] Phrase 2, like phrase 1, conceals a regular four-bar hypermeter beneath a slightly irregular surface. The reader can test this analysis by playing it: simply excise bar 5, take a slight ritard at the end of bar 4, and excise the first beat of m. 9. Of course, this recomposition, while plausible, undermines the phrase flexibility of these measures.

Mm. 10–17 affirm the tonic with cadences on B♭ in m. 14 and in m. 17. The eight-measure structure of mm. 10–17, however, results from eliding a five-

Example 2.15. Piano Sonata no. 8, op. 84/I, cadential similarities in mm. 13–14, mm. 19–21, and mm. 24–25

measure first phrase with a four-measure second phrase. The first period (mm. 1–9) had a nine-measure surface resulting from a 4 + 4 model transformed into a 5 + 4 surface. In the second period, Prokofiev, as though exploring the 5 + 4 scheme, creates an eight-measure surface by eliding the phrases. Only period C, mm. 18–25, is rhythmically regular; it is eight measures long, comprising two 4-bar phrases.

Subsequent periods pick up two aspects of period A's cadence. First, period C concludes in m. 25 with the E♭ arrival which was set up but avoided in m. 9. M. 26, beginning period D, follows with a B♭ chord, completing the subdominant-tonic progression implicit in m. 9.

Second, three cadences expand upon the F♯–B♭ bass motion which closes period A. Example 2.15a shows how double neighbor motion deriving from m. 9 embellishes G♭ in the bass of m. 13. The stems mark on-beat bass notes, and the dotted line indicates a shift in register. "UN" denotes upper neighbor, and "LN" denotes lower neighbor. The cadential motion in the bass from m. 13 to m. 14 is enharmonically equivalent to the bass in m. 9's cadence.

Example 2.15b shows how the bass approaches the cadence in m. 21. After dipping down a diminished octave from B♭ to B♮, the bass embellishes B♮ with a filled-in neighbor motion. Then the bass climbs up chromatically to E♭, shown by the downward stems and the slur from B♮ to E♭; from above, the bass moves from the dominant B♭ to the local tonic E♭, shown by the upward stems. A related cadence occurs over mm. 24–25, shown in example 2.15c.

3 Analytical Categories

I n the present chapter I organize the results of the analyses in Chapter 2 into analytical categories. After outlining the categories, I apply them in analyses of the Piano Sonata no. 4, op. 29, last movement, and the *Sarcasmes,* op. 17/2.

While Prokofiev's lines articulate important qualities in his work, the distinctions between lines are surprisingly indifferent to pitch structure. A line such as the grotesque may depend for its identity more upon distorting a type than upon expressing a particular collection of quintessentially grotesque pitches. Similarly, the toccata line clearly relies upon features of surface rhythm more than upon particular harmonies or melodies. Of course, not all aspects of a line are independent of pitch structure, and some lines may be strongly dependent on it. For instance, the lyric line may depend upon stepwise motion, which will impose some constraints upon its melodic pitch collections, and harmonies that feature perfect fourths and fifths. But, in general, pitch structure is remarkably consistent across all five lines.

Not only are the five lines surprisingly independent of pitch structure; they are not strictly correlated with particular periods, either. Lyric music can be found in works of all three periods, including the early works, where, however, grotesque and modern lines are, on the whole, more common. The toccata line can also claim a representative in each style period, though the middle, contrapuntal period is characterized less by extroverted lines, such as the toccata and grotesque lines, than by what one might interpret as classical restraint.

Not all of Prokofiev's pitch and rhythmic practice is fixed. The mutable aspects of his music were studied in the second part of the previous chapter. In the realm of pitch structure, despite a preference for a small number of certain set classes in all of the music, there was a shift from overtly harmonic music, through overtly contrapuntal music, to the balance between the two which Prokofiev achieved in his later works.

Prokofiev's control of phrase structure and large-scale form evolved gradually. Early on, his control over some of the problems posed by the toccata line was already in place. For music in the toccata line, a line which demands a high degree of regularity in the rhythmic surface, Prokofiev usually preserves some hypermetric level of rhythmic structure while altering a lower level. For example, a hypermeasure may contain four hypermetric beats in an established quadruple scheme, but the attack points may be unevenly spaced because the timespan between a hypermetric upbeat and the succeeding downbeat is smaller than that between any other pair of contiguous hyperbeats.

In contrast to his handling of surface rhythm in the toccata line, Prokofiev sometimes had difficulty, in his first period, in producing phrase flexibility. The hypermetric regularity in the *Scythian Suite* is predictable and distracting, while the flexible phrase structure of a later work such as op. 84's first movement is elegant and absorbing.

From the analyses of Chapter 2 one can draw five significant conclusions.

1. The surface of Prokofiev's music differs from the surface of traditionally tonal music.
2. Triads alone do not constitute the recurring characteristic sonorities of any given piece.
3. The individuality of a given piece is usually defined by a small number of set classes, which occur often and prominently and which include non-triadic collections.
4. If triads are present in the music, they usually occur with added notes, as in op. 33a, where a minor triad with an added note produces a form of 4−19 [0148]. Another commonly occurring set class is 4−17 [0347]; it includes 3−11 [037], the major or minor triad, in its subset structure. Non-tertian collections, often 4−23 [0257] as in op. 9/1, are also commonly heard in Prokofiev's music. The set class 4−23 [0257], while not containing a triadic subset (3−11 [037]), does emphasize interval class 5, a quintessentially tonal interval.

5. Some single structure or some single process often drives different aspects of the music. For instance, the first sonority in the Quintet, op. 39/IV, is 6–22, which helps structure the phrase ambitus in section A (see examples 2.7 and 2.8). A set may be deployed in more than one dimension or play more than one role in the music. But it is equally common for a collection of pitches or pitch classes to generate a process with broad application. For example, in the *Scythian Suite,* over R4, the process associated with a chromatic line raises the melody at the same time that it lifts the axes of inversion linking the harmonies. In the minuet from *Romeo and Juliet,* the ordered root succession Ab–Db–Ab–Gb–Ab over mm. 37–41 reflects the large-scale key structure of part 1. The set which generates such processes I will refer to as a structural set.

Types of Structural Sets

There are two general types of structural sets, those with tonal affiliations and those without. Of those with tonal affiliations, members of the largest category contain a triadic subset. This is not surprising since many of Prokofiev's characteristic harmonies are built upon triadic subsets—they contain a form of 3–11 [037]. However, rather than having the extra, non-triadic elements arising from stacking thirds, a scheme often advanced for late nineteenth-century harmony and jazz harmony, Prokofiev often attached extra elements chromatically to one of the triadic elements. In the stacked-thirds model, a chordal element's relation to the root is measured by stating how many thirds away from the root it lies. For example, a chordal seventh lies three thirds away from the root. Where the stacked-thirds model depends upon a consistent building scheme, the same is not true for Prokofiev's extended triads. The chromatically attached element (or elements) thus can sound pasted on, giving rise to the perception that it is a wrong note. Example 3.1 shows such an instance from the beginning of the Piano Sonata no. 4, third movement. Here, the Ab in the right hand of m. 3 does not arise out of any sort of chromatic context; it does not sound like a chordal thirteenth whose connection to the C triad is mediated by a chordal seventh, ninth, or eleventh. Rather, Ab sounds as though it has been glued on to the C triad.

Further investigation into this piece (to be undertaken later in this chapter) reveals that, together with the C triad, Ab forms a structural set, a form of 4–19 [0148], a commonly occurring sonority in Prokofiev's music. Besides 4–17 [0347] and 4–19 [0148], other possibilities for such chromatically enhanced triads not deriving from a stacked-thirds model are 4z29 [0137] and 4–18

Example 3.1. Piano Sonata no. 4, op. 29/III, mm. 1–13

[0147]. Another possible member of this category of chords is 4–14 [0237], but without much difficulty it can be heard (depending upon its particular realization) as a minor triad with an added major ninth, even without a chordal seventh as a mediating chord factor.[1]

The opening motif of the Symphony no. 3/I gives a form of 4–17 [0347] in the form (1458), another type of embellished triad. The highest and lowest pitches are A♭ and D♭, respectively, suggesting a D♭ arpeggiation. The metrically accented notes, F and E (enharmonically F♭) make up the shifting chordal third, now major, now minor. Beginning from the major third above that root, the violin traverses an ascending minor third up to the chordal fifth; then the violin reverses direction and, beginning on the minor third above the root, traverses a descending minor third down to the root. Inversional balance, here occurring about F/E♮ and highlighted by the two opposed minor thirds, is a regular feature of Prokofiev's music.

The form 4–23 [0257] owes its tonal sound to its emblematic ic5, which it maximizes uniquely for its cardinality. We encountered 4–23 [0257] in op. 9/1, analyzed in the previous chapter.

Like op. 9/1, the Piano Concerto no. 5, op. 55, fourth movement, owes much of the opening relaxed character to the sound of 4–23 [0257], a collection penetrating the bass, the melody, and the harmony. As we shall see in the analysis in Chapter 7, the collection of bass notes from mm. 5–12 is a form of 4–23 [0257], (57to). The same pitch-class collection occurs as the distinctive opening harmony.

The second general type of structural set lacks specifically tonal affiliations. Its largest, most commonly occurring category contains the chromatic set, usually small, and appearing as a form of either 3–1 [012] or 4–1 [0123]. The small chromatic structural set in Prokofiev's music is most often realized as a series of unit pitch intervals in continuously increasing or continuously decreasing order; its chromaticism is thereby expressed in virtually the most straightforward manner possible.

As we shall see in Chapter 4, the Piano Sonata no. 7's second movement relies heavily on the small chromatic set (I discuss a motive labeled "v") in many different guises.

In the fourth and final category of structural set belong remainders, whose members contain neither triads nor fifths and are not chromatic. While these sets are relatively rarer in Prokofiev's music than are members from the other three categories, they are by no means negligible. Later in the present chapter, I shall examine this type of set in op. 17/2, a piece in which 3−4 [015] predominates.

A frequently occurring progression encountered in Prokofiev's music, the triadic flip, needs to be mentioned here. There are two species of triadic flip. A "fifth flip" is that inversion which exchanges the root and the fifth. A "third flip" inverts the triad about its mediant. In both cases, the triadic flip changes the mode of the triad. The fifth flip only changes mode, whereas the third flip changes mode as well as moves the chordal root either a half step up or a half step down.

An especially clear instance of the triadic flip occurs in op. 62/3, mm. 1−2. A third flip takes the E-minor triad of m. 1 to an E♭-major triad in m. 2. Thus the process is I^G [I^G (47e) = (37t)]. The triadic flip is a pitch-class operation. The third flip I^G exchanges E (pc4), the root of the E-minor triad, and B♭ (pc10), the fifth of the E♭-major triad; IG exchanges B (pc11), the fifth of the E-minor triad, and E♭ (pc3), the root of the E♭-major triad; G (pc7) is held invariant by I^G.[2]

Triadic flips can be alternately chained together. Example 3.2 shows the four possibilities and their results. Examples 3.2a and 3.2b begin with a major triad; examples 3.2c and 3.2d begin with a minor triad. Examples 3.2a and 3.2c alternate third flip with fifth flip; examples 3.2b and 3.2d alternate fifth flip with third flip. Instances of these progressions are surprisingly common, as in the Piano Sonata no. 2/II, mm. 35−37, where fifth flips are alternated with third flips (a

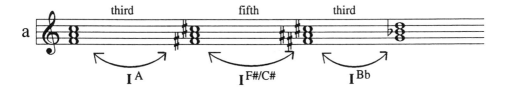

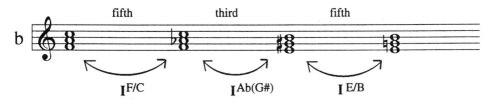

Example 3.2. Triadic flips

passage not discussed in this book). In Chapter 5 (example 5.14) I discuss alternating fifth and third flips in the Symphony no. 6/I.

Listening to Wrong-Note Music: A Model

Chapters 1 and 2 addressed the apparent "bad fit" of traditional and innovative
elements that is a feature of Prokofiev's grotesque line. More generally, that bad
fit appears under the heading "wrong note"; in the guise of a wrong note it can
cut across all five lines, not only the grotesque. Not all of Prokofiev's music is
wrong-note music. In fact, many pieces display a contextual homogeneity which
is inconsistent with the contextual heterogeneity advanced by the wrong-note
model. The advantage of studying wrong-note music is that it offers a convenient introduction to Prokofiev's music precisely because distinctions such as
those between right note and wrong note and between tonal and non-tonal are
so clear.

By acknowledging contingently the status of some notes as wrong, we will
also be able to account for coherence in the music. Below I interpret the experience of wrong-note music, following over the course of the piece the changing
status of the wrong note as it becomes an "integrated" note and even a right
note.

In this model the musical context of the opening establishes a tonal center as
well as a goal. The context generates some sort of expectation, deriving from
the listener's familiarity with similar goals in other pieces. The expectation may
be of a general nature, as in "I expect this piece to continue in the key of D" or
"the bass in this style of music will alternate between $\hat{1}$ and $\hat{5}$." The expectation
may be more specific, as in "I expect the next note to be C♯."

The expectation is contradicted when an element appears which seems to be
either a contextual superfluity or an impediment to achieving the expected goal.
The anomalous element is the "wrong note." Because the wrong note sounds
foreign in the setting in which it first appears, its relation to the other notes in
that context is indefinite and unclear. The wrong note (along with other elements) produces a motive—the structural set—which has significance either as
a pitch-class set or as the source for more broadly applicable processes which
derive from the structure of the motive itself. As the music unfolds, it teaches us
how the wrong note may be integrated into the context, thereby making concrete certain hitherto indefinite relations.

The structural set bridges the space between familiar contexts and wrong
notes. By analyzing how the structural set behaves in a piece and how its occurrences are related, we can understand how it embraces wrong notes and shows
their impact beyond the local context in which they first arise. These wrong

notes are not, in fact, wrong. Usually they insinuate themselves into many different musical levels, and we discover that the sounds and relations they create actually form both the piece's structural underpinning and its characteristic surface sonorities. We can follow this model as it is realized in the third and final movement of Prokofiev's Piano Sonata no. 4, a movement very well behaved according to our model.

PIANO SONATA NO. 4/III

In the Piano Sonata no. 4, op. 29, subtitled "From Old Notebooks," Prokofiev reworks earlier material and integrates both a movement from a juvenile symphony, composed during his years at the Conservatory, and a juvenile piano sonata.[3] Let us concentrate on mm. 1–17, part of the first thematic group in a rondo form (the first thematic group continues over mm. 18–25, which repeat mm. 10–18). The opening tonal context of C major is set out by several different tonal gestures, above all by the C-major scale of the introductory flourish. The flourish ends on the fortissimo C triple octave in m. 2, which marks the registral upper limit of the passage. When the movement gets fully under way in m. 3, the widely spaced C-major triad arpeggiated in the left hand of mm. 3–5 confirms the tonal center.

Consequently, we have a clear sense of this as a piece in C major. But intruding upon the C-major tonality are several wrong notes. In m. 2, F♯ and A♭ enter at the end of an upward sweep through an arpeggiated C triad. F♯ tops off the arpeggiation in m. 2, beat 2. A♭ enters on the next downbeat, answering motivically the downbeat of m. 2 and sounding starkly against the C triad arpeggiated beneath in the left hand.

We can analyze F♯ and A♭ as chromatic neighbors encircling a deeper-level dominant scale degree, G. However, G does not entirely absorb the weight of the decorative chromatic notes. As the goal of m. 2's upsweeping arpeggiation, A♭'s prominence is imperfectly captured in its embellishing, neighbor status. A♭'s metric accent reinforces its registral accent. G, on the other hand, is an upbeat beginning; it initiates a drive toward the downbeat of m. 4. That the composer does not slur A♭ to G helps confirm their separateness. Too, the octave doubling and the textural relief provided by the left-hand arpeggiation mark the A♭ as a prominent note left hanging even after G's entrance. A♭'s prominence is inconsistent with the prevailing C-major tonality. Indeed, A♭ and F♯ are not easily disposed of, for they resurface in mm. 10–13 to inflect the triads connecting an F triad in m. 10 to a C triad in m. 13.

The upbeat to m. 4 initiates the first of a series of four downward arpeggiations in the right hand, each of which is phrased together in the music. G–to–E in the upbeat to m. 4 creates an expectation that the music will continue on and, following the lead of the left hand, completely arpeggiate a C-major triad. But at the third note the music overshoots the expected goal by a half step, landing on B instead of C, thereby contradicting expectation. The C-major context demands the dissonant B resolve, and it would be understood to do so on the melodic C three sixteenth notes later. But, again, Prokofiev's phrasing does not support such a reading: to hear B as an appoggiatura to C, one would expect the B, the octave E, and the C to be grouped together by a slur as well as a beam. Prokofiev expressly does not do so; instead, he marks the B tenuto and legato and begins a new slur (non leggiere) on the octave E. The composer continues motivically in this manner in each successive arpeggiation, overshooting the expected pitches of the C triad without resolving the legato, tenuto, dissonant notes. The second arpeggiation overshoots G and hits F♯, the third overshoots E and hits D♯, and the fourth overshoots C and hits B. The result is that the metrically stressed tenuto pitches concluding each local arpeggiation themselves arpeggiate a larger-scale B-major triad, pressuring the C-major tonal center downward.

Like B4 in m. 4, the staccato B3 in the right hand of m. 5, beat 2, could begin restoring the C tonic by resolving upward to C4. But instead, B3 avoids the resolution and passes through C4, landing on D♭, another "wrong note," now a half step too high. The right hand of m. 6 affirms that arrival by accenting and then arpeggiating a D♭ triad.

The D♭ triad of m. 6 is a kind of pivot, with two functions. On the one hand, as chordal roots, D♭ and B balance inversionally about C. On the other hand, in the musical flow from m. 6 to m. 8, D♭ is a tritone substitution for the dominant.

The six-three chord over B in m. 7 weakly cadences on m. 8's tonic. The F-minor chord in m. 10 (inflected by A♭) initiates an elaborated plagal cadence which passes through an E-minor triad and a D triad in mm. 11–12 (inflected by F♯) on its way to C. The plagal cadence is followed by the authentic cadence which closes this opening statement in m. 17 and again in m. 25 when the passage is repeated.

C major is reposeful: with varying degrees of success it absorbs and resolves dissonances. In addition to its role as a point of tonal focus, the tonic C participates in three important inversional schemes, all of which were adumbrated in mm. 2–3, where F♯ and A♭ encircled G. The root C is the midpoint between a B-major triad and a D♭–major triad (which contain, respectively, the chromatic inflections F♯ and A♭ from mm. 2–3). More conventionally, the root C is the midpoint between subdominant and dominant, as that relation is realized in the plagal cadence over mm. 10–13 and the authentic cadence closing this thematic statement.

C continues its inversional role in mm. 10–13: C5 exchanges E5 (four half-steps above C5) and Ab4 (four half-steps below C5). C5 is embellished by an arpeggiation in m. 11. The inversional symmetry about C is reflected rhythmically as well. In the melody, C5 occupies the strong beats of the central two measures, mm. 10–11, framed by E5 in m. 10 and Ab4 in m. 13.

F♯ and, in particular, Ab scratch the otherwise pure C-major diatonic surface more deeply than traditionally tonal chromatic embellishments would, and in several different ways. While this music is not traditionally tonal, C major is nevertheless projected by the introductory scalar flourish, the arpeggiated C chord in the left hand, and the cadential bass progression in mm. 16–17. Each of these three gestures is a tonal interpreter.

In perceiving some note as wrong in Prokofiev's music, a listener virtually always discerns it against a tonal background (this is the "bad fit" of traditional and innovative elements). The concept of tonal interpreter captures those aspects of a passage which create tonal stability without also asserting that all components of the passage so contribute. By a tonal interpreter I shall mean a harmonic triad, a diatonic scale segment, or a functional bass segment or progression whenever such a set is heard to organize pitches around it into a locally tonal scheme.[4]

Tonal interpreters may occur anywhere in a composition, but they characteristically occur in the beginning of a piece, where they create and anchor a tonal context. Tonal interpreters appear transparent, permitting "wrong notes" to shine through. The meaning of the wrong notes at such an early point in the piece may be obscure. Almost invariably, the meaning of the apparently wrong note depends upon further working out of musical material.

In this third movement of the Piano Sonata no. 4, the pitch-class set 4–19 [0148] appears in two segmentations, which are characteristic of this work as well as many others. The first segmentation presents 4–19 as a form of 3–11 [037], that is, as either a major or a minor triad, plus one more note attached chromatically to an element of the triad. The second segmentation presents 4–19 as an augmented triad (3–12 [048]), plus one more note attached chromatically to an element of that augmented triad. In this movement, 4–19's constituent elements rarely resonate with a democratic equality. Instead, one or another of its subsets predominate: tonal contexts highlight 3–11; non-tonal contexts highlight 3–12.

The set 4–19 in the form (0478) makes its first, very prominent appearance in m. 3 when the octave Ab sounds against the C-major triad arpeggiated in the left hand. Also, mm. 10–13 begin and end with two different forms of 4–19, both of which contain Ab: m. 10 comprises (0458), and m. 13 comprises (0478). The two forms share the common subset (048), the augmented triad—precisely the form of the augmented triad in the melody of mm. 10–13 (E–C–Ab). The

Example 3.3. Piano Sonata no. 4, op. 29/III, mm. 14–17, 4–19 [0148] and 8–19 [01245689]

two forms of 4–19 are inversions-about-C, each of the other. The arpeggiated figure in the left hand of m. 10 segments that 4–19 into a tonal-interpreting F-minor triad plus the "wrong note" E; the texture of m. 13 analogously segments its I-related form of 4–19 into a tonal-interpreting C-major triad plus the "wrong note" Ab. The F-minor and C-major triads enjoy an inversional relation; as pointed out above, the "wrong notes" E and Ab are inversionally related, balanced about C.

Example 3.3 shows how, at the end of the first section, 4–19 and its complement, 8–19, saturate the texture of mm. 14–17, a variation of mm. 3–6. The notes stemmed and beamed together in the top treble analytical staff are forms of 4–19 in the right hand. In the lower treble analytical staff brackets show that the tenuto pitches together form 8–19 in the form (45789e01).

The set 4–19 and its subset 3–12 are ubiquitous over mm. 1–25. Of 4–19's two characteristic segmentations, that which features 3–11 predominates as expected within the C-major context. The set 8–19, the abstract complement of 4–19, then emerges in the closing measures. Despite being featured in the melody of mm. 10–13, the other characteristic subset of 4–19, the subset 3–12, is otherwise submerged over this first thematic area. However, as I explore below, 3–12 soon emerges prominently.

The transition connecting the first and second tonal areas of the Piano Sonata no. 4/III extends over mm. 25–42. The bass pitches of this passage are analyzed in example 3.4, which displays two local arpeggiations of 3–12 (048), shown slurred together with the headnote of each local arpeggiation stemmed. These arpeggiations are nested within a larger one, also a form of 3–12, created by the headnotes along with G♯ in m. 33.

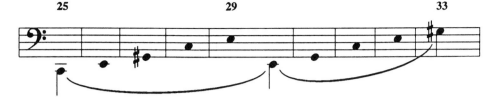

Example 3.4. Piano Sonata no. 4, op. 29/III, mm. 25–33, 3–12 [048] in the bass

As discussed earlier, 3–12 is a characteristic subset of 4–19. Even without an explicit statement of 4–19, the pitch-class intersection of (048) in the transition with (0478) in m. 3, for example, strongly binds together the two passages. In this sense, 3–12 and 4–19 are closely related sets, and 3–12 (048) can be said to descend from 4–19.

Mm. 43–50 constitute the first eight measures of the second thematic area. The G-major chord on the downbeat of m. 43 creates a dominant foil that plays against the tonic C major in the first thematic area. Large-scale dominant-tonic tension is, however, perhaps less effective than texture at distinguishing the two thematic areas. The confined soft trill of the second thematic area contrasts vividly with the expansive, bravura writing of the first thematic area.

In the right hand of m. 43, the lower neighbor F♯ leads to G by octave transfer while in the left hand E♭ is upper neighbor to D. M. 44 brings in a neighboring chord to m. 43, a move made especially clear when G/B in m. 43 slides up to G♯/B♯. As indicated in example 3.5a, each measure contains a form of 5–21 [01458], a superset of 4–19. In example 3.5b I identify in these same measures five forms of 4–19, the structural set originating in the first theme area whose descendant 3–12 occurred in the transition.

In the transition, 3–12 does not occur as a bald chord; the arpeggiation which expresses 3–12 is a forward-driving action whose completion marks the end of the passage. Hence, in addition to conceiving of a structural set as a collection of elements which are transposed, inverted, increased or decreased in number, or complemented, we can also view it as a particular realization of a process. Such processes, abstracted from their expression within the structural set, may considerably influence other sets or other domains. We can look at how a structural set is transformed throughout a piece and follow the way derived processes structure the piece.

There are three ways to read the trill figure over mm. 43–44. First, we could hear the metrically accented eighths as main notes, decorated by neighbors on the intervening sixteenth notes. This reading brings out a G-major dominant and thus affirms a conventional tonal response to the first thematic area. Alternatively, we might hear a lower neighbor D (in m. 43) and an upper neighbor E♮

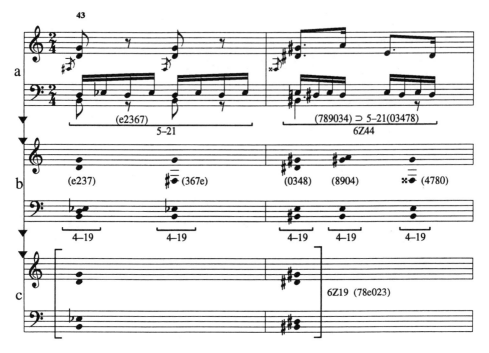

Example 3.5. Piano Sonata no. 4, op. 29/III, mm. 43–44, set structure

(in m. 44) circling E♭/D♯. This second hearing finds support in the earlier analysis of chromatic double neighbors: F♯ and A♭ circled G, and B and D♭ triads circled C. In the first hearing we understand the passage as a decorated G-major triad in first inversion moving to a decorated E-augmented triad in second inversion. As is shown in example 3.5c, in the second hearing we understand the harmonies underlying the passage as a form of 4–19 in m. 43 (from the bass up: B–E♭–D–G) moving in m. 44 to a G♯-major triad in first inversion. In both readings, an augmented triad emerges strongly, the precedent for which can be found as early as the second measure of the movement. One might also strive for a more neutral stance, shown at the bottom of example 3.5a. This third reading stresses the transformation T1 in m. 44; T1 embeds (e2367), which is formed by all the notes in m. 43.[5]

All three of these hearings recognize an interplay between a major triad and an augmented triad which share a common dyad. The first two hearings settle on either a major or an augmented triad as an underlying harmony; the last reading recognizes all the elements in the measure (except for A in m. 44) as equally weighted. Whether we read the major triad, the augmented triad, or the larger set 5–21 as fundamental to these measures, we are naturally led to the topics of structural sets and descendants.

The set 4–19 in this movement is a structural set. A structural set occurs frequently and recognizably throughout a piece, either unordered or in a preferred ordering and often at important points of articulation.

By a point of articulation is meant either the onset or the termination of some formal event, such as the beginning or ending of a phrase. Points of articulation are often marked by dynamic, registral, or agogic accents. On a larger scale, structural sets may be formed by summing up points of articulation. For example, in the Piano Sonata no. 4/III, the B-major triad over mm. 4–5 is formed from points of articulation: phrasing and agogic accent isolate B4, F♯4, D♯4, and B5.

In heterogenous contexts, such as the one we have been studying, the contrast of a traditionally tonal background with wrong notes places in relief the structural set that unites these apparently dissimilar musical domains. Specifically, in the Piano Sonata no. 4/III, the set 4–19 unites the familiar C-major triad with the apparently anomalous A♭.

The structural set may occur as harmony or melody, and it may occur literally or it may be represented by one of its subsets, one of its supersets, or its complement. For example, as a harmony, 4–19 permeates the first thematic area, as in m. 3, mm. 10–13, and mm. 14–17. The set 8–19, the complement of 4–19, occurs in mm. 14–17. As a melody, the structural set 4–19 is represented by one of its subsets, 3–12, over mm. 10–13. In the second thematic area, 4–19 is represented by one of its supersets, 5–21, whose ubiquity in the second theme area is analogous to 4–19's in the first thematic area. In all these instances, the structural set is primarily a surface phenomenon.

The structural set may also contribute processes that occur in the piece. For example, one of 4–19's distinctive subsets is 3–12, the augmented triad, whose intervallic content consists of a single interval class, ic4 (see the Appendix). The transition derives its series of repeated, nested transpositions at T4 from this characteristic interval class. We think of processes or a web of intervals, rather than a catalogue of items such as collections of pitches or pitch classes. Thus, the structural set, based on its intervallic makeup, provides a store of potential transformations upon which the music may draw.

There is no strictly methodical procedure for determining structural sets; structural sets emerge after one studies the entire piece. To determine the structural sets, one searches for a congruence between characteristic surface features and aspects of voice leading which play out and express processes inherent in those surface features.

The structural set captures the peculiar and distinctive character of a piece. Along with familiar signs of tonality, the wrong notes form large-scale and small-scale structural sets which are disposed linearly and harmonically. The wrong notes do not become absorbed into traditionally tonal structures.

Structural sets projected linearly over large spans may remind one of the work of Edward T. Cone or, more recently, Joseph Straus.[6] In analyzing Stravinsky's *Symphonies of Wind Instruments,* Cone suggests that Stravinsky's well-known juxtaposed blocks of sound arise from a vertical counterpoint; they result from formal sections that abruptly interrupt one another, that are cut and pasted in a way that obfuscates their underlying integrity. Cone shows that reassembling the blocks produces coherent, continuous threads. Straus suggests that in Stravinsky's music, set classes of characteristic sonorities on the surface are reproduced in larger-scale articulative points. Thus, one can take the surface structures as a model in order to gauge when the large-scale structures are incomplete.

Both theorists imply that a psychological principle operates in the music which one might term expectation of continuation or expectation of completion.[7] Cone suggests that each abrupt interruption of an integral musical idea disturbs the listener and engenders the expectation that the musical idea will return or continue. Straus suggests a similar idea but focuses the listener's attention on pitch-class sets. A listener will wait impatiently for a set to be completed: hearing only three elements of a four-element set creates such an expectation.

According to the models proposed by Cone and Straus, a listener is able to determine aspects of incompleteness in the music. Listening then becomes a kind of search for the missing elements. But the listening model for Prokofiev's music outlined earlier is differently motivated. Where one can differentiate between traditionally tonal background and wrong note, musical coherence is often denied because of the "bad fit" of the wrong note. An otherwise complete and coherent context is undermined by an apparently foreign element or gesture. Such a context is "super-complete" rather than incomplete. One's listening becomes relatively less guided than it is in, say, Stravinsky's music, because the listener in Prokofiev's music may have to wait for the music to show how an unexpected event may be integrated. Only at that point is the listener able to retroactively interpret the music and understand its coherence.

To analogize the difference between the two models, one might imagine two detective stories. In one, on the basis of the clues, a clever reader may be able to provide the solution before the story does. But in the other, evidence is withheld (for a while), thus preventing the reader from drawing a conclusion. Christopher Hasty, in analyzing temporal and formal aspects of twentieth-century music—Stravinsky's *Symphonies of Wind Instruments* in particular—eloquently expresses a point of view encompassing both of the models outlined here. He suggests that "instead of regarding expectation as a determination of what can be, we understand it as an openness to the possibility of relating events."[8]

A structural set may or may not itself be a tonal interpreter. However, in certain characteristic motivic, thematic, rhythmic, or registral dispositions, the structural set often highlights one of its subsets (more rarely a superset) as a tonal interpreter. In these cases, listeners may experience the remaining note or notes of the structural set as "wrong." The interplay between 4−19 and a C-major triad in the Piano Sonata no. 4/III's first thematic area is between structural set and tonal interpreter.

Tonal interpreters, as subsets of structural sets, depend on context to activate their tonal-interpreting function. Some subsets of structural sets have the potential to interpret a passage tonally. Such subsets, however, do not of necessity so function; tonal interpreters can be activated—switched on or switched off—by context.

A structural set may be transformed in several ways which preserve its character while altering either its cardinality or its intervallic structure. These transformed sets, derived from an original structural set, I will call descendants to distinguish them from their progenitor.

Prokofiev typically generates a family of descendants by increasing or decreasing the size of the structural set. Where n is the cardinality of the parental structural set, the descendant is usually of size $n − 1$ or $n + 1$. In the Piano Sonata no. 4/III, the set 4−19 is a structural set; 3−12, an $(n − 1)$-sized descendant, drives the transition (mm. 25−33); 3−11 and 3−12, $(n − 1)$-sized descendants, play central roles in the first and second theme areas; and 5−21, an $(n + 1)$-sized descendant, structures the second theme.

The structural set, in generating the descendant, resembles somewhat a "nexus" set in Fortean theory.[9] Forte develops nexus sets and pitch-class set complexes abstractly and then investigates their application to specific pieces. In contrast, structural sets and descendants are first given by the piece; the structural set is contextually and empirically determined.

By a constellation of sets, I mean a family of sets descended from some particular structural set by complementation, subset or superset relations, or fragmentation (discussed later) with the proviso that the compositional presentation of these sets justifies grouping them together.

I conclude this chapter by examining op. 17/2 from *Sarcasmes*. It is more contextually homogenous than the opening of the Piano Sonata no. 4/III. By analyzing it we can see how structural sets operate in contexts less dependent upon distinctions between tradition and innovation.

SARCASMES, OP. 17/2

Prokofiev indulges his innovative inclination in *Sarcasmes* (1912−1914), pieces in which he explicitly sought a more modern musical language. Prokofiev speaks of them in the *Autobiography*: "The pieces were a big success with the 'modernists,' perhaps because the search for a new musical language was more strongly evident in them than in other works of the same period."[10] Experimentation is evident in even the orthography. For example, op. 17/4 has a dual key signature: the right hand is written in three sharps, the left hand in five flats. Enhancing the harmonic and melodic progressiveness in several of these pieces, evidence of the modern line, is a powerful rhythmic drive (especially in numbers 1, 3, and 5).

Unlike the Piano Sonata no. 4/III, whose heterogenous context so clearly contrasted wrong-note with traditionally tonal background, the *Sarcasmes* are contextually homogenous. Experimentation penetrates all levels of the structure, effectively blurring the distinction between traditionally tonal background and wrong notes. Yet structural sets still guide the music.

The second piece of the collection features dense, relatively dissonant harmonies; extensive parallel motion in the voice leading; dramatic shifts in register; and slow-moving, closely packed chords alternating with flurries of gossamer figuration. Binding together these diverse features is a motivic fabric woven from the structural set [015].

There are three basic motivic sources in this piece: the first is derived from the melody of mm. 1–2, the second from the wide-ranging twelve-tuplet in m. 3, and the third from the grace notes in m. 5 (the grace notes are themselves related to the tuplet in m. 3). The form of the piece, diagrammed and annotated in figure 3.1, is closest to being a loose series of variations. Each of the four sections develops the motives in slightly different ways, and each introduces some new material. Section 2 introduces the ponderous, dense forms of 4–24 [0248] over mm. 21–24, as well as the sequential passage over an E pedal in mm. 26–36. Section 3 picks up on mm. 21–24, combining the dense chords with a motive derived from m. 1's melody. Section 4 is a closing passage; the only new material it contributes is the scalar flourish over mm. 49–50, whose fresh quartal harmonies are a clear signal that the piece is about to conclude.

Mm. 1–12, in the first section of the piece, divide in half after m. 6. Example 3.6 shows the melody notes over mm. 1–6. F and D♭ from mm. 1–3 are ana-

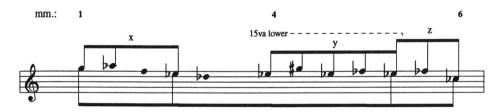

Example 3.6. *Sarcasmes, op. 17/2, mm. 1–6, melodic analysis*

phrase 1: mm. 1–6
phrase 2: mm. 7–12

Section 2: mm. 13–28

mm. 13–21 (chaining)
mm. 21–25 (dense chords built around [0248])
mm. 25–28 (chaining)

Section 3: mm. 28–45 (sequential treatment of m. 1's motivic idea, pedal E)

Section 4: mm. 45–52 (closing material)

Figure 3.1. *Sarcasmes, op. 17/2, form outline*

lyzed as auxiliaries and appear in the example as unbeamed, filled-in noteheads. F steps down to the E♭ goal from above, while D♭ is a neighbor note below that goal. The notes G, A♭, and E♭ over mm. 1–3 form the structural set [015], a set class which is realized twice more as (378) in the melody of the following three measures, mm. 4–6. The notes with upward stems beamed together show the three forms of [015], labeled x, y, and z, which are embedded in this melody: x = (378), y = (348), and z = (e34). Only in the opening three measures is [015] embellished, but there the structural set (378) captures the beginning and the ending of the melody as well as its high point.

The overall melodic motion in mm. 1–6 is downward, from G to C♭, accomplished in two increments of a major third each. The beamed-together notes with downward stems show the descent through an augmented triad, whose pitch classes, 7, 11, and 3, are contained in the first chord of the piece and also return in the left hand in mm. 21–24.

Example 3.7 is an analysis of the three forms of [015], x, y, and z, as a pair of overlapping dyads with each constituent dyad beamed together. The elements of x, y, and z are shown in the middle C octave for convenience. The forms x and y and the forms y and z are inversionally related, with each inversionally related pair sharing two invariants, the maximum possible under inversion. Thus we can represent the inversional relations in terms of the invariant dyads. An arrow above example 3.7a shows $I^{E\flat/A\flat}(x) = y$; similarly, example 3.7b shows $I^{E\flat/F\flat}(y) = z$. The arrows labeled "R" (for retrograde) in example 3.7 complete the order transformation of x into y (in example 3.7a) and y into z (in example 3.7b). When we conceive of each three-note set as a pair of dyads, there is a serial regularity to the succession of these dyads, though within a dyad there is free treatment of note repetition and order: G and A♭ in x are heard in the music before E♭ and A♭; E♭ and A♭ in y are heard before E♭ and F♭; and E♭ and F♭ in z are heard before C♭ and F♭.[11]

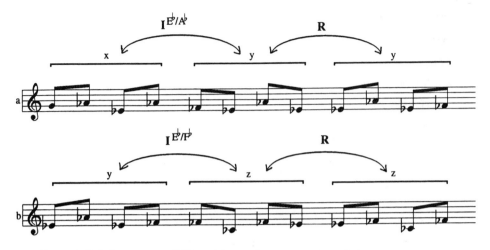

Example 3.7. *Sarcasmes,* op. 17/2, motivic transformations in the melody

The influence of [015] is not limited to melody. The spare, registrally isolated gesture in m. 4 states [015] harmonically, first as (t23) and then as (891). The structural set [015] also occurs in m. 10, which transposes m. 4 up a half step.

Example 3.8 shows the [015]s embedded in the melody over mm. 7–12 and labeled x', y', and z'. Only y' and z' are related in the same way as y and z in example 3.7, that is, by an inversion operation which produced two invariants and by the dyadic retrogression discussed above. In mm. 7–12, the inversion operation taking x' to y' is not IF/B♭ (= T₃I), which would begin to reproduce the chain of example 3.7. Instead, T₂I(x') = (y') [T₂I(59t) = (459)], an adjustment which eventually steers the melody of example 3.8 to C♯5 rather than to B♭4, as would have been the case had mm. 7–12 been strictly analogous to mm. 1–6. That adjustment, however, creates a powerful link between sections 1 and 2 (mm. 1–12 and mm. 13–28, respectively).

M. 13 launches section 2, in which transpositionally related [015]s are again chained together. With arrows, I show in example 3.9 how [015], in the form (7e0), summarizes the melodic targets of the first two phrases, C♭ in m. 6 and C♮

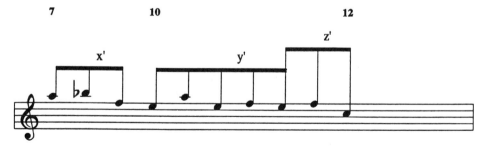

Example 3.8. *Sarcasmes,* op. 17/2, mm. 7–12, melodic analysis

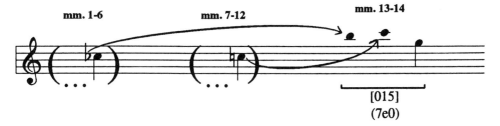

Example 3.9. *Sarcasmes,* op. 17/2, 3–4 [015] in the melodic structure of mm. 1–14

in m. 12. The form (7e0) then concludes on G in m. 14 and in doing so completes a large-scale form of the structural set [015], which connects mm. 1–12 to mm. 13–21.

Example 3.10 charts the chain of descending [015]s over mm. 13–21. Each form of [015] is stemmed and beamed together above the staff; the notes stemmed and beamed together below the staff link the tail notes of each form of [015]. The entire passage spans G5 down to G♯4 (A♭4), thus recalling the identical interval that occurred harmonically in the first chord of the piece.[12] The beamed-together notes below the staff, a form of 5Z37 [03458], embed 4–19 [0148], a commonly occurring structural set in Prokofiev's music.

The [015] meets the criteria for a structural set. It occurs frequently on the surface of the music—for example, as the melodic contour of mm. 1–3 and as a harmony in m. 4. On a deeper level, [015] connects the two phrases over mm. 1–12 to the section beginning in m. 13. The structural set's identity in this view is based on traditional equivalence under transposition or inversion. But later in the piece, over mm. 26–28, a powerful motivic association links [015] to [016]. Let us investigate this association.[13]

Not just superset and subset transformations of the structural set can generate descendants; so can fragmentation. Equating a set class with a structural set may impart to the structural set a too-rigid identity, based on transpositional or inversional equivalence. Fragmentation is a way to seek the identity of a structural set in its individual components, not only in their sum.

Fragmentation exhaustively partitions a pitch-class set X set into subsets,

Example 3.10. *Sarcasmes,* op. 17/2, chain of [015]s in the melody of mm. 13–21

which may or may not overlap. If the subsets overlap, they may overlap partially or completely. These subsets are then reassembled to produce a different set class than pitch-class set X. In the descended pitch-class set, as in the original pitch-class set X, the subsets must exhaustively partition the set, and the subsets may or may not overlap. Unlike superset and subset transformations, fragmentation does not necessarily change the cardinality of the structural set. Fragmentation will, however, alter its intervallic structure and hence its Tn/TnI-type.[14]

An example of fragmentation occurs over mm. 25–28 of op. 17/2. As example 3.7 showed, the constituent overlapping dyads which form the structural set [015] can be conceptualized as a dyad which spans a half step and a dyad which spans a perfect fourth (or, more precisely, ic1 and ic5). We can imagine the structural set [015] realized in the pitch set (E, F, C). E/F spans a half step and is included within the span C-up-to-F, a perfect fourth. Fragmentation can generate the descendant pitch set (C, F, G♭), which preserves both a perfect fourth and a half step, by attaching the half step, the dyad F/G♭, outside the perfect fourth C-up-to-F. Rearranging the dyads transforms [015] into [016].[15]

In example 3.11 I return to op. 17/2 and reproduce the melodic material of mm. 25–28. These measures combine and develop sequentially the three main motives of this piece (the melody of mm. 1–2, the twelve-tuplet in m. 3, and the grace notes in m. 5). A single form of [015] begins the passage in m. 25. But beginning in m. 26, brackets above and below the staff identify instances of the descendant [016]. Brackets above the staff mark Tn-type [016]; brackets below mark Tn-type [056].[16] In this example, as in example 3.7, inverted forms of a trichordal set are chained together; each contiguous pair of sets shares two invariants. The parallelism created by chaining in example 3.7 and example 3.11 reinforces the connection between [015] and [016] which fragmentation asserts.

Example 3.11. *Sarcasmes,* op. 17/2, mm. 25–28, fragmentation

4 Piano Music

For most of his life, Prokofiev was a concertizing pianist as well as a composer. His account of his graduation from the Conservatory is emblematic in this regard, for it illustrates both his compositional and his pianistic abilities. By deliberately provoking a conservative portion of the faculty, he also exhibited important personality traits, including a high degree of self-confidence and a desire to challenge tradition.

In the spring of 1914, at the age of twenty-three, I graduated from the Conservatoire. . . . There was a sporting interest involved too [in graduating], for the Rubinstein Prize, a grand piano, was to be awarded for the best performance. . . . For the competition, instead of a classical concerto, I chose one of my own [the First Piano Concerto—Prokofiev judged the Second to be too modern for the competition]. . . . I bought twenty copies [of the piano score from the publisher, Jurgenson] and distributed them to all the examiners. When I came out on the stage the first thing I saw was my concerto spread out on twenty laps—an unforgettable sight for a composer who had just begun to appear in print! My most serious competitor was Golubovskaya . . . a very subtle and intelligent pianist.[1]

Prokofiev won the competition, even though "the older professors, headed by Glazounov, the director of the Conservatoire, voted against."[2] The anecdote reveals an artist who is eager to participate in a traditional activity but who insists on doing so on his own terms. It is reminiscent of the play of tradition and innovation.

Prokofiev's list of works, which begins and ends with piano compositions, extends from the Piano Sonata no. 1, op. 1 (1907; revised in 1909), through the Piano Sonata no. 9, op. 103 (1947), and the revised Piano Sonata no. 5, op. 135 (1952–1953).[3] The large quantity of works for piano which Prokofiev composed during all three periods of his creative life documents his compositional activity consistently and accurately.

Prokofiev's output for piano includes sonatas, short character pieces, and transcriptions. At the pinnacle stand his nine piano sonatas.[4] The Piano Sonata no. 1, with its bravura and virtuosic writing, owes a stylistic debt to late nineteenth-century romantic piano music. Its one-movement form also shows a spiritual kinship to the kind of organicism aimed at by many romantic composers, such as Liszt (in the B-minor Sonata, for example) and Scriabin (as in the Piano Sonatas nos. 5–10). Yet despite its derivative nature, the Piano Sonata no. 1 is a remarkable composition for an eighteen-year-old boy. Prokofiev himself was well aware of the youthfulness of the work:

> That summer [1906; Prokofiev was fifteen] I decided to write a long piano sonata. I was determined that the music would be more beautiful, the sonata interesting technically, and the content not superficial. I had already sketched out some of the thematic material. In this way I began to work on the F minor *Sonata No. 2,* in three movements, and wrote a good deal of it in a very short time. It proved to be a more mature work than my other compositions of that period, and for several years it towered above them as a solid opus. Later I discarded the second and third movements, then reworked the first and made it into *Sonata No. 1, Opus 1* [Prokofiev completed the revision in 1909 at the age of eighteen]. But alongside my serious numbered works, that sonata seemed too youthful, somehow. It turned out that, although it was a solid opus when I was fifteen, it could not hold its own among my more mature compositions.[5]

In the Piano Sonata no. 2, op. 14, Prokofiev makes a remarkable leap from the first sonata and moves surely toward establishing his mature and distinctive compositional voice. His habit of economical recycling is evident in the composition of the Piano Sonatas nos. 3 and 4, opp. 28 and 29; in these sonatas he reworked material that he had kept in notebooks which dated back to his Conservatory years. The Sonata no. 3 is the only other sonata to return to the one-movement form of the first. With the Piano Sonata no. 5, op. 38, Prokofiev struck out on the most experimental path of any of the nine sonatas. Later in his life, in 1952, Prokofiev returned to the Piano Sonata no. 5, revised it, and listed the new, longer work as op. 135.[6]

The Piano Sonatas nos. 6–8, the "War Sonatas" (composed between 1939 and 1944), cap Prokofiev's achievement as a composer; they are monumental in scale and quality. The ninth and final sonata, which is dramatically different in character from the War Sonatas, was composed in an effort to achieve his new simplicity. Sviatoslav Richter, the dedicatee of the ninth sonata, "was surprised—and even disappointed—at its remarkable 'simplicity,' but he later came to regard it as one of his favorite Prokofiev sonatas."[7] Prokofiev himself seems not to have worried about the work being too simple, a worry he did, in fact, express about the Symphony no. 7.

Besides the nine piano sonatas, character pieces occupy the most significant position in Prokofiev's piano music. Perhaps the best known of the character pieces are the two collections *Sarcasmes,* op. 17 (1912–1914), and *Visions Fugitives,* op. 22 (1915–1917), but the lively and fancifully titled pieces of opp. 3 (1907–1908), 4 (1908), and 12 (1906–1913) pave the way for opp. 17 and 22. Complementing the extroverted and often animated mood of the earlier works are the serious, introspective opp. 45 (1928) and 62 (1933–1934).

The remaining music for piano solo, excluding the piano sonatas, includes the early *Etudes,* op. 2 (1909), and *Children's Music,* op. 65 (1935).[8] Prokofiev also made various piano transcriptions of his other compositions. The transcriptions include the Symphony no. 1, op. 25 ("Classical"), the Andante from the String Quartet no. 1, op. 50, and probably his most famous transcription, the *March* from *Love for Three Oranges,* which Prokofiev often played in his own recitals.[9]

Works of Prokofiev's first period, such as op. 3, op. 4, op. 17 (*Sarcasmes*), and op. 22 (*Visions Fugitives*), rely on the dynamic interplay between harmonic experimentation and traditional tonality, between wrong notes and right notes. Earlier discussion showed how that interplay created a convenient gateway through which one could be easily led to salient aspects of Prokofiev's music, especially its pitch and pitch-class structure. The many compositions relying on types like march, allemande, gavotte, and mazurka, which include op. 32 (*Four Pieces* [1918]), offer examples of how right and wrong notes interact.

Symmetrical Pitch Structures

Considering the Russian heritage of octatonic pitch structures, particularly in the music of Rimsky-Korsakov (one of Prokofiev's teachers) and Stravinsky, one might not be surprised to find that it plays a role in Prokofiev's music as well.[10] Op. 22/3, mm. 13–22, is a purely octatonic passage, not a common phenomenon in Prokofiev's music. Several clues attest to the music's symmetric octatonic structure. These clues include major seconds separated by a tritone in the left hand and melodic fragments in m. 13 and m. 17 which are forms of [0134] related at T3. Still, octatonicism is not a defining characteristic of Prokofiev's music in the same way as it is of Stravinsky's, for example.[11] Somewhat more common in Prokofiev's music are non-octatonic symmetrical formations and especially whole-tone structures and an important derivative, the augmented triad.

PIANO SONATA NO. 5, OP. 38/I

In the Piano Sonata no. 5, first movement (1923), whole-tone structures are represented by the tritone. The first movement is a sonata form. In the exposition a transition (m. 20) connects theme 1 with theme 2 (m. 26), and a closing theme (m. 46) leads to the end of the exposition in m. 61. The development extends over mm. 62–139; the retransition begins in m. 155 with a B♭ chord, which is eventually replaced by a B-minor chord (or quasi G major seventh chord). The recapitulation proceeds traditionally: theme 1 (m. 140), transition (m. 156), theme 2 (m. 161), closing 1 (m. 178), and closing 2 (m. 190), based on theme 1.

In m. 7, the Lydian-inflected bass line creates a whole-tone segment, (0246), spanning a tritone. Each element of the whole-tone segment is the root of one of a series of major triads ascending from C, through D and E, up to F♯, where the whole-tone segment breaks off. F♯ defeats the C-major bass line by displacing the expected F♮ and continuing whole-tone motion one more step past C, D, and E. F♯ is unexpected and stands out as a wrong note within the C-major context. The outer voices then move from F♯ in m. 7 up by a half step to the dominant G in m. 8. But F♯ in an inner voice is also held over into m. 8. There it balances the outer voice's upward move from F♯ to G by moving down to F♮, the chordal seventh of the dominant G.

Numerous passages later in the movement derive from the bass of mm. 7–8. In mm. 20–21, the motion from A3 down through D♯3 to D3 inverts C–F♯–G from mm. 7–8 [T9I(670) = (923)]. The descending scale in the melody of mm. 31–32 develops the whole-tone motion of the bass in m. 7. In each of mm. 65–66 a form of [0246] returns in the left hand: (79e1) occurs in m. 65, and (0246) occurs in m. 66. G♯ in the bass of m. 67 expands by one element the whole-tone collection in the bass of m. 66. G♯ then persists in the bass of mm. 67–76 (G♯ is respelled as A♭ in mm. 73–76).

M. 77 moves A♭ (= G♯) from the bass of m. 76 to the upper voice, where it is harmonized in the right hand by an E-major chord. Over mm. 77–87, the E-major chord is juxtaposed against a Bb-major chord, thus expressing the tritonal relation which originated in m. 7 between C and F#.

The Bb-major triad which is developed over mm. 76–87 explicitly denies C major's leading tone, B♮. A Bb-major triad reappears in m. 125, where it cuts short the music of mm. 121–124 and displaces B♮. In mm. 121–124 the texture grows thick and highly chromatic. The upper voice features B on the beat and its lower neighbor A# off the beat. The left hand alternates between G dominant seventh and B dominant seventh chords, each of which harmonizes the common tone B. Besides G7 and B7, one more familiar chord is detectable in m. 123. There one can hear the right hand arpeggiating up through an F#-major chord toward B♮. The C# which begins that arpeggiation is already present in mm. 121–122. The combination of all three of these chords, G dominant seventh, B dominant seventh, and F# major, creates a form of 9–12 (1235679te), a symmetrical set and a complement of the augmented triad.

The primary function of mm. 121–124 is to introduce B♮ and prepare for the return to C major through its leading tone. Beginning in m. 125, a Bb-major triad enters and successfully fends off B♮, imparting to pitch class 10 a stability which it lacked in its guise as A# in mm. 121–124. In m. 138 Bb eventually yields to what appears on the printed page to be a B-minor triad. In fact, the B-minor triad is a dominant-function chord, with F# added (and G omitted). In preparing the recapitulation, F# leads up to G, as it also did in m. 8.

Voice leading in the movement's opening interprets F# tonally, that is, as a passing note aiming at G. But F# also generates an important tritonal relation with the tonic C. That tritonal relation is expressed as the root relation Bb-E in the development section, mm. 77–87.[12] At the end of the development section Prokofiev manages to interpret aspects of the Bb-E chord pair in a tonal light, for the Bb triad returns in mm. 125–136, where it explicitly delays the appearance of the leading tone B♮, sweetening the onset of the recapitulation.

VISIONS FUGITIVES, OP. 22/4

In Prokofiev's music the augmented triad is a common derivative of the whole-tone scale which divides the octave symmetrically. Though division by major thirds promises symmetrical structure, Prokofiev virtually always introduces some sort of a "balance-tipper" to disturb the symmetry. *Visions Fugitives,* op. 22/4, exhibits a typical development of the augmented triad. Example 4.1 is an analysis of its first four measures as an ornamented, descending arpeggiation of an augmented triad, elements of which are stemmed and slurred to lower neighbors. The range from C6 down to C2 is traversed in equal increments of eight half-steps each.

M. 5 begins by embedding example 4.1's symmetrical collection, (048), in a

Example 4.1. *Visions Fugitives*, op. 22/4, (048) in mm. 1–4

characteristic asymmetrical tetrachord, (4580) (4–19). In example 4.2a I analyze the left hand of m. 9, which expands upon (4580) from m. 5 and begins a varied repeat of mm. 1–4. The left hand plays (048), as shown, but pairs it with an arpeggiated D♭-major triad. In example 4.2b I analyze the left hand as a form of 5–21 [01458]. In examples 4.2c and 4.2d I extract the two forms of 4–19 contained in 4.2b. Example 4.2c is made explicit when m. 16 gives a C augmented triad along with only the root of the D♭ triad.

Many of Prokofiev's works rely on symmetrical tonal schemes. Division of the octave by major thirds seems to predominate, but minor-third divisions and octatonic structures are by no means rare. In general, a concern for self-contained formal equilibrium motivates these symmetrical tonal schemes.

Works of the First Period

Grafting Prokofiev's modern harmonic practice onto traditional types can produce music in the grotesque line, as in the *March* from *Love for Three Oranges*. However, the same structural sets which in the grotesque line meld the divergent impulses of conservation and experimentation also occur in music in the modern line, where the harmonic context is more homogenous. Prokofiev's modern harmonic practice is well represented in op. 22/13.

Example 4.2. *Visions Fugitives*, op. 22/4, analysis of m. 9

Example 4.3. op. 22/13, inversional balance in mm. 1–8

OP. 22/13

Inversional balance is a recurring feature of Prokofiev's music. Op. 22/13, a piece in the modern line, explores inversions, specifically common-tone inversions. The piece is a ternary ABA form: section A covers mm. 1–5; section B covers mm. 5–21; and section A returns in mm. 22–26. Example 4.3a shows mm. 1–8, containing the A section and the beginning of the B section. Aligned below 4.3a are several staves with analyses of inversional relations. In example 4.3b I analyze the melody of mm. 1–2, which moves from B4 through E5 to A5, highlighting the pitch inversional center E5 with chromatic double neighbor motion. Slurs connect pitches which invert about E5.

Pitch class 4, realized as E4, is also the center of a harmonic inversion in the left hand. In the accompaniment, the diminished chord over G♯ (enharmonically D six-four) inverts in pitch space around D4/F4 and arrives at a diminished chord on D (B six-three), as is shown in example 4.3c.

The bass of mm. 1–4 spans the interval from G♯3 to G♯4. In m. 2 it moves through D4, which is chromatically enclosed by C♯4 and D♯4, very much as E5 in the right hand is enclosed by D♯ and F. Arrows in example 4.3d invert the overlapping three-note fragments about D4. The inverted fragments share the two common pitch classes D and G♯.

Pitch inversion in mm. 1–4 (discussed in connection with examples 4.3b and 4.3c) becomes pitch-class inversion in section B. Section B's melody begins in m. 6 with a straightforward chromatic descent starting from D4. In m. 7, B♭3 reverses the melody's downward progress and helps highlight the tail-fragment B3–B♭3–E4, a form of [016]. Another common-tone inversion, I^{B/E} (in pitch-class space), ties (te4), the melodic tail-fragment, to the left hand's collection in m. 7, (45t).

The melody's measured expansion over mm. 6–8 reveals another striking inversional relation. It begins by spanning the interval from D4 (pitch class 2) down to Bb3. The melody then expands outward to E4, a step above D4, and concludes on G#3 (pitch class 8), a step below Bb3. Section B continues to stress the pitch classes 8 and 2. The left hand plays a slow ostinato pattern while the right hand's melodic strands either begin or end on G# or D, taking over their articulative function from the first phrase of section B.

In the inversional relations shown in examples 4.3c and 4.3d, an n-sized set inverts into its partner through $n - 1$ common tones (where the tone is either a pitch or a pitch class). While these inversional relations are not unknown in tonal music, they are a common feature of the language of early twentieth-century music, as in the music of Berg, Webern, and Schoenberg.[13] Here, the linked inversions illustrate the modern side of Prokofiev's compositional style.[14]

PIANO SONATA NO. 2, OP. 14

The compositional maturity displayed in the Piano Sonata no. 2 is startling when we consider that Prokofiev was only twenty-one when he wrote it.[15] The sonata marks the structural beginning, as it were, of Prokofiev's cycle of piano sonatas.

In addition to elevating genius to a high position in Prokofiev's aesthetics, Romanticism bequeathed the notion of organic unity. I have already mentioned the one-movement forms of the Piano Sonatas nos. 1 and 3 and their late nineteenth-century heritage. In the Piano Sonata no. 2, a work with four separate movements, features of organic unity are aired less loudly, more subtly. This intermovement unity is most obvious when the last movement quotes the first movement's lyric theme.[16]

The third movement is a once-repeated, slightly varied binary: A (mm. 1–22), B (mm. 23–30), A' (mm. 31–52), B' (mm. 53–60). In example 4.4 I analyze the underlying structure of mm. 3–4 as a once-repeated neighbor motive,

Example 4.4. Piano Sonata no. 2, op. 14/III, mm. 3–4, melodic analysis

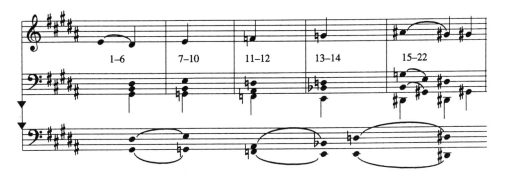

Example 4.5. Piano Sonata no. 2, op. 14/III, mm. 1–22, retrograde relations in outer voices, aspects of harmonic structure

E-D♯; in the lowest analytical staff I distill motion from the analytical staff above it. The neighbor motive is first set out from the upbeat of m. 3 to its downbeat. The slurs below the notes show that both the neighbor E and the main note D♯ are embellished by a downward skip of a third. In the middle of m. 3 the upper neighbor reappears and becomes stretched out by passing downward through a third, each element of which is also embellished by a downward third skip. The main note D♯ finally returns in the middle of m. 4.

Over section A, the melody is systematically transposed upward in stepwise increments. Each step in the melodic transposition is matched by a change of harmony. The grand staff in example 4.5 shows a distillation of the main melodic notes and their match against the harmonic progression. Comparing the stemmed melodic notes with the stemmed bass notes reveals their retrograde relation, disturbed in the melody only in m. 15, when A♯ is interposed between G♮ (= F✗) and G♯.

The outward wedging which governs the outer-voice structure is also featured in three of the harmonic progressions. The bass clef aligned below the grand staff in the example has opposed slurs to show the voice pairs participating in the wedging.

Section B (mm. 23–30) carries over the tonic from section A, expressing it as a low-register octave pedal. Two distinct parts emerge over this G♯ pedal. Example 4.6 is a sketch of the right hand, which begins on G and moves downward through three major triads. The major triads are spaced a whole step apart and glued together by a serpentine chromatic line in an inner voice.[17]

In m. 23, after reaching E♭, the melody retraces its steps and returns to its starting point, G, before leaping down through a perfect fifth to conclude on C, producing a cadential feel. A linear chord leads to m. 24 by collapsing inward to m. 24's G-major chord; the inward wedging derives, by retrograde, from the

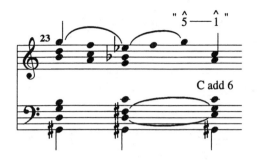

Example 4.6. Piano Sonata no. 2, op. 14/III, m. 23, harmonic structure

bottom staff of example 4.5. M. 24 then repeats m. 23 but begins from a different position of the right-hand triad, placing the chordal fifth rather than the root on top.

The left hand accompanies the melody over mm. 23–24 with the stemless chords shown in the bass of example 4.6. While the chords appear to be so-called primary chords from G major (in order: I, V7, IV), example 4.6 shows them within the domain of a C tonic. G is therefore a dominant, while the "D7" chord is a neighbor chord whose third D/F♯ resolves stepwise to E/G, shown by the slurs on the example. Both the right-hand and left-hand parts converge and conclude on the 5th eighth-note of m. 23. Example 4.6 is an analysis of that sonority as an added-sixth chord whose added-note A does not materially alter the identity of the C-major chord. The C "tonic" chord and the pedal G♯ create a form of 4–19 [0148], a superset descended from 3–12 [048], which structures this movement.

In example 4.7 I abstract the G♯ tonal focus from section A, follow it with the C-major "tonic" with G♯ pedal from mm. 23–26, labeled "b1," and follow that with b2 (mm. 27–30), a transposition of b1. In the middle of the staff the letters G♯–C–E show how the augmented triad (048) governs points of articulation for section A through sections b1 and b2. The two diagonal arrows show

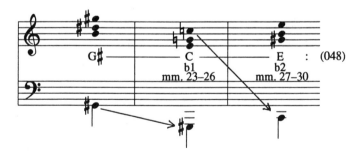

Example 4.7. Piano Sonata no. 2, op. 14/III, mm. 1–30, large-scale harmonic structure

how sections b1 and b2 recall previous sections: the pedal G♯ of section b1 recalls the tonal focus of section A, while the pedal C of section b2 recalls the tonal focus of section b1's upper parts.

Works of the Middle Period: Pensées, *op. 62/2*

Ten years separate op. 32 (1918), the last piano solo work in Prokofiev's first period, from op. 45, *Choses en Soi* (1928), the first solo piano piece in his next phase of compositional development. The extroversion found in earlier music like op. 4/4, op. 11, op. 17/5, and op. 22/10 is absent. Instead, in the two pieces of op. 45, along with op. 62, *Pensées* (1933–1934), the composer impresses self-control and introspection on the music, traits not popularly associated with Prokofiev.

The manifestation of this self-control and introspection is a turn toward counterpoint and away from the dense, dissonant harmonic surfaces which so attracted the composer earlier. Relatively lighter textures and transparent polyphonic surfaces are especially evident in opp. 45, 54, and 62. One perceives the "serious" counterpoint as being arrived at somewhat self-consciously by the composer. Prokofiev's turn toward this style of composition seems tacitly to indicate the adoption of an aesthetic stance in which contrapuntal skill marks intellectual depth.

Prokofiev alludes to the serious demeanor of *Pensées* in the short autobiography. He comments: "In 1933 I wrote a rather large orchestral piece which I called *Symphonic Song,* op. 57. This was a serious piece of work and I took great care in choosing the thematic material. . . . The music [of op. 57] is similar in character to that of op. 62, three pieces for piano under the general title of *Thoughts.*"[18] Prokofiev goes on to make a rather laconic comment about op. 62/2, saying, "The second of the three [pieces of op. 62] I consider one of the best things I have ever written."[19] Unfortunately, he gives no further explanation about what is so special about op. 62/2, and one is left to speculate on which characteristics Prokofiev so admired. Certainly the textural transparency and the clear, distinct, and independent voices are wholly consistent with Prokofiev's new contrapuntal concentration.

Like many of Prokofiev's shorter piano pieces, op. 62/2 is a ternary ABA' form. Section A' is an embellished recapitulation of section A, and for the purposes of this analysis I shall regard it as essentially identical to section A. The diagram of the form given in figure 4.1 includes phrase structure and points of articulation (phrase beginnings and stressed cadential points in the bass).

Section A, a three-phrase period, is predominantly in three voices, with four voices appearing briefly in mm. 9–11. The melody-and-accompaniment texture features a relatively slow-moving melody, proceeding in quarter and half notes, with very little eighth-note motion, and a bass moving even more slowly.

Phrase	Measure Numbers	Points of Articulation
Section A: mm. 1–12		
1	1–4	F♯–B♭
2	4–7	B♭–D
3	8–11	D–B♭–G♭–E
Section B: mm. 12–22		
1	12–15	G–G
2	15–19	G–B
3	20–22	B–G
Section A: mm. 23–35 (varied repetition of mm. 1–12)		

Figure 4.1. Op. 62/2, form outline

The first two phrases, A1 and A2, begin in parallel fashion, forming an antecedent phrase-pair which is answered by the consequent phrase A3. Phrase A1 actually concludes on the downbeat of m. 3, with the remainder of m. 3 through to m. 4's breath mark affirming and extending the arrival of the B♭-minor chord. The beginnings of phrases A1 and A2 are separated by ip4, a constructive interval of an augmented triad. As I discussed earlier, the augmented triad often suggests some type of whole-tone structure.

As is evident in figure 4.1, the bass in the first two phrases explicitly maps out the augmented triad F♯–B♭–D, which is hinted at by the ip4 separating the beginnings of the first two, parallel phrases. The augmented triad is present in complete form in the bass of phrase 1 as well, sketched in example 4.8. Registral accent brings out the boundary pitches F♯2 and D3, while structural accent brings out the first and last notes, F♯2 and B♭2. Whole notes in the example show that the pitches thus emphasized form the augmented triad and duplicate the pitch classes of section A's points of articulation through m. 10.

That augmented triad is yet easier to hear if we regard m. 3's bass G, shown as a filled-in notehead, as a decorative skip, embellishing B♭, a goal already reached. In that case, C♯ and B, also filled-in noteheads, are species of passing notes, filling in stepwise the space between D and B♭. (Later I shall reexamine phrase A1's bass line from a different point of view.)

Example 4.8. *Pensées*, op. 62/2, mm. 1–4, analysis of bass

The bass of phrase A3 begins on D, a pitch class still within the augmented triad (26t); in its points of articulation phrase A3 retrogrades and undoes the motion of the first two phrases. M. 8 begins on D2 and passes down to B♭1 in m. 9. B♭1 in m. 9 then releases an inner voice which arpeggiates upward to activate a higher register. M. 10 returns the favor, arpeggiating from B♭2 down to B♭1, returning to the register left at the beginning of m. 8, and finally bringing in G♭ on its last beat. On m. 10's final beat we return to the identical bass octave on which the piece began. But the cadential m. 11 settles down two more half steps to E, a pitch not belonging to the augmented triad which has been structuring the bass up to this point. E thereby upsets the balance of the symmetrical augmented triad.

The cadence in m. 11 is solidified by a set-class relation which recalls the opening and helps round off section A. The first measure sets out C/F♯ in the outer voices, embellished by lower neighbors B/E♯, with C and E in the inner voice. C, F♯, and E, (046), create a form of [026] (3–8), a set class deriving from the same whole-tone scale which provides the augmented triad (26t), the F♯ whole-tone scale. Phrase A3 moves to its cadence through (46to) on the last two beats of m. 10. The (46to) set contains (046) from m. 1, as well as two additional forms of 3–8, (to4) and (6to). In approaching m. 11, the bass itself moves through a form of 3–8, (46t), an inversion of (046) from m. 1, with which it shares two common tones, the maximum possible under inversion.

While section A's final cadence removes the large-scale structure from the explicit control of the F♯ augmented triad, the structure nevertheless remains in the world of the F♯ whole-tone scale from which that augmented triad derives. Because the whole-tone scale remains intact through the points of articulation of section A, a certain symmetry yet prevails. Section B, however, settles on G and B as the points of articulation, thereby displacing section A's F♯ whole-tone scale altogether.

Section A hints several times at G and B, subtly foreshadowing their appearance in section B. The first hint occurs in the bass line over mm. 1–4, for whose analysis we return to example 4.8. Metric accent brings out the embedded F♯-major triad (strictly, a form of 3–11 [037]), beamed below the staff. Taking as a model m. 1's chromatic neighbor gesture, the beams above the staff show a G-major triad as an upper neighbor to an F♯-major triad.

Phrase A2's cadence also stresses G. While phrase A2 cadences on the bass note D, that bass supports a G triad in six-four position, whose relatively pure diatonic sound contrasts with the darker whole-tone-dominated structures in phrase 1. One might therefore hear the arpeggiated F♯-major triad in phrase 1 move in phrase 2 to the cadence on a G-major triad.

Like section A, section B contains three phrases. From figure 4.1 it is evident that in section B all phrase beginnings and endings are either on G or B and that ic4 separates these points of articulation. Section A foreshadows ic4 in the relation between the beginnings of phrase A1 and phrase A2.

Section A also duplicates two more relations of more global importance. Example 4.8's opposing beams separate the F♯-major (6t1) and G-major (7e2) triads a half step apart. On a larger level, T11 maps section B's points of articulation, (7e), into those of section A, (6t1), excluding m. 11's cadential E. Again excluding E in m. 11 and m. 35, the neighbor relation F♯–G–F♯ produced by the ABA form derives, by inversion, from m. 1's neighbor relation. By disrupting perfect motivic parallelism and [048]'s symmetrical division of the octave, the cadential E chord in m. 11 and in m. 35 is that much fresher and more effective.

With example 4.9 we return to a more foreground level to analyze some contrapuntal relations in phrase B1. The motives labeled "MOT A" (motive A) and "I (MOT A)" (inversion of MOT A), both of which are tetrachordal pitch-class sets, are contour inversions: while MOT A steadily increases in pitch height, I (MOT A) steadily decreases. Further, motion from MOT A's first to second and second to third elements is by ascending step, labeled "ST" in the example, while the approach to MOT A's last element is by ascending skip, labeled "SK." I (MOT A) preserves the order of steps and skips, but it reverses direction. MOT B and MOT B' are both approached by a note repeated across the barline, so that metric placement helps to emphasize their similarity.

MOT B, like MOT A and I (MOT A), is a tetrachordal pitch-class set. The bracketed numbers above the beam on MOT B identify its first, third, and fourth elements as a form of [012], a structure repeated in MOT B'. MOT B', as shown by numbers within square brackets, has the contour segment <0312>, identical to the contour of MOT B (which is not labeled in the example)— another reason to hear the two motives as similar.[20] I (MOT B') is the contour inversion of MOT B', and its contour is shown within the staves. Enhancing

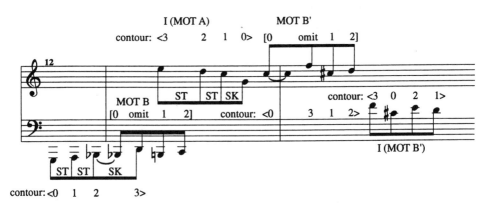

Example 4.9. *Pensées*, op. 62/2, mm. 12–14, aspects of contrapuntal structure

the similarity between the two motives produced by contour inversion is the ordered pitch-class segment $(5-1-2)$, held common between MOT B' and I (MOT B').

As Prokofiev explores nontraditional structures and sonorities, he characteristically clings to many signs of tonality, including triadic harmony and stepwise melody. In op. 62/2 he blurs the distinctions between traditional and modern contexts and invites us to hear the piece first one way and then another. For example, we can tune our hearing of the opening bass line to pick out either an augmented triad or a major triad as the underlying structure.[21] Similarly, the bass D concluding phrase A2 completes a bass arpeggiation of an augmented triad even while it supports a G-major triad, and that sonority emerges as the tonal focus of section B. In this sort of smoothly blended and homogenous context the grotesque line does not appear. The partition which the grotesque line raises in some music (such as the *March* from *Love for Three Oranges*) is replaced by cooperation between familiar tonal structures and nontraditional ones.

Works of the Last Period: Piano Sonata no. 7, op. 83/II

The third and last period of composition began around 1936, roughly coincident with Prokofiev's return to the Soviet Union. Music of this period melds Prokofiev's harmonic and contrapuntal experimentation with his experience, by this time considerable. Where in the first two periods he favored either the vertical or the horizontal domain, in music of the third period he struck a balance, emphasizing harmony no more than counterpoint.

The shorter piano works extend only into the middle period: *Three Pieces*, op. 59 (1933–1934), *Pensées*, op. 62 (1933–1934), and *Children's Music*, op. 65 (1935). Except for arrangements and transcriptions of his music, Prokofiev's only works for piano solo composed after 1936 are the Piano Sonatas nos. 6–9. As I mentioned earlier, among the very greatest music from this period and, indeed, in Prokofiev's entire output, are the Piano Sonatas nos. 6–8, opp. 82, 83, and 84. All three are very large works, with the Piano Sonata no. 6 lasting nearly twenty-seven minutes.

The Piano Sonata no. 7 features the classical line in the simplicity and tunefulness of the opening theme of its slow movement. However, the development and subsequent treatment of this theme is decidedly modern, so much so that the soft character of the opening is nearly effaced by the dissonant, aggressive middle section. The very juxtaposition of these stylistic extremes recalls the grotesque line, whose analysis reveals the essential feature of contrast. In the *March* from *Love for Three Oranges*, the grotesque arises when the listener acquainted with tradition—with preexisting knowledge of a march—encounters the actual music which distorts the tradition: the grotesque arises in the interaction between expectation and reality. In the Piano Sonata no. 7, tradition abides in the music itself, expressed in the conservative and almost atavistic tunefulness of the opening theme. Whereas the *March*'s traditional element is largely present in the listener's mind and therefore external to the piece, in the sonata's slow movement both tradition and modernism are present, existing as formal sections of the music.

The slow movement of the Piano Sonata no. 7 has elicited extensive and varied response from audiences, critics, and composers. William Austin catalogues some of these reactions:

> In the slow movement of the same sonata [no. 7], the "innovating line" is evident in the unpredictable form, while the very commonest chord progressions, with smooth, sweet, chromatic ornaments, take a prominent place in the opening phrase. Diverse judgments of this phrase are useful touchstones to the attitudes of the judges. For Nestyev this is "a beautiful singing theme" in contrast to the outer movements, where "boldness and stunning power" are "so exaggerated as to make it difficult for the listener to perceive any features of Soviet reality." For the American author of a preface to the sonatas, Irwin Freundlich, and the author of a thesis on them, D. L. Kinsey, the sweet phrase is a "reversion to an obsolete romanticism," marring what would otherwise be their favorite sonata. For Francis Poulenc, writing a swift survey of all Prokofiev's piano music, the same melody is "ah! marvelous . . . one of those melodies of which Prokofiev has the secret," and an essential part of the whole sonata.[22]

Nestyev seems to find comfort in the opening phrase's simplicity, tunefulness, and conservative sound, especially when compared to the outer movements. For Freundlich and Kinsey, however, the opposite is true: where the outer movements make a coherent and aesthetically justifiable statement, the middle movement vitiates the sonata because it commits the sin of epigonism by resorting to an atavistic style. Certainly the charge of "obsolete romanticism" carries the implication of either failed or absent innovation. Poulenc alone hears in the entire sonata an arcane integrity which eludes the other critics.

Though all the judgments of the opening theme phrase differ, the critics agree that there exists a considerable contrast between the opening phrase's relatively traditional demeanor and much of the rest of the movement, such as mm. 52–68, measures full of insistent, repeated dissonance and an aggressive, full texture. Yet the entire movement, including mm. 52–68, draws on features of the opening theme. Accordingly, the main thrust of this analysis will be to

Section	Measure Numbers	Performance Indications	Comments
First Thematic Group	mm. 1–8	Andante caloroso	Theme A1; E-major tonal interpreter
	mm. 9–16		Theme A2; D-major tonal interpreter
	mm. 17–23		Theme A1 returns in E; variation on theme A2 ends the section
	mm. 24–31		Transition
Second Thematic Group	mm. 32–39	Poco più animato	Theme B1 Theme B2
Second Thematic Group Variation	mm. 40–45		Non-synchronous octaves begin in m. 44
Development	mm. 46–52	Più largamente	Development of theme A2
	mm. 50–51		Development of motive b
Denouement	mm. 52–59		Alternating chords begin; dramatic chords follow
	mm. 60–61		Development of theme B1
	mm. 62–64		Alternating chords resume
	mm. 65–68		Development of theme B1
	mm. 69–78	Un poco agitato	Most extensive development of theme B1
	mm. 79–97		New pair of alternating chords
Recap of First Thematic Group	mm. 98–107	Tempo I	Third flip in final cadence

Figure 4.2. Piano Sonata no. 7, op. 83/II, form outline

show how material originating in the opening phrase is treated subsequently.

Two constellations of sets structure this piece. The first includes the small chromatic sets 2–1 [01], 3–1 [012], and 4–1 [0123], as well as [04] (2–3), a subset descended from [0123]. The second constellation is organized around the structural set 5–21 [01458]. This second constellation includes 3–11 [037], a subset descended from 5–21, and two supersets of 5–21, 6z19 [013478] and 6–20 [014589].

Figure 4.2 is an outline of the movement, a varied sonata form which includes two thematic groups, a development, a denouement, and a recapitula-

Example 4.10. Piano Sonata no. 7, op. 83/II, catalogue of themes and motives

tion that omits the second thematic group. *Più largamente* marks the beginning of the development section, which is based on ideas from both thematic groups. *Un poco agitato* marks the special development of a motive from the second thematic group, a motive I shall later call *x*. Example 4.10 is a catalogue of the themes and motives cited in figure 4.2. Themes A1 and A2 belong to the first thematic group; themes B1 and B2 belong to the second thematic group. Particular motives *v*, *v* −, *vi*, *x*, and *b* are shown in brackets below the staff. Let us turn first to two related structural sets, an ordered form of 3 − 1, labeled motive "v" in example 4.10, and 5 − 21, a harmonic set shown in example 4.10a.

Motive *v* first occurs as theme A1's chromatic upbeat F♯–F×–G♯, labeled "v(F♯)", and is counterpointed by D–D♯–E, labeled "v(D)"; motive *v* permeates the entire movement. Example 4.10c shows that the untransposed pitch classes of motive *v* also introduce the second thematic group at m. 32. Motive *v* also occurs in transposed, retrograded, and inverted forms. For instance, example 4.10d shows inverted motive *v* (labeled "inv v") in the next-to-last measure of theme B2.

Motive *v* directly generates much of the movement's chromaticism, as in the left hand's inner voices in m. 14. By reading the position of the D♯-minor chord on the last eighth of the measure as the result of octave shift, we can extract two linear components of the progression: C♯4–D4–D♯3 represents C♯4–D4–

Example 4.11. Piano Sonata no. 7, op. 83/II, motive *v* — in mm. 13–16

D♯4, a transposed form of motive *v*, while G3–G♯3–A3–A♯2 represents G3–G♯3–A3–A♯3, a motive we can label "v+."

Two other descendants of motive *v* are 3–2 [013] and 2–1 [01]. The set 3–2, an ordered descendant labeled "v1" in example 4.10d, occurs as a component of motive *b*. Three factors link motives *v1* and *v*. First, like motive *v*, *v1* makes a continuous stepwise ascent. Second, motive *v1* retains motive *v*'s function as an anacrusis: both motives comprise two eighth notes leading to a downbeat. And third, motive *v1* moves stepwise through small intervals.[23]

A second descendant of motive *v* is an ordered form of the subset 2–1, labeled "v—" in example 4.10a. Example 4.11 gives a sketch of the bass of mm. 13–16. The notes beamed together, G and G♯, form motive *v—*. G–to–G♯, pitch class 7 to pitch class 8, echoes the pitch classes of the original motive *v*, F♯–F×–G♯ (pitch classes 6–7–8). The beams below the staff indicate that the interval E/G in mm. 13–14 expands to E/G♯ in mm. 15–16 with E, G, and G♯ each standing out as a bend in the contour. The interval E/G♯ in mm. 15–16 recalls the same interval in mm. 1–3 in the right hand.[24]

E/G♯, prominent in example 4.11, is prepared in the first thematic statement. E, the tonal center, returns regularly every two measures in the bass of mm. 1–6. G♯ is the goal of motive *v* in mm. 1–3, where it is the highest pitch (occurring as G♯4); it is also the lower bound and a point of stability for the right hand's melody. Through m. 5, E and G♯ anchor the music. Then in m. 5 and m. 7, D♮ transforms the tonic E into an applied dominant seventh, V(7)/V, in D major to prepare m. 9's thematic restatement. (M. 7 moves to m. 8 through an E dominant $\frac{4}{2}$ chord, V$\frac{4}{2}$ of V in D.)

Tugging gently against the low, reposeful G♯3 is an upper line, slowly ascending from C♯ through D♯ to E, a rhythmically augmented form of motive *v1*. The right hand in m. 5 brings in E4 via a retrograded form of motive *v* which occurs simultaneously with a retrograded and inverted form of motive *v1* in the left hand. Forms of retrograded motive *v* lead m. 6 into m. 7, at which point V/V in D appears. A brief circle-of-fifths progression then takes E dominant $\frac{4}{2}$ in m. 7 to A dominant $\frac{6}{3}$ in m. 8 and finally to the D tonic in m. 9.

The insistent F♯4 first heard in m. 9 initiates an extensive rhythmic augmentation of motive *v* at the same pitch-class level as the right hand's upbeat to

m. 1.[25] F♯ enters in m. 9, G enters in m. 13, and G♯ enters in mm. 16–17. Besides using the crescendo to help bring in G5 in m. 13, Prokofiev carefully activates the C5 octave each time a new increment lifts motive *v* from F♯ in m. 9, through G♮ (F×) in m. 13, to G♯ in m. 17.

Like the first thematic group, the second also features motive *v* as an anacrusis. Mm. 29–32 contain two interlocking forms of motive *v*: the left hand brings in E–F–G♭ in mm. 29–30 and follows with G♭–B–A♭ in mm. 31–32. Motive *v*'s presence in these measures recalls the successive forms of motive *v* in mm. 7–9. The form of motive *v* leading to *Poco più animato* in m. 32 is pitch-class invariant with the anacrusis of m. 1.

By introducing the second thematic group as well as the first, the original form of motive *v* helps us hear that the A♭ expressed in the bass of mm. 32–35 expands upon G♯, so prominent in the first thematic group. The second thematic group also refers to the first when it begins by marking out the intervallic span from A♭2 to D♭3, recalling the identical pitch interval and the same pitch classes in the melody of mm. 1–2.

In example 4.12 I extract a two-voice counterpoint from the second thematic group. The counterpoint is based on two forms of motive *v* which move away from A♭ in contrary motion and then return to A♭ by the same type of contrary motion. In the bass, the elements of retrograded motive *v* are stemmed where A♭ in m. 32 slowly makes its way down to G in m. 36 and finally to G♭ in m. 37. The bass marks orthographically the change from retrograded motive *v* to motive *v* when m. 38 respells G♭ as F♯.

Despite the four-flat key signature, mm. 32–33 focus harmonically on D♭ because the melody begins and ends on D♭, because the chord in the middle of m. 33 is a D♭-major triad (albeit in six-four position) and because G♭, the flat missing from the key signature, is provided by the upbeat to m. 32. G♭ has also been sounding persistently in the bass ever since m. 25.[26] D♮ on the downbeat of m. 34 begins to disturb the D♭ tonality, and then in m. 35 the melodic pause on A♮ continues the move away from diatonic purity. A♮3 displaces A♭3 from m. 32 and begins an ascending form of motive *v*, which aims toward its completion on B♭3 in m. 35, beat 3, a goal reiterated in m. 37. In example 4.12 I stem and label

Example 4.12. Piano Sonata no. 7, op. 83/II, motive *v* in mm. 32–39

this form of motive *v*. At the end of m. 38, the melody presents a compact form of retrograded motive *v* which retraces its steps B♭–A–A♭ before landing on G, at which point the bass reaches the same pitch-class goal. As though joining forces on the final G, the bass relinquishes its low-register G1 to the melody, where motive *v* continues through to A♭3 at the end of m. 39 and a varied statement of the second theme begins. The final A♭ in example 4.12 completes motive *v* and dovetails with the beginning of the varied second theme (marked "varied repeat" in the example).

The E-minor triad of m. 39 (not shown in the example) finds weak first-inversion support in the bass. Still, it does recall the "tonic" E-major tonal-interpreting triad of the opening theme. Further, mm. 12–13 and mm. 21–22 also imply the minor mode. The bass of mm. 12–13 moves C–B–E, outlining a tonal interpretive motion $\hat{6}$–$\hat{5}$–$\hat{1}$ in E minor. And if we freeze the music at the downbeat of m. 13, we do in fact hear an incomplete E-minor triad, E/G. As mentioned earlier, the interval E/G gets special treatment in the bass of mm. 13–14. (Later, in the denouement, we shall see more interaction among E, G, and G♯.) In mm. 21–22, measures parallel to mm. 12–13, the bass even more strongly suggests the minor mode, moving $\hat{4}$–$\hat{3}$–$\hat{2}$–$\hat{5}$–$\hat{1}$ in G♯ minor and containing a complete "D♯ dominant seventh" on beat 3 of m. 21.

In the development section Prokofiev combines and interweaves motives from the two thematic groups without introducing any new motivic material. The insistent B (or C♭ in m. 51) in the bass over mm. 46–51, while not the keynote of a conventional dominant tonal area, is nevertheless a sign of traditional tonal design. As the bass of this passage pushes up and away from B, it unfolds a form of motive *v* (D) identical in its notes to the occurrence in m. 1. D2 in m. 47 rises to E♭2 in m. 49 and finally to E4 (two octaves higher) in m. 52.

The melody superimposed on this passage has two sources. From m. 46 to the 5th eighth note of m. 49, the melody is a transposition at T7 of the melody in mm. 13–16. Then the last beat of m. 49 to the end of m. 51 is a transposition of m. 36 (including its upbeat) through m. 37 at T5. Development for Prokofiev is very often a matter of combining and recombining thematic material from the exposition (as, for example, in the Symphony no. 3/I and the String Quartet no. 1, op. 50/I). The thematic material is often taken over virtually intact. Less common developmental strategies for Prokofiev are the kind of motivic development which depends on disassembling thematic material into motivic components or sequential treatments of themes or motives.

The bass motion in mm. 51–52, from C♭ (B) to E, is a tonal-interpreting dominant-to-tonic gesture in which the dominant chord is spelled enharmonically, with C♭ and E♭ in place of B and D♯, and in which A♭ (G♯) displaces the expected chordal fifth, F♯.[27]

Example 4.13. Piano Sonata no. 7, op. 83/II, mm. 69–79, motivic and harmonic structure

In the form outline in figure 4.2, mm. 52–97 constitute a denouement rather than, say, a continuation of the development, because of the static, ostinato-like character of the section. During the denouement the energy built up in the dense chromatic texture and expansiveness of the development is slowly and somewhat fitfully dissipated by the various pairs of alternating chords. To continue working within this interpretational scheme: theme B, in m. 60 and mm. 65–68, bursts through the alternating chords with yet-to-be-dissipated energy, as though inadvertently forgotten by the development. Along with the passage in mm. 69–78, theme B disrupts the alternating chords so severely that when they return in mm. 79 ff. the alternating chords are changed.

Un poco agitato, beginning at m. 69, features a three-voice framework, sketched in example 4.13. In the lowest voice, beginning in m. 69, F♯ sets in as a pedal. The pedal F♯ does not relinquish its hold on the bass until m. 79, where it settles down to E to begin a new set of oscillating chords. A registrally isolated upper voice descends from B in m. 69 to A in m. 72 and to G in m. 74. We can transform motive *v* (G) into this upper voice by first doubling the intervallic distance between its elements, so that half steps become whole steps: (G–G♯–A) times 2 = (G–A–B). Then we retrograde the result: R(G–A–B) = (B–A–G).[28] An inner voice shown in example 4.13 traces out a descending (retrograded) form of motive *v,* moving F♯–F–E. The inner voice draws considerable attention when F♮5 in mm. 71–72 defeats F♯5, a pitch that has been in force for nearly three measures, mm. 69–71. Both the inner and upper voices are completed in m. 74, where they arrive at the interval E/G.

The bottom staff of example 4.13 shows the tonal-interpreting harmonies of mm. 69–71, mm. 72–73, and mm. 74–79.[29] In those measures, two dominant-function harmonies, G major and B half-diminished seventh, lead to the C tonic (of which the interval E/G is obviously a part). The movement's conclusion will recall this tonal focus on C.

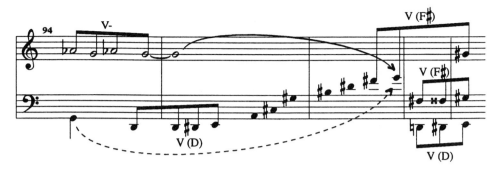

Example 4.14. Piano Sonata no. 7, op. 83/II, mm. 94–97, motivic structure

There are two different pairs of alternating triads which occur in the denouement. For convenience I shall refer to forms of 3–11 by their conventional tonal names without thereby necessarily implying tonal function. Tonal-interpreting structures will be pointed out as they arise.

The first pair of alternating chords, occurring over mm. 53–54, 56–59, and 62–64, is E major / C minor. In m. 56, this chord pair introduces an inner voice C–B–A♯, a retrograded form of motive *v*, C–B–A♯.

M. 79 introduces the second and final pair of alternating chords, whose inner voice now alternates between G and A♭, the two pitch classes forming motive *v*–, a motive first encountered in the bass of mm. 13–16 (see example 4.10). Example 4.14 is a sketch of mm. 94–98, which conclude this passage. The pitches of motive *v*– are labeled and beamed together. In m. 95 the inner voice G/A♭ finally halts on G. Rocking between G and A♭ is a tease, a contest to decide which pitch will triumph. At the end of m. 94, G appears to win: the rocking ceases as G is held for four and a half beats. But the pause on G only forestalls the arrival of A♭. As the solid arrow in example 4.14 shows, G4 sustains through the beginning of m. 96, at which point the left hand ascends to pick it up. In fact, the left hand's voice converges on the right hand's G4 within a form of complete motive *v*, labeled in the example. Hence, G's original tonal-interpreting character is ultimately revealed when the reprise gets under way at m. 98 and we hear G as F×.

The recapitulation of the first thematic group begins with motive *v* and follows G4 on the last beat of m. 97, where motive *v* finally, definitively pushes up to G♯ (A♭). The form of motive *v* comprising F♯4, G4, and G♯4 in mm. 96–98 is considerably altered rhythmically. The literal motive *v* occurs an octave lower in the upbeat to m. 98, also shown in example 4.14.

Example 4.15 shows the notes from m. 81 on the middle system, which is analyzed on a treble staff and a bass staff aligned above and below. These framing staves show a distillation of E tonal-interpreting elements from the

Example 4.15. Piano Sonata no. 7, op. 83/II, mm. 81, tonal-interpreting structure

middle system. (E♭5, respelled as D♯5, can also be heard as a major seventh above an E root.) In particular, the E tonal-interpreting elements E2, G2, G5, and G♯5 (A♭5) delimit the registral extremes, making them especially easy to hear. The major-minor chord (4–17 [0347]) which these elements form is a favorite sonority of Prokofiev's.[30] While the musical presentation blurs the mode, the tonal focus on E prepares for the recapitulation of the opening theme.

We can now turn our attention to those aspects of m. 1 shown in example 4.16a. The open noteheads on the example show the E-major triad, the local tonic. The union of the E-major harmony and the third D/F✕, shown as filled-in noteheads, is (3478e), a form of 5–21 [01458]. The melodic voice of example 4.16a is motive *v—*, F✕–G♯, which is already familiar to us. In example 4.16b I interpret (3478e) in this context as a tonal-interpreting major triad whose lower third is embellished by chromatic lower neighbors, shown as filled-in noteheads which are beamed and flagged.

In mm. 12–13 theme A2 embeds 5–21 within its opening. In example 4.17a

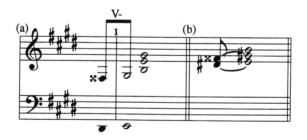

Example 4.16. Piano Sonata no. 7, op. 83/II, m. 1, motive *v—* and 5-21 [01458]

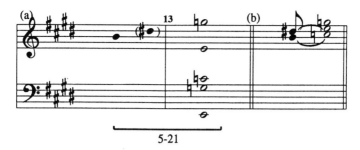

Example 4.17. Piano Sonata no. 7, op. 83/II, mm. 12–13, 5-21 [01458]

I isolate the notes forming 5–21 at this juncture. In example 4.17b I analyze m. 13 the way I analyzed m. 1 in example 4.16: a major triad's lower third is embellished chromatically.[31]

The structural set 5–21 generates the descendants 6–20 and 6z19 through a unit increment in cardinality. In this piece, 6–20 is formed either by the union of two augmented triads whose roots lie a minor third apart or by the union of a major and a minor triad whose roots lie a major third apart. The descendant 6z19 is formed either by the union of two minor triads whose roots lie a half step apart or by the union of two major triads whose roots lie a half step apart.

Mm. 28–29, part of the transition from the first thematic group to the second, are a varied repetition of mm. 26–27. Leading into the large bracket in example 4.18 are two forms of motive *v*, one on A♭ and one on G♭. Motive *v* (G♭) brings in the repeated inner voice, A♭3, which arrests the forward motion so that mm. 28–29 hover, nearly motionless, in anticipation of the second thematic group (as I have already discussed, the insistence on A♭ carries over into the second thematic group).

The opposing stems in example 4.18 separate melodic strands in the right

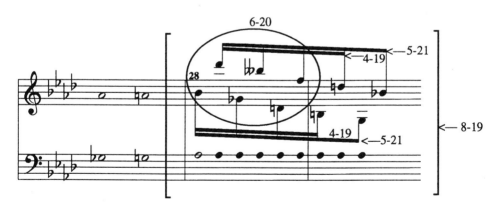

Example 4.18. Piano Sonata no. 7, op. 83/II, mm. 27–29, set structure

Example 4.19. Piano Sonata no. 7, op. 83/II, m. 1 and m. 53, set structure

hand, each of which unfolds an augmented triad within m. 28. The union of these augmented triads forms 6–20, shown within the circle. The double beams in the example connect two forms of 4–19, whose complement, 8–19, is formed by all the pitches shown in the example over mm. 28–29. Finally, the total content of each strand is a form of 5–21.

In the denouement, 6–20 emerges again where, like 5–21 in m. 1, it arises from a triad embellished by chromatic auxiliaries. For ease of comparison, example 4.19 reproduces 5–21 from m. 1. We find a related structure in the alternating triads from m. 53, shown on the right side of example 4.19. The C-minor triad chromatically displaces the entire E chord, not only its lower third.

A tonal interpretation of the alternating triads is not the only one possible, however. In mm. 79ff., a new pair of alternating triads occurs, namely C major and A♭ minor. Example 4.20 shows a comparison of these two pairs, revealing that, in fact, they are identical in pitch-class content. Both pairs of triads project (3478e0), 6–20 [014589]. The partitioning of 6–20 into its triadic subsets is different in each case. In mm. 53 ff. the subsets are (48e) (E major) and (037) (C minor); in mm. 79ff. the subsets are (047) (C major) and (8e3) (A♭ minor).[32]

The inner voice of the C-major / A♭-minor pair expresses in pitches its pitch-class center of inversion; those pitches are A♭ and G, motive $v-$: $I^{G/A♭}(047) = (3e8)$.

At the beginning of this analysis we surveyed various different published responses to the movement's main theme. Though the critics evaluated the appropriateness of the opening theme variously, they did believe that it was, at least to some extent, stylistically anomalous when compared to the outer movements or to the central portion of the middle movement itself. The foregoing analysis has shown that the opening theme, and indeed the brief opening ges-

Example 4.20. Piano Sonata no. 7, op. 83/II, mm. 53ff. and mm. 79ff., partitionings of 6-20 into triadic subsets

ture, contributes material that, in several different guises, significantly structures the entire movement.

Motive v, the chromatic upbeat beginning the movement, and pitch-class set 5–21, the harmonic set associated with motive $v-$, account for the bulk of this analysis, clearly demonstrating their status as structural sets.

Three features help motive v stand out. First, motive v is ordered: when it occurs, its elements continually ascend by half step (or descend, in retrograded form). Second, motive v is stubbornly "pitch-loyal." It most often appears at the pitch level of the two original forms, beginning on D or on F♯. For example, the form beginning on F♯ introduces the second thematic group; the form beginning on D occurs in the bass of the development. Motive $v-$ is truly pitch-loyal since it is never transposed. Finally, each of the various formal sections usually preserves a single function of motive v. In the expository sections motive v is anacrustic, introducing both the first and the second thematic groups. In the development section motive v structures the bass line and determines the transposition levels of the harmonies derived from mm. 13–16. The development unfolds a rhythmically augmented, untransposed form of motive v which is completed, in dramatic fashion, on the first beat of m. 52, beginning the denouement. (Here too, then, motive v retains a sort of anacrustic function.) In mm. 79ff. motive $v-$ inverts the chord pair C major/A♭ minor.

Pitch-class set 5–21 enjoys distinctly more plastic treatment than motive v: it occurs melodically as well as in several different harmonic forms. Prokofiev is especially adept at showing off both 5–21's inherent tonal structure—say, as an embellished major triad, as in m. 1—and its inherent non-tonal structure— say, as a superset of an augmented triad, as in mm. 26–29. The 5–21 also generates two significant hexachordal supersets, 6–20 and 6z19. In the denouement, embellishing structures project 6z19. The 6–20 occurs in the transition from the first to the second thematic group and in the denouement, where the alternating chord pairs project it. We may recall as well that those chords relate via an inversion whose I-center (inversional center) directly associates with motive v.

As we have seen, motive v itself occurs as an upbeat and as a structuring motive. Motive $v-$ is an I-center and the "descant" of 5–21. The 5–21 contributes pitch material shaping much of the music. The broad impact on the music of a single motive suggests another shade of meaning of the word "motive," that is, as a driving force. As we have heard, whether the opening theme and its opening motive are "a beautiful singing theme" or a "reversion to an obsolete romanticism," they intimately connect with the other parts of the movement, bridging any perceived stylistic differences.

5 Orchestral Music

Prokofiev naturally invested much time in composing ballet music during his years of association with Diaghilev. In the passage from *Chout* examined below, the music is relatively compressed, direct, and nondigressive. In general, the composer eschews lengthy and complex development of thematic material. But Prokofiev's ballet music still exhibits relations familiar from the previous chapters in this book. In particular, we shall find that the same structural sets which are prominent on the musical surface also control longer-range tonal structure.

Suite du ballet Chout, *op. 21 bis/II*

Prokofiev's ballet *Chout* (composed in 1922, premiered in 1924) was the first of his three ballets for Diaghilev; the other two were *Le Pas d'acier,* (composed in 1926, premiered in 1927) and *The Prodigal Son* (composed in 1929, premiered in 1931).[1] The suite made from *Chout* was also a regular feature of Prokofiev's concert repertoire and remains one of his best-known works.[2]

Figure 5.1 is a diagram of the form of the second movement, a binary A– B1–B2, whose second part, comprising sections B1 and B2, receives special emphasis through a varied repetition. Section A is tonally circular, beginning and

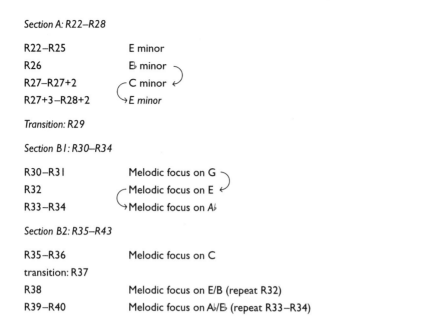

Section A: R22–R28

R22–R25	E minor
R26	E♭ minor
R27–R27+2	C minor
R27+3–R28+2	E minor

Transition: R29

Section B1: R30–R34

R30–R31	Melodic focus on G
R32	Melodic focus on E
R33–R34	Melodic focus on A♭

Section B2: R35–R43

R35–R36	Melodic focus on C
transition: R37	
R38	Melodic focus on E/B (repeat R32)
R39–R40	Melodic focus on A♭/E♭ (repeat R33–R34)
codetta: R41–R43	Melodic focus on C (completes symmetrical division of the octave over section B2: C–E–A♭–C)

Figure 5.1. *Suite de ballet Chout*, op. 21 bis/II, form outline

ending by focusing on E minor. Section B1, on the other hand, exhibits progressive harmonic movement, concluding on a point of articulation, A♭, which is a half step higher than the one on which it began, G. Section B1's goal is the melody of R33, which will be discussed below. In the figure the tonal goals of each section are in italics. Though section A is harmonically circular and section B1 is progressive, they both approach their goals through transpositions of T9 followed by T4. These transpositions are marked by arrows.

Several factors create the E-minor tonal focus in R22–R24. In each of the first five measures, the strings sweep downward through a fifth to land on E. The E-minor chord at R22+2 is approached by the stepwise fragment $\hat{6}$–$\hat{7}$–$\hat{1}$ in the bass. A descending circle of fifths in the bass concludes on E at R23. The second harp relentlessly plucks the constituent thirds of an E-minor triad on the beat over R22 to R23+6. And finally, an E-minor triad confines the motion of the piano and the harps: E4/G4 is the lowest interval and G4/B4 is the highest.

Disturbing the lower pentachord of a conventional E-minor scale E–F♯–G–A–B are two wrong notes, F♮ and A♯. F♮ drives down to the tonic E in the grace note flourish, and balancing that, A♯ drives up to the dominant B in the piano-harp ostinato. A♯ receives greater emphasis than F♮ because of repetition and relatively greater durational accent. The augmented second it forms with G stands out clearly within the texture, as does the repeated ordered fragment G–A♯–B and its retrograde. G–A♯–B is a form of the structural set 3–3 [014].

A D♯-minor triad is hinted at in R23+1 when the flutes and violins trace out the fifth D♯/A♯. That D♯-minor triad prepares E♭ minor of R26 (enharmonically D♯ minor), where the music slips down a half step. R26 then sustains E♭ minor just as the previous music sustained E minor. At R27, the music moves down a major third and focuses on C minor. The prominent motive in the violins in R22–R24, (G–A♯–B), and the succession of tonal centers through R27+1, (E–E♭–C), are both forms of [014]. Hence, part of the context which produced the "wrong note" in the beginning (G–A♯–B) actually portrays on a local level the tonal progression of the movement's first twenty-seven measures.

R30, beginning the binary's second half (section B1), introduces a new melody, a diatonic modal melody centering on G. Variations on this melody enter at R32, centering on E, and at R33, centering on A♭. The melody at R30+2 is the simplest of the three, and its total pitch-class content (02479) is a form of 5–35, the pentatonic scale. Each of the two melodic variants embeds a form of 5–35: R32 embeds (93146) [=T9(02479)], and R33 embeds (1358t) [= T4(9e146)].

Each melody also focuses on a particular chord, determined primarily by melodic structure. The melody in R30 focuses on G. Three stressed attacks on G5, in the first oboe and first harp, begin the melody at R30+2. D5, G major's chordal fifth, concludes the first phrase at R31 in a melodic half cadence, reinforcing the G-centricity. Like G5 in the melody's first two measures, D5 is dynamically stressed in the next two. The treble staff of the second harp, clarinets I and II, and high strings reinforce with a G triad the melody's G tonal center.

I also note that here the bass alternates between A and E, reproducing at a different pitch level the intervallic relation between the melodic G and D. Together the bass and melody project a form of 4–23 [0257], one of Prokofiev's characteristic tonal tetrachords.[3]

The melody of R32, like that of R30+2, from which it derives, stresses pitches a perfect fourth apart, here E and B. In the first two measures E always draws the melody back before it can move away; B plays the same role in the following two measures. The bass, however, begins supporting the melodic focus on E, but by the passage's third measure moves down to C♯ in preparation for an upward step to E♭ at R33. R33 brings in the third melodic statement, focusing on A♭5 in its first two measures and then, immediately preceding R34, ending on a half-cadential E♭ a fourth below.

Example 5.1a reproduces from R22 the original structural set (7te), a form of [014], and displays two order operations which permute it. The first arrow

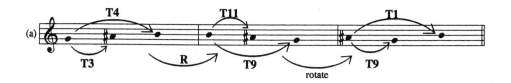

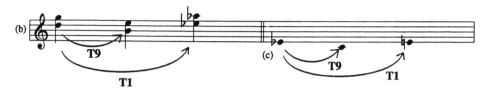

Example 5.1. *Suite de ballet Chout,* op. 21 bis/II, generating the arrow structure T9–T11 and applying it to melodic variations over R30–R35 and to the tonal structure of section A

across a barline, labeled "R," shows retrogression; the second one, labeled "rotate," shows a circular permutation. The curved arrows within barlines show ordered pitch-class transpositions. Example 5.1b shows that the arrow structure which is the final result of the analysis in example 5.1a also governs the succession of melodic variations over R30–R35, so that those melodies embody a large-scale projection of the structural set [014], a set first heard in m. 1's accompaniment pattern. In example 5.1c I return to the succession of tonal areas in section A to show that they, too, are organized according to example 5.1a's final arrow structure.

A new section follows R33's extended stop on E♭, a stop sufficiently long and weighty to close R30–R34. A melody focused on C and G then enters at R35 and extends through R36. A brief transition at R37 leads to R38, whose melody, a repetition of R32's melody, features E and B. R39 repeats R33, centering on A♭ and E♭, and this entire section, beginning with R35, then extends through R40. As can be seen in figure 5.1, section B2 cycles through the elements of an augmented triad, C–E–A♭–C, to create its circular tonal progression. These points of articulation, italicized in figure 5.1, summarize the large-scale tonal scheme: the goal of section A is E, which moves by T4 to section B1's goal, A♭; section B1 then also moves by T4 to section B2's goal, C.

Symphony no. 1, First Movement

Touring Prokofiev's seven symphonies in order from beginning to end is not a smooth ride. Very different forces motivated each symphony's production. As is well known, the Symphony no. 1, the "Classical" Symphony, was an intended poke in the ribs of the classical style. As Prokofiev predicted, it achieved considerable popularity as a witty filtering of an anachronistic style. With the Symphony no. 2, Prokofiev wished to demonstrate his compositional depth and to combat any possible impression of a lack of serious intent that the "Classical" Symphony may have left.[4] In both the Symphony no. 3 and the Symphony no. 4 Prokofiev reworked earlier material. The Symphony no. 3 is a reworking of music from the opera *The Flaming Angel,* which Prokofiev was unsuccessful in getting staged; the Symphony no. 4 is a reworking of music from the ballet the *Prodigal Son,* a piece which enjoyed considerable success.[5] The Symphony no. 7 was composed by Prokofiev in the hope of rehabilitating himself in the eyes of the government following the Decree of 1948. In this intent it belongs with the Cello Sonata, op. 119, and the Piano Sonata no. 9, op. 103.

Of all the symphonies, the Symphony no. 5 and the Symphony no. 6 seem most free of external motivating factors. In them, Prokofiev sought neither to salvage earlier music nor to soothe the Soviet government.[6] The initial reception for each symphony was very positive.

The Symphony no. 1 (1916–1917), though a pastiche, shows Prokofiev's highly refined compositional skill.[7] One senses in this work a composer comfortable with his materials and confident in his product. While remaining within the tradition of the classical symphony, which he understood and revered, Prokofiev twisted and distorted it without destroying it. The play of tradition (represented by the obvious classical line) with innovation (represented by Prokofiev's witty interpretation of the classical line) produces a piece in the grotesque line. But Prokofiev's respect for the classical style sets bounds on the grotesque quality and prevents it from crossing into malicious parody.

The interaction between tradition and innovation is evident in the first movement's rhythmic and pitch structure, aspects of which we shall examine. Square regular hypermeter, which is also evident, is a typical feature of a first movement allegro in a classical style. But Prokofiev makes subtle changes in the hypermeter and manipulates it to keep the listener off balance, in effect creating in the rhythmic domain a parallel to wrong notes in the pitch domain. Each distortion of the hypermeter is slightly different, and each consistently contradicts the listener's expectations. In the exposition, rhythmic irregularity is purely a matter of hypermetric distortion. In the development, rhythmic interest derives from syncopation, the untangling of which leads directly into the recapitulation.

The first movement, diagrammed in figure 5.2, is a sonata form. Minus the two-bar introduction, both mm. 1–10, in D, and mm. 11–18, in C, use the same melodic material, labeled "theme A1" in figure 5.2; theme A1 is given in example 5.2a. The material beginning at R2 is in D, like mm. 1–10, and rounds out the first thematic area tonally. But R2 relies on a slightly different melodic idea,

First thematic area: m. 1 to R3

    R0: theme A1, key of D

    R1: theme A1, key of C

    R2: theme A2, key of D

    R3: theme A2, key of B minor

    transition spinning off from first theme: R4 or so to R5

Second thematic area: R6–R8 (theme B, key of A)

Closing: R9–R11 (variation on theme A1)

Development: R12–R19 (D minor–G dominant–C major; focus on material from the first thematic area)

Recapitulation: R20–R29

    R20: theme A1, key of C

    R21: theme A2, key of D

    R22–R23: theme A2, key of B to V/D

    R24–R27: theme B, key of D

    R28–R29: closing (variation on theme A1)

Figure 5.2. Symphony no. 1 ("Classical"), op. 25/I, form outline

theme A2, reproduced in example 5.2b. In particular, the stepwise descent in m. 4, labeled "y_1" in example 5.2a, recurs at R2+1, where it is shorn of its embellishing thirds. This new incarnation of the motive is labeled "y_2" in example 5.2b.[8] M. 4 and R2+1 are also similar rhythmically, occupying the second hyperbeat of a four-bar hypermeasure.

After the two-measure introduction, the music proceeds in regular four-bar hypermeasures. Over R1, quadruple regularity penetrates the next higher level of rhythmic structure so that four 4-bar hypermeasures carry into R2, at which point the flutes state the melodic fragment shown in example 5.2b. Besides motive y_2, the melody contains a second four-beat motive, labeled "x" in example 5.2b. The first four bars of R2 associate motive x with strong beats and motive y_2 with weak beats.

But the second hypermeasure of R2 (R2+4 through R2+8) repeats motive x one time, as shown in example 5.2b. This repetition creates metric ambiguity and suggests two possible interpretations. The upper row of hypermetric beat-numbers in example 5.2b continues a four-bar hypermeasure through mm. 23 – 26. In this reading, motive x's repetition neatly divides one hypermeasure in half within an already established four-bar hypermetric norm. However, by repeating motive x, motive y_2 is shifted from its previous position on a hypermetric weak beat to one on a strong beat. The group closes at R2+8 on a hypermetric downbeat, thereby combining metric and structural accents. R2+8 poses

Example 5.2. Symphony no. 1, op. 25/I
a. mm. 3–6, theme A1
b. mm. 19–36, theme A2

two challenges to metric regularity. First, R3 clearly initiates a hypermeasure when it restates theme A2, thus making R3 and the previous measure into two successive downbeats.[9] That irregularity is enhanced because one measure before R3 the meter changes from $\frac{2}{2}$ to $\frac{2}{4}$. Thus, as a downbeat closing off mm. 23–27, m. 27 arrives on time but endures too briefly.

The lower row of hypermetric beat-numbers in example 5.2b gives a second interpretation. Here, R2+5 expands the phrase by repeating the previous bar, as though a needle on a turntable had skipped. The expansion is shown on the example as "(1)." Though this reading disrupts regular four-bar hypermeter, it preserves the placements of motive x and motive $y2$ as metrically strong and weak beats, respectively. There are now no successive downbeats, as in the first interpretation. One measure before R3 is now a fourth hypermetric beat, but, as in the first interpretation, it still endures too briefly.

As can be seen on example 5.2b, R3 restores hypermetric regularity in its first four bars. By repeating motive x, R3's second hypermeasure, beginning at R3+4, feigns a parallel repetition of R2's second hypermeasure; but instead of delivering a five-bar group, R3's second hypermeasure takes in four bars. Following motive $y2$, R3's second hypermeasure omits a bar parallel to R2+7, but it preserves the too brief bar of $\frac{2}{4}$. The effect is to disrupt metric regularity (even if one had adjusted to R2's metric irregularity and was now prepared to perceive it as regular) and accelerate forcefully into R4 (m. 36), a hypermetrically regular passage leading into the second thematic area.

Examples of wrong notes are not difficult to find. One instance is shown in example 5.3, which displays the outer-voice structure in the second theme, beginning at R6. Its dainty, restrained character is a virtual parody of the textbook description of a second theme. It is here that we can imagine the composer chuckling over traditional sonata-form etiquette and poking fun at it most vigorously. While the first theme is also stylistically correct, marking out the tonic key with a forceful arpeggiated melody, it is not as exaggerated in its demeanor as the second.

The second theme comprises three parallel phrases: R6 through R7+2, R7+3 through R8, and R9 (which leads smoothly into R10's closing theme). A variety of strategies for distorting the phrase parallelism enables Prokofiev to string the phrases together without losing forward momentum. Both harmonic and rhythmic repose are restored only in the cadence which closes the exposition, two measures before R12.

The simple progression beginning the second theme is shown in the first four bars of example 5.3: I–V$^6_5$ in A major plainly aims at a resolution on A/C♯, harmonized by an A-major chord, in the fifth measure of the example. But in the fifth measure wrong notes enter: instead of a C♯ in the melody, Prokofiev gives us the chromatic inflection C♮; and instead of a bass A, Prokofiev gives us F♮, whose awkward approach through the leap of an augmented ninth (G♯3 down to F♮2), makes its appearance all the more jarring. The F-major triad lingers as a tonal problem to be addressed by the following two phrases. The first phrase goes on to close on a sort of half cadence on a B-major triad, V/V within the local A-major tonality.

The beginning of the second phrase (at R7) simply begins anew on A major.

Example 5.3. Symphony no. 1, op. 25/I, mm. 46–74, second theme, analysis

The B-major cadential triad moves directly to A.[10] The second phrase varies the latter part of the first. Borrowing a technique used in theme A2, Prokofiev lops off half of phrase 2's eighth hyperbeat to make a written bar of $\frac{2}{4}$. That shortening pushes the music into phrase 2's last hypermeasure, where an F#-minor chord corrects what was previously an F-major chord. The F#-minor chord then leads more "properly," as ii/V/V, to the half cadence on B in phrase 2's twelfth bar. Still, by the end of phrase 2 the very active V$^6_5$, and especially its G#, continues to be unresolved.

The third phrase begins, like the other two, with the progression $I-V^6_5$, and then goes on to correct the jarring and "wrong" F-major triad by omitting it altogether. Five measures into phrase 3 the upper voice finally delivers the long-withheld C♯ to resolve D, but the bass continues to eschew A (which would resolve G♯), opting instead for D, which creates a new dissonance against C♯ in the upper voice. For the next three measures the upper voice holds to C♯, a pitch made more prominent by a trill and its placement on the downbeat. At the same time the bass makes its way to the dominant, an E-major triad at the end of m. 73, immediately before R10. In m. 74 (at R10) the A-major chord toward which the theme has been struggling finally arrives, approached by G♯ in the upper voice. The slur below the staff in example 5.3 indicates that the unresolved dominant chord, expressed as V^6_5 (in phrase 3's third written measure), recurs immediately before the closing theme, at which point it resolves. The closing theme, which begins at R10, confirms that arrival with an arpeggiation figure reminiscent of the opening theme, and the exposition ends twelve measures later.

In addition to withheld harmonic resolutions, rhythmic distortions also keep the phrases forward-oriented. Phrase 1, while surprising in the move from E dominant $^6_5$ to F ($^5_3$), is hypermetrically regular: an 8-bar phrase comprises two 4-bar hypermeasures. Though phrase 2 is longer than phrase 1, its parallel structure only reinforces an expectation of continued hypermetric regularity. However, phrase 2's overeager second hypermeasure shortens its final hypermetric beat from a four-beat written measure to a two-beat written measure. The deletion propels the phrase into its third and final hypermeasure (mm. 62–65).

The third phrase is the longest of all. Like the first, it is hypermetrically regular. The third phrase, including the extension over R10 and R11 (mm. 66–86), comprises five 4-bar hypermeasures, plus a *Generalpause* which separates the exposition from the development (example 5.3 ends at the downbeat of m. 74). Phrase 3's hypermeasures themselves organize into a larger level with the first four 4-bar groups forming into a 4-bar hypermeasure on a higher level. The fifth bar is a large-scale hypermetric downbeat. The coincidence of structural accent and metric accent at that point makes the arrival particularly strong.[11]

After the *Generalpause*, the development begins at R12 in the parallel tonic minor; the modal contrast further helps to delineate the boundary between the exposition and the development. Example 5.4 gives a harmonic sketch of the development section. Considering the entire span of the development, the opening D-minor tonal area can be heard as a pre-dominant area in the key of C, as indicated by the lowest line of chord labels in the example.

At R13, the flutes superimpose the melodic note E♭ over the deceptive progression G–to–A♭ (V–♭VI in the key of C). E♭ is in force for two measures, and it is set as the main note within a form of motive *x*. Forms of motive *x*, each

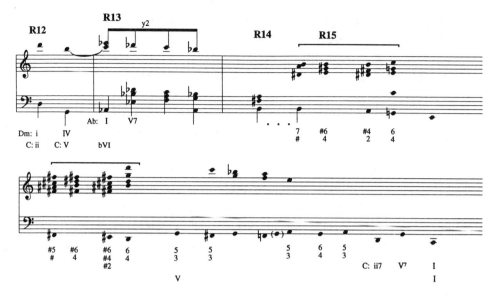

Example 5.4. Symphony no. 1, op. 25/I, development, harmonic sketch

two bars in length, continue to the end of R13. The main notes together are a large-scale projection of motive *y2*, beamed and labeled in the example.

R14 brings in B in the bass, expanded over the course of R14, as shown by the ellipsis, so that a B minor seventh chord becomes a B dominant seventh chord. R15 then initiates a $\frac{5}{3}$–$\frac{6}{4}$ motion above the B bass; a B dominant four-two follows and leads deceptively to a C-major triad in second inversion. The first bracket in the example shows this passage. The second bracket shows a transposed repetition, occurring at T7. The goal of the repetition is the G chord, labeled by the "V" in the lowest row of chord labels. That G chord then returns immediately preceding R19; at R19 the G dominant resolves to C, completing the large-scale progression initiated by the D-minor chord (= ii/C) at the beginning of the development.

The hypermetric structure of the development is completely regular, proceeding in four-bar hypermeasures. Rhythmic interest peaks over R17, where high strings are pitted against the rest of the orchestra to produce a powerful syncopation, a hitherto unused device for creating rhythmic tension. The syncopation straightens out at R18 in order to prepare the G dominant chord immediately preceding R19.

Evident in figure 5.2 is the reordering of themes in the recapitulation relative to the exposition. Sonata-form developments in the classical style typically lead to a dominant harmony. This dominant harmony plays two roles: it divides the sonata form in half harmonically and is thus a kind of ending, and it "resolves" to the recapitulation and is thus also a kind of beginning.[12] But Prokofiev's plan

is unusual from a classical point of view, for the development leads to a dominant (not V of the tonic D, but V of the subtonic C); however, the dominant
cadences before the onset of the recapitulation. Rather than teetering on the
brink of resolution and resolving only when the recapitulation begins, Prokofiev's development ends by affirming a cadence, not by delaying it.[13] R20 is
thus only a thematic return, not a tonal one. Because the recapitulation begins
neither in the tonic nor with theme A1, the development empties into the recapitulation as though coming upon an event already in progress. In fact, the
development's emphasis on material from the first thematic area to some degree
plays the role of the missing portion of the recapitulation.

Symphony no. 5, First Movement

The Symphony no. 5 might have claim to be a true Soviet "war" symphony, a
work of art reflecting the involvement of the Soviet people in the Second World
War. The Symphony no. 5 does have a heroic quality, and it was composed
during the war, in 1944, and premiered in 1945.[14] But its date of composition
and its expansive, heroic feel are not in themselves convincing evidence of a
Socialist Realist program that depicts the war. Boris Schwarz feels that "the Fifth
. . . simply does not lend itself to a martial interpretation."[15] Harlow Robinson
points out that a compositional ease is perceptible in the Symphony no. 5, and
implies that Prokofiev could not have achieved this if he had been composing
an occasional piece: "[The Symphony no. 5's] heroic tone and large scale conformed to what was expected of Soviet composers at the moment, but also
emerged spontaneously and naturally, as though Prokofiev was writing for himself alone."[16] Indeed, Prokofiev was at this point in his life less taken with modernism and novelty than he had been early in his career, and the oppressive
atmosphere of 1948 was still three years away, so that, for Prokofiev, governmental and ideological pressures had not yet become factors in his professional
life.

The exposition is traditional: the first thematic area brings in themes A1 and
A2 (at R3), both in B♭; the second thematic area brings in themes B1 (at R6),
theme B2 (at R8), and a closing theme (at R9), all in F, the dominant.

The expansive quality of the symphony as a whole is a feature at the outset,
and it owes as much to flexible phrase rhythm as it does to pitch structure. In the
opening eleven measures of the movement, while one can hear duple hypermeter, several aspects of the surface rhythm are far more prominent to the ear
and prevent the melody from locking into a regular pattern. For instance, the
first two measures contain a hemiola (if one can hear a hemiola against a triple
meter which has not yet been established) created by the two-beat rhythmic pat-

terns. Also, points of articulation in m. 3, m. 5, and m. 7 all arrive on the weak second beat, thus preventing metric and structural accent from coordinating.

The first convincing cadence is the half cadence in m. 7 (which arrives on a weak beat). The path to that cadence is somewhat indirect, with asymmetrically placed caesuras enabling the seven-measure phrase to breathe. The melodic pause on F in the third measure, punctuated by the onset of accompaniment, is followed by two more measures leading to a slightly weightier articulation, making an opening subphrase five measures in length. A short two-bar subphrase follows, moving to the dominant. Attention shifts from melody to harmony as the cadence thus reached in m. 7 is explored. M. 11 returns the music to the dominant from which it began four bars earlier. In all, the first eleven measures comprise a seven-measure phrase, articulated as 3 + 2 + 2, followed by a four-bar elaboration of the cadence.

Irregular 3 + 2 + 2 phrase construction and unhurried phrase "respiration" work nicely with the expansiveness resulting from a pitch structure highlighting perfect fourths and fifths. The fifth in the accompaniment of mm. 3–6 very conspicuously contributes to the open sound, but metric, registral, and structural accents in the melody also contribute. In the first subphrase, the downbeats of m. 1 and m. 2 project F and C, registral accent brings in B♭5 in m. 2, and structural accent highlights F5, which concludes the first subphrase. M. 2 also emphasizes C5, F5, and B♭ on the beat. Registral accent returns B♭5 in m. 6, and structural accent returns F5 in m. 7. Thus, permeating these measures is the pitch-class set (to5), a form of [027], a set class which maximizes ic5.

Now let us concentrate on a structural set which arises from the chromatic inflection of the otherwise undisturbed diatonicism of the opening. M. 3 contains the structural set whose appearance and behavior follow fairly closely the listening model outlined in Chapter 2. Our attention is first drawn to m. 3 because there is a small but obvious contextual change: accompaniment (except for the pedal F in the flutes) and chromaticism enter simultaneously and for the first time. M. 3's E♮ hardly has the force of a wrong note and sounds neither incongruous nor unexpected; it does, however, disturb the smooth diatonic surface.

Following the opening statement of theme A1 in B♭ major (mm. 1–11), the music moves through several keys before R3 brings in theme A2, also in B♭. Connecting the two themes is a series of modulations making a circular progression away from B♭ and back. The modulations support varied statements of theme A1, and all are influenced by the unobtrusive half-step slide from E into F first heard in m. 3. That gesture is the clue to a structural set whose influence gradually increases. M. 3 brings in an open fifth in the accompaniment, B♭/F. E♮ embellishes, chromatically inflecting F.[17] By taking a fragmentation approach, we can analyze this three-element structural set as a pair of overlapping dyads, one a form of 2−5 (B♭, F), realized as a perfect fifth, and one a form of 2−1 (E, F), realized as a minor second. We can think of the resulting structure as a perfect fourth with a half step attached outside. The set class thus created in m. 3 is (45t), a form of [016]. By placing the half step inside the perfect fourth, we can rearrange the two dyadic types into a form of [015].[18]

In m. 3, E♮, the clue to the structural set's presence, lasts but a sixteenth note. In m. 6, however, the E♮, at this point still a melodic phenomenon, enjoys a slightly longer duration. Through a shift in register, three beats later E resolves to F, a minor ninth above, thus duplicating the pitch-class motive from m. 3.

Theme A1 is restated beginning at R1. The theme becomes slightly distorted when, in stepping up to its third note, G♯ enters in place of the expected A♮. A's replacement by G♯ depresses the tonal center a half step, from B♭ to A. In a harmonic guise, E♮ now introduces the new key area. As the dominant of A major, E♮ acquires the status of a chordal root.

Thus, from the movement's beginning to the end of R1, successive thematic statements unfold tonal areas related by half steps; one can listen for key relations between B♭ and A playing out on a larger scale the local gesture E-F, which gave rise to the structural set [016]. In later passages, Prokofiev explores relations by half step which are expressed simultaneously, as well as chromatic neighbor motions generally.

Example 5.5 sketches the bass of R1 to the beginning of R3, isolating the modulatory mechanism in the bass, the structural set [015]. Beginning with R1's slide from B♭ into A, [015] directs a succession of tonal areas which lead back to B♭ at R3. The [015] lowers each local tonic a half step to become the dominant of the next area. At R1+4, the bass A slips to A♭, and A♭ supports V/♭III to guide the music into D♭ major. From the D♭ chord, Prokofiev moves back to F, B♭'s dominant.

In brackets in the example is the chromatic gesture in which E♮ is introduced

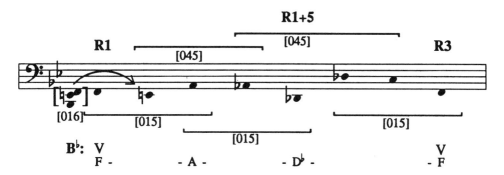

Example 5.5. Symphony no. 5, op. 100/I, R1–R3, harmonic and bass structure

as an inflection of the dominant scale degree. The arrow signifies E♮'s change in status from melodic embellishment to chordal root. The "V" below the staff marks the departure from and the return to the dominant. Taken together, the brackets above and below the staff labeled "[045]" and "[015]" denote Tn-types in a linked inversion chain which connects the dominant chord in m. 8 with the dominant scale degree at R3.[19] The last bracket below the staff isolates D♭–C–F, a contrapuntal line leading into R3 in bass clarinet and bassoons. Unlike the previous two brackets, the last one denotes a melodic fragment and not a succession of chordal roots; nevertheless the last bracket shows a continuation of the pattern of chained-together [015]s.[20]

Each of the three [015]s contains a dominant-to-tonic gesture, making a total of three upward transpositions of a "fourth."[21] Each of the three [015]s also contains a downward chromatic slip. Thus the chromatic slides offset the ability of successive T5s to cycle through all twelve pitch classes. Prokofiev therefore composes a relatively compact circular progression: the music ends where it began, on F (= V/B♭). Dividing the octave equally by moving F-A-D♭-F (shown below the staff in example 5.5) thus arpeggiates the augmented triad, whose influence in Prokofiev's music is already familiar.

Theme A2, reproduced in example 5.6, arrives at R3. Like theme A1, theme A2 is buttressed by a triadic skeleton, but theme A2's profile is more jagged and more manifestly triadic. In example 5.6's analytical staff I isolate, with stemmed noteheads, the underlying arpeggiation up and down of a B♭-major triad. Stemless noteheads, labeled "N" and slurred to main notes, are chromatic neighbors. In another striking similarity to theme A1, theme A2 recycles the E-F chromatic neighbor and develops it by pairing it with C♯–D.

As in traditional sonata form, the second thematic area is in the dominant key, F major. Its outer voices are sketched in example 5.7. In harmonic structure, theme B1 is strongly reminiscent of theme A1, above all by its displacement of the dominant downward by a half step to target a tonal center built on the leading tone. The notations below the staff in the example show the first three measures of the theme in F and a progression from tonic to dominant.

Example 5.6. Symphony no. 5, op. 100/I, R3 through R3+1, melodic analysis

Example 5.7. Symphony no. 5, op. 100/I, R6 through R6+9

The bass begins by stepping downward through the lower third of the F-major tonic triad, A–G–F, and then continues until it arrives at B. In the third measure of the theme, the melody loosely imitates, a third higher, the bass's descent into the new key: a bracket above the staff isolates C–B–A–G–F–E–D♯ in the melody. The scalar descents in both the melody and the bass converge at the downbeat of the fourth measure of the theme, where the harmonic rhythm slows to whole notes and the outer voices reverse direction. The bass then moves up in half-step increments from B, the root of E's dominant, to D♯, B's chordal third. In the ninth measure of the example a register shift in the bass, the beginning of a crescendo, and a pause on G♯ in the melody all mark the arrival of an E-major tonal interpreter. However, the tonal-interpreting V–I motion (in E) is not unadulterated. While the low strings and winds reinforce the interval E/G♯ through registral and durational accent, E and G♯ arrive at the top of arpeggiations of an A-major triad and a C♯-minor triad, respectively; those arpeggiations are shown in the inner voices in example 5.7.

Below the staff in the example, a bracket after the key change indicates that a tonal-interpreting B-major dominant triad is expanded as the bass moves from B to D♯ and the upper voice moves from D♯ to F♯. Parallel tenths guide the music into and out of the bracketed passage: C/E leads down to B/D♯ at the key change and D♯/F♯ leads up to E/G♯ when the E chord arrives following the bracket. Within the bracket, beginning with the bass B♯, parallel sixths control the measure-to-measure motion. (Prokofiev will return to using parallel imperfect intervals when he maneuvers the end of the development into position for the recapitulation.) Extracting the bass C preceding the key change, the bass B beginning the bracketed passage, and the E tonic resolving the B dominant makes explicit the underlying form of [015] which structures the motion. The [015] is familiar from the first thematic area, discussed in connection with example 5.5.

R8 brings in theme B2, which highlights the dotted rhythm that is an integral component of all the themes so far, especially themes A1 and B1. The F pedal, which also enters at R8, remains steadfast to the end of the exposition (that is, to the end of R9).

The nervous, rapid sixteenth notes of the closing theme present a contrast, especially with the unhurried opening. On the surface, the closing theme also displays much more overt chromaticism than the other themes of the exposition. Structurally, however, like the two themes in the first thematic area, the closing theme is built solidly upon a triadic arpeggiation. Example 5.8 shows the closing theme at R9. To the right, the underlying structure is compressed and analyzed as an F-major triad whose upper third, A/C, is displaced chromatically by G♯/B. Example 5.6 can be analyzed similarly, as a B♭-major triad whose upper third is displaced chromatically by C♯/E. Besides sharing an underlying structure, both themes span the same interval, an octave plus a fourth.

In figure 5.3 the development is divided into three subsections. Each subsection is associated with one or two themes and one or two tonal areas. The first subsection is initiated by theme A1's return, in the tonic B♭. As at the beginning of the exposition, theme A1 comes to rest on a half cadence. During the exploration of this half cadence a C half-diminished seventh chord enters; this chord is a modally inflected supertonic seventh expanding the dominant function at hand. But the modal inflection which transforms G into G♭, and a minor seventh into a half-diminished seventh chord, is somewhat unsettling. In the exposition that chord was simply abandoned, and the music went on to make its way through a symmetrical division of the octave and a large-scale expansion of the F dominant. But there is a sense in which the C half-diminished seventh chord which results from the chromatic alteration is, in mm. 8–10, mysterious and unresolved; it seems to point toward a path that, since the exposition, remains unexplored.

In the development the strings take notice of the half-diminished seventh

Example 5.8. Symphony no. 5, op. 100/I, R9 through R9+1, closing theme, set structure

Part 1

R10: Theme A1 in B♭. This section leads to a C half-diminished chord, a chord upon which the orchestra seizes to introduce a new texture. The chord progression underlying this passage is E♭ minor–E♭ major–E major (against E♭ in the bass).
R11: A tonal-interpreting focus on E♭ emerges.

Part 2

R12+5: The closing theme enters (and dominates until R14, where theme B1 enters in E♭).
R13+1: Frozen closing theme chords.
R13+3: Closing theme, version from R9+4.

Part 3

R14: Theme B1 in E♭.
R14+3: Parallel sixths and tenths, derived from theme B1, move into the key of A but quickly become unstable; at R15+4, theme A2 enters in inversion.
R15: Last half of theme B1, in F.
R15+6: Theme B1 in C.
R16: Preparation for the recapitulation.

Figure 5.3. Symphony no. 5, op. 100/I, development, form outline

chord immediately after it arrives. In response to it they introduce a new orchestral texture featuring a quiet triplet motive. This new motivic idea begins tentatively, extracting the E♭-minor triad embedded within the C half-diminished seventh chord. The E♭ root which emerges then becomes the controlling tonal focus of the development until R15, a point in the form partway through the development's third subsection.

At R11's *un poco animando* theme A1 enters in E♭, and one measure later E♭ minor (derived from the C half-diminished chord) switches mode to E♭ major, an instance of the fifth flip. But rather than continuing this progression systematically from E♭ minor to E♭ major to E minor to E major, the music skips the link in the chain from E♭ major to E minor, and at R11+6 the harmony moves straight from E♭ major to F♭ (= E) major, in the winds and brass, against E♭ in the bass (the bass E♭ carries over the tonal focus of the previous measures). By moving directly from E♭ major to F♭ major, the music highlights the half step which separates the two chords. The half-step juxtaposition, here simultaneously expressed, is emblematic of chromatic relations that we have already encountered: it recalls the first thematic area, which unfolded the tonal succession B♭ (beginning in m. 1) to A (which entered at R1+1), and the second thematic area, which moved from F (beginning at R6) to E (which entered at R6+8).

E♭-against-E specifically reproduces a relation first heard in theme B2, at R8+2, where the brass, piano, and bass sound a G♭ triad against F. The piano

Example 5.9. Symphony no. 5, op. 100/I, R8+2 and R13, set structure

part of that passage is given in example 5.9a; particularly distinctive is the deliberate rhythm. The motivic idea introduced at R8+2 is developed later at R13,
which is analyzed in example 5.9b. There the notes of the closing theme are
condensed into a chord and a bass and set according to the model of R8+2;
half-step displacements are thus explicitly connected with the closing theme.

Beginning at R12+5 and continuing until the beginning of R14, the closing
idea is developed extensively. To the basic underlying structure in example 5.8,
the music beginning at R12+6 adds a chromatic upper neighbor to the chordal
fifth. This gesture is analyzed in example 5.10a. Evident in the analysis of the
underlying structure is the chromatic double neighbor motion about C. This
idea is picked up later in the measures leading to the recapitulation.

Example 5.10b shows a second incarnation of the closing idea beginning at
R13+3. The analytical format to the right is slightly different from that in
example 5.10a, and it attempts to follow the theme more chronologically
(example 5.10b also shows B♮ in a single octave rather than two). F♮ is shown par-

Example 5.10. Symphony no. 5, op. 100/I, R12+6 and R13+3 through R13+4, set structure

enthetically since it is an extra note, unlike in the model in example 5.8. Below the theme, brackets designate the same form of 7–13, (35679te), that is shown in example 5.9b.

The final development of chromatic neighbor motion occurs immediately preceding the recapitulation and continues into its beginning. The double neighbor motion around the chordal fifth introduced at R12+6 leads to theme A1's reprise. E–F is already familiar from m. 3. To that, the recapitulation adds G♭, the note so important in theme A1's first cadence, where it helps create the C half-diminished seventh chord. G♭ is the chromatic upper neighbor to F and balances E♮, F's chromatic lower neighbor. E and G♭ (= F♯) emerge very prominently in the measures immediately preceding the recapitulation. Four measures before R17, E is in force in the bass, and then two measures before R17, E moves up to F♯, enharmonically G♭, which remains for the next two measures. Contrary motion in the outer voices brings back G♭/E immediately before R17, the beginning of the recapitulation. At that point, G♭ and E converge on F and theme A1's return. Over the first seven measures of the recapitulation, the counterpoint vigorously celebrates the inversional balance of G♭ and E about F and, in so doing, creates a texture contrasting in its contrapuntal activity with the movement's opening.

Figure 5.4 is a diagram of the recapitulation, which begins at R17. In the order of its events, the recapitulation offers no significant deviations from traditional sonata form. Of special interest, however, is the retransition, for in designing the recapitulation of the first thematic area, Prokofiev borrowed the tonal plan he used for expanding theme A1 by equal divisions of the octave. As figure 5.4 shows, the arpeggiation B♭–D–G♭–B♭ is spread over R17 through R21 and links the first and second thematic areas. At R19+6 a prominent G♭ emerges in the bass, where it is explicitly pitted against F♮ in the melody, recalling

R17: theme A1, B♭
    R18+3 (touches on G)
    R18+5 (touches on B)
R18+10: B♭
R19+2: theme A2, D
R19+6: variation on theme A1, G♭ in bass
R21: theme B1, B♭
R22: theme B2, B♭
R22+5: closing theme, B♭
R23: extended closing section (varied theme A1), B♭
R24: varied repeat of R23

Figure 5.4. Symphony no. 5, op. 100/I, recapitulation, form outline

previous expressions of half-step displacement (or expressions of interval class 1), as at R8+2, where G♭ is also pitted against F, or R11+6 (E against F♭).[22]

The recapitulation moves on to restate expository themes in order, and then, beginning at R23, the tonic key is firmly set to conclude the movement. As is common practice with Prokofiev, the final chord is a plain B♭-major triad. But standing out in the final cadential progression is E−to−F in the upper voice, against a held B♭ in the bass, thus producing a pitch-class repetition, one last time, of m. 3's original structural set, (45t).

Symphony no. 6, First Movement

Prokofiev began work on the Symphony no. 6 in 1945, one year after the completion of the Symphony no. 5. Because the two symphonies are so chronologically proximate and because they are both large and ambitious works, the Symphony no. 6 has acquired a reputation as the Fifth's darker companion, a reputation deriving primarily from its first movement, which seems more serious and somber than the joyous and affirming opening movement of the Fifth. The Sixth's last movement, however, compensates for its first one and strives to restore to the symphony a positive spirit; considered as a whole, then, the Sixth's pessimistic reputation is not completely deserved. Nevertheless, the first movement's solemnity may have been an ominous portent for Prokofiev; its lack of blatant buoyancy likely contributed to the composer's troubles with Andrei Zhdanov.

The Moscow premiere of the Symphony no. 6 occurred on December 25, 1947, just days before Zhdanov launched his brutish attack on the leading Soviet composers. The premiere was eagerly anticipated, and it was preceded by positive estimations of the work from critics who were already familiar with it. However, as though precipitated by the premiere, the events leading to the Decree of 1948 followed almost immediately, forcing a rapid and dramatic reversal of the Sixth's official status. Zhdanov's attack began with the musicians' conference in January 1948 and culminated with the Decree of 1948 in February.

To gauge how quickly and radically opinions changed, we can examine reactions to the Symphony no. 6 before and after Zhdanov's attack. Alexander Werth describes an encounter with Grigori Sneerson, who wrote the program notes for the Moscow premiere. Sneerson commented enthusiastically about the new work and told Werth, "It [the Sixth Symphony] is wonderful; better than the usual Prokofiev. It is philosophic, has the depth of Shostakovich."[23] Sneerson's program notes, equally ebullient, are quoted by Werth: "It [the Sixth Symphony] is one of the most beautiful, most exalted of his works, imbued with the creative spirit of Soviet humanism. . . . It is a great landmark not only in the art of Prokofiev, but in the whole history of Soviet symphonism. . . . This great work shows once again how immeasurably superior Soviet music is to the music of the capitalist West, where symphonism has long ceased to be an art of lofty ideas and high emotionalism and is now in a state of profound decadence and degeneration."[24] Sneerson praises the symphony in part by comparing superior Soviet music to inferior Western music, a critical line which would seem to be ideologically correct and pleasing to Soviet authorities. But despite the political content of Sneerson's analysis, this view of the symphony as exemplary Soviet music—as free of subversive Western influence and as continuing a Soviet tradition—was clearly not shared by Zhdanov. Read as an attack on the Symphony no. 6, the Decree of 1948, ironically, seems to characterize the work as lacking precisely what Sneerson finds it possessing. In the Decree of 1948, Zhdanov (its presumed author) says: "Particularly bad are the conditions in symphonic and operatic production, with reference to composers who adhere to the formalistic anti-national movement. This movement had found its fullest expression in the works of composers such as Comrades Shostakovitch, Prokofiev, Khatchaturian, Shebalin, Popov, Miaskovsky, and others, in whose music formalistic distortions, and anti-democratic tendencies which are alien to the Soviet people and its artistic tastes, are represented with particular obviousness."[25] It is difficult to believe that Prokofiev's new work was not very fresh in everyone's ear and mind at the time; "bad conditions in symphonic production" must certainly have extended to include the Sixth Symphony. In saying that Prokofiev's symphonic production is "anti-national" Zhdanov both ignores and contradicts Sneerson's belief that the Sixth Symphony is "imbued with the creative spirit of Soviet humanism." Evidently Zhdanov was unconcerned with and insensitive to substantive musical issues. His purpose in meddling was political and not musical, and his desire to totally control Soviet music brooked no obstacles.

The following passage from the Decree of 1948 placed Prokofiev securely in Zhdanov's vise, with one jaw tightening down on epigonism and the other on false novelty. For Prokofiev, who spent much of his career trying to reconcile innovation with tradition, Zhdanov's charge must have felt absolutely suffocating.

> Trampling upon the best traditions of Russian and western classical music, rejecting these traditions as supposedly "obsolete," "old-fashioned," and "conservative"; haughtily snubbing those composers who are conscientiously trying to absorb and develop the concepts of classical music as adherents of "primitive traditionalism" and "epigonism," many Soviet composers, in their pursuit after a false conception of novelty, have in their music torn themselves away from the ideals and artistic tastes of

the Soviet people, have cloistered themselves in a narrow circle of specialists and musical epicures, have debased the lofty social role of music and narrowed its significance, limiting it to the gratification of the perverted tastes of esthetizing egocentrics.[26]

The charge is nominally aimed at any composer who strives toward novelty purely to avoid epigonism. Zhdanov's point is that such art cannot be relevant or meaningful to the Soviet people because the artist leaves them out of any precompositional consideration. In fact, as was discussed in Chapter 1, Zhdanov's position is downright illogical: he condemns both novelty and epigonism when it suits his purposes.

But Zhdanov's charge, if one treats it seriously and not just as a political product, carries for the romantic a menacing implicit message. Pursuing novelty as a goal only for its own sake implies that some sort of reflection precedes artistic production; one must plan to produce an innovative work. In a romantic view, pursuing novelty consciously is therefore irreconcilable with genius's unmediated production of great art, art that has not been before. To admit to a conscious pursuit of novelty is to admit to insincere motives. It is tantamount to admitting to compositional craft without compositional soul.

Ironically, Prokofiev's composition had not grown more avant-garde since his return to the Soviet Union; it had grown more conservative. Much of that more conservative music, before the Decree of 1948, was composed relatively freely and without direct government interference. If one assumes that Prokofiev thoughtfully and sincerely considered the Decree of 1948 and did not simply dismiss it, then it must have produced tremendous conflicts in him.[27] No conclusion to be drawn from the document was reconcilable with any facts as Prokofiev knew them.[28]

Figure 5.5 outlines the form of the first movement of the Symphony no. 6. In later discussion themes A and B will be compared in more detail, and specific similarities between the two themes will be developed. For now, I need only note that the close resemblance of those two themes suggests hearing music from the beginning of the movement to the end of R17 as an expanded first thematic area in a sonata form. Theme C is the main theme of the second thematic area. Besides hearing two thematic areas in the exposition, we also hear a clear development section (R20–R32) and a recapitulation, which permutes the exposition's ordering of the themes.

But rather than regarding themes A and B as a single entity, I am more comfortable recognizing them as distinct. Despite thematic resemblances, to my ear, sectional boundaries, and hence form in this movement, are largely determined by the music's denying an idea its completion: the music sets out on a certain

mm. 1–10: Introduction
R1: Theme A, A♭ minor–V/E♭ minor
R2: Theme A, D minor–melodic close on 5/A minor
    R2+7: Theme A, variation–form 1 (vii°7/E♭)
    R3+8: Theme A, variation–form 2 ([012] in melody)
  R4+7: Theme A, A♭ minor to melodic close on 5/E♭ minor
      R5: Theme A, variation–form 2 ([012] in bass)
    R5+3: Theme A, variation–form 3 (truncated)
      R6: Theme A, variation–form 2 ([012] in bass)
    R6+3: Theme A, variation–form 3 (truncated)
        R7: E♭ minor–E♭ major–E minor ([012] in harmonic progression)
      R8+3: Theme A, variation–form 3
      R8+3: transition to theme B
R10: Theme B (B minor = C♭ minor)
  R13: upward string sweep leading to variation–form 2 ([012] in melody)
R15: Theme A, variation–form 3 (truncated)
  R16+5: transition to theme C
R17: Theme C (E♭ minor)
R20: Development (beginning with theme A)
R33: Recapitulation, theme B
R36: Recapitulation, theme C
R37: Recapitulation, theme A

Figure 5.5. Symphony no. 5, op. 111/I, form outline

course only to abandon it and begin anew. Over and over, thematic statements begin as though to make a clear and tonally closed statement only to fail, either by not following through on a promised direction or by meeting an interruption. For instance, the two statements of theme A contained in R1 and R2 are strongly articulated, first, because R1's statement finishes open-ended on a half cadence and, second, because R2's statement begins in the distant key of D minor.[29] The result is a marked open-endedness in the form. Phrase and sectional beginnings are strong and clear; but cadences tend either to be half cadences or not to have strong closure. Half cadences in themselves do not produce such open-endedness when they occur within a period structure. But in the case of theme A, for example, period structure is avoided in favor of a single phrase.

Because theme A appears before and after both theme B and theme C, one can interpret figure 5.5 as demonstrating characteristics of sonata-rondo as well as sonata. But, unlike many classical period rondos, the refrain (theme A) in this movement does not mark out an unambiguous tonal area, and it is surprisingly developmental from its very first appearance. Theme A, in fact, gives rise to several variation-forms. Variation-form 1, the "vii°7" variation, occurs at R2+7;

Example 5.11. Symphony no. 6, op. 111/I, R2+7, variation-form 1

variation-form 2, the "[012]" variation, occurs as melody at R3+8, as bass at R5+1, and as structure for the harmonic progression at R7; variation-form 3, "truncated theme A," occurs at R5+3.

Within the initial statements of themes A, B, and C (which begin at R1, R10, and R17, respectively) Prokofiev employs several strategies for achieving flexible phrase rhythm, wholly commensurate with his mature style and in marked contrast to some of his early music.

Example 5.11 gives an example of Prokofiev's expanded range of techniques of phrase rhythm. It shows the melody from the music's return to the six-flat signature at R2+7; this is variation-form 1. The return here is vigorous: it is marked forte, it employs increased orchestral forces, and it initiates a contrapuntal dialogue between winds and strings—all features contrasting with the preceding statement of theme A in D minor. The arabic numerals below the staff indicate the regular four-bar hypermeter, but Prokofiev's afterbeat melody softens the arrival of hypermetric downbeats.[30] Indeed, the third hyperbeat is more forceful than the first. Such details of phrase construction help deflect any bad effect of regular hypermeter.

At R5+3, the solo viola plays variation-form 3, truncated theme A. As in its previous statements, here theme A is set in a regular four-bar hypermeter. But the bass phrase beginning at R5+7 shifts to a triple meter. And at R6+3, theme A responds and squeezes into the prevailing triple meter. Duple regularity returns two measures before R7. At that point, the shift from triple to duple meter accelerates toward E minor, the tonal focus of R7+6. E minor helps prepare the upcoming B-minor tonal area of theme B.

The somewhat tentative introduction lays out two musical ideas. The first consists of two descending scalar fragments separated by a brief rest in mm. 2–3. The scalar fragments introduce stepwise chromaticism, a feature picked up

Example 5.12. Symphony no. 6, op. 111/I, R1 through R1+6, melodic analysis

in subsequent thematic material. The second idea consists of two triadic arpeggiations over mm. 5–8, the first one of C♭ major and the second of A♭ minor. Each arpeggiation moves tonic-third-fifth, with contour <120>, which we shall explore later.

The introduction, however, only exposes each of the two ideas; it does not develop them. That task falls to theme A, shown in example 5.12, which changes the introduction's scalar descent into a partially filled-in ascending arpeggiation, shown under the bracket labeled "w." Theme A also develops the introduction's contour <120>. As marked in the example, the contour <120> reappears in theme A in the second and third measures and in the last two measures. The retrograded form <021> appears in the third measure. To this developed contour material, theme A now adds a distinctive rhythmic shape, for the first time clearly showing the triple beat-subdivision of the $\frac{6}{8}$ meter.

As mentioned earlier, theme A's tonal focus is somewhat elusive. The six-flat signature and the dark sound of the theme hint at an E♭-minor tonic. But considered as melody alone, the triad outlined by the beginning of the theme, metrically stressed, more strongly projects A♭ minor, not E♭ minor. The A♭-minor hearing is reinforced when Prokofiev harmonizes the beginning of the theme with an A♭-minor triad in first inversion, the only harmony in an otherwise monophonic passage.

Despite the shift in meter from $\frac{6}{8}$ to $\frac{9}{8}$ in the example's last measure, duple-quadruple hypermeter remains in force, shown by the arabic numerals below the staff. Hypermeter draws one boundary between example 5.12's fourth and fifth measure. But in its pitch structure, the seven-measure theme shows a careful balance between its first three and its last four measures. A brief pause on E♭ in the third measure prepares mm. 4–7, each measure of which develops m. 4's figure (which is a rhythmic repetition and a rough contour inversion of the theme's first measure). Continuous upward motion in the first two measures is balanced by downward motion in m. 4 and m. 5 and from m. 5 to m. 6.

Theme A's single phrase ends at R1+6 in a clear half cadence on B♭, E♭'s dominant. The E♭-minor tonic sounds nowhere more convincing than here, as one can test by playing up to the half cadence and then playing an E♭-minor triad. While theme A is tonally progressive, moving from A♭ minor to V/E♭ minor, what follows is not: R1+6 through R1+13 expand the B♭ half cadence. Two statements of a fragment developing theme A's first measure lift the melody up to D♭, enharmonically C♯, the leading tone of R2's new key of D minor. Upon achieving D♭, the harmony rocks between F minor seventh four-three, a "minor" dominant of B♭, and a B♭-minor chord whose chordal fifth is displaced by a 5–6 motion.[31]

By the end of R1, no conclusive tonic cadence has been heard, raising the possibility that theme A's phrase is the first in a period structure which will eventually conclude on tonic. But before that can happen, R1 leads into R2, almost as if the music is trying again, searching for a pitch level conducive to tonal stability. The two measures leading into R2 accelerate the pace of events and transform the introductory stepwise bass descent into a whole-tone (A♭–G♭–E–D) fragment. R2 then enters with a statement of theme A in D minor.

As at R1, R2 supports its melody with a subdominant of the key signature's minor tonic: a D-minor triad initiates R2's melody, written in a key signature of no sharps and no flats, though A minor is suggested in the following bar. R2 is no more successful than R1 at delivering a convincing and conclusive cadence. The D-minor detour, while prominent, is brief. A downward rush in the strings follows the melodic close at R2+6 and brings back the original six-flat tonal area at R2+7. Beginning with variation-form 1, the music over R3 begins to fracture and develop theme A, whose disassembly into component parts is accomplished in large part through the orchestrational division between winds and strings.

In example 5.12, brackets designate components of the theme, two of which are "x" and "y." R2+7's material, shown in example 5.11, already develops theme A within the exposition. The music beginning at R2+7 develops *x* into *x1*, labeled in example 5.11, by inserting and holding C♭ in the descent from E♭, thereby shifting the metric and pitch placement of *y*, a chromatic trichord. In *x* and *x1*, a descent leads to C♭, but in *x1* C♭ becomes an element in an arpeggiated vii°7/E♭ as *x1* extends *x* by two full measures.

The vii°7 chord gives variation-form 1 a built-in instability. Conclusive cadences continue to be avoided, and the music continues to roll forward. The first variation-form leads into the second one at R3+8, where the [012] fragment, labeled "y" in example 5.12, receives expanded treatment.

Example 5.13. Symphony no. 6, op. 111/I, R3+8 through R3+12, the structural set 3–1 [012]

As I discussed earlier, [012] plays a structural role in melody, bass, and harmonic progression. Example 5.13 shows the melody which begins at R3+8. A motivic component of the melody, bracketed and labeled "w1," derives from example 5.12. Comparing the two examples shows how R3+8 expands the intervals of R1's melody while preserving rhythmic and metric structure.

In the analytical staff in example 5.13, a form of [012] is picked out—a form of retrograded motive *y* created by the melodic peaks which occur every other measure. The [012] next occurs in the bass at R5 and remains a prominent feature to the end of R6. A version of that bass begins at R5+7.

Finally, [012] structures the underlying harmonic progression beginning at R7. Embedded in R7's first measure is E♭ minor; E♭ major arrives two measures later, and E minor arrives at R7+6. Example 5.14 is a comparison of the melodic fragment E♭–E–F from theme A with the progression E♭ minor–E♭ major–E minor, which demonstrates the isomorphism between the pitch-class succession (moving in the smallest possible increments) and the progress of inversional centers controlling the chord succession (also moving in the smallest possible increments).[32]

In its complete seven-measure form, theme A is not heard again until R4+7. As at the movement's beginning, R4+7 states theme A with minimal harmonization. What then follows is a miniature development. In this development Prokofiev concentrates on several aspects of theme A: he explores [012], as, for example, beginning at R6; he explores the theme's first-measure figure, as at

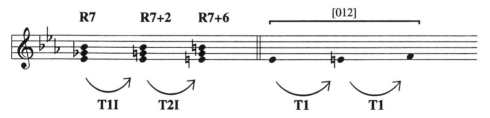

Example 5.14. Symphony no. 6, op. 111/I, isomorphism between alternating triadic flips and the structural set [012]

R6+9; and he develops arpeggiations featuring the quarter-eighth beat subdivision so characteristic of theme A, as in the passage beginning at R7. The music beginning at R8+3 rounds off the miniature development by echoing R5+3, thus leading into theme B.

Prokofiev here relies more on motivic development than on a contrapuntal interweaving of several complete themes. Indeed, this movement is notable for its classical approach to development.

Theme B enters at R10, tonally focused on B minor, and realizes the suggestion of a complete theme that has been denied since R4+7's statement of theme A. This is another instance of Prokofiev's mature and subtle control of pacing, achieved here through harmonic means rather than purely rhythmic ones. Theme B's tonal stability gives it a mass that is in high contrast to theme A's mobility.

Theme B is analyzed in example 5.15. The music of example 5.15 is continuous, but each of theme B's five varied statements is set on a separate line. Theme B shares several features with theme A. Beyond showing similar metric and rhythmic structures in themes A and B and their avoidance of chromaticism, a comparison of examples 5.12 and 5.15 shows numerous duplicated contour segments. Especially easy to hear are the similarities between contours of three-note groups and the stair-stepping contour <34120> which closes theme B and occurs within theme A.

Phrase b1 serves as a model for the rest of the variants. Phrase b1 begins on a downbeat with a bar of $\frac{9}{8}$, which feels slow and stretched out in comparison with the following two bars, where constant eighth-note motion and a duple meter set in. The melodic activity ceases in the fourth bar, where the $\frac{9}{8}$ meter returns and, as in the first bar, an extra beat expands a bar of $\frac{6}{8}$ into a bar of $\frac{9}{8}$. The switching between $\frac{9}{8}$ and $\frac{6}{8}$ that is so characteristic of theme B is another strategy Prokofiev uses to let his melody breathe and flex. That switching is a local application of the similar strategy that he uses in R5 – R7, which also shifted between duple and triple meter.

In all of the phrases following b1, the change to $\frac{6}{8}$ meter internally, and the resulting deliberate and duple feel, is motivated by a repeated rhythmic pattern, either ♩♫ (four times), as in phrases b1, b2, and b3, or ♪♩ (six times), as in phrase b4. Phrase b3 apparently veers from the model of $\frac{6}{8}$ meter setting constant eighth-note motion. In an analytical staff below phrase b3 the melody is rebarred to show how it, too, may be heard as consistent with the other phrases. The $\frac{6}{8}$ meter also sets the upbeat measure which is prefixed to b1's five-bar model in phrases b2, b3, and b5.

The final phrase, b5, breaks the five-bar model for the only time in all of theme B. Discounting the "upbeat" bar of $\frac{6}{8}$, there are only four bars, not five.

Example 5.15. Symphony no. 6, op. 111/I, R10 through R12+9, rhythmic and melodic analysis

Phrase b5 never switches back to $\frac{6}{8}$ once the $\frac{9}{8}$ meter arrives in its second bar. Together, these deviations help mark the cadential role of theme B's final phrase.

The prefixed upbeat measure slightly intensifies phrase b2, as though hinting that the music is moving toward some goal, perhaps away from B minor. But no other change is made. Phrase b3 departs furthest from phrase b1 by transposing the melody up a third, but despite the change, the harmony remains resolutely fixed on B minor; no harmonic progression occurs. Phrase b4 then repeats phrase b2, as though conceding all hope of motion and progression. And then the last two phrases, played by the horn, provide some melodic variation to compensate for the absolutely static B-minor harmony which has been maintained since the theme's beginning. By the end of R12, the afterbeat cadence (C#-A) has closed five of the six phrases, and the burst at R13 simply relies on force to escape the stasis of theme B and return to the mobile and varied theme A.

Theme B closes with a rest in all parts two measures before R13. R13's energetic, interrupting burst features [012] from theme A. Soft, sustained chords through R14 transfer [012] to an inner voice, and then R15 restates theme A at the original pitch level (though with a key signature of five sharps and a written-in E#, rather than a key signature of six flats). Still, statements of theme A are unable to complete themselves, and, following the model of R5+3 (variation-form 3), they state only the original theme's first three measures.

R17 begins theme C, a long and expansive passage, whose continuity is in high contrast to virtually all the music since theme B. Yet after a faithful repetition beginning at R19, theme C's continuity is abruptly disrupted at R20 by the beginning of the development, which brings in theme A, altered now by a quasi-sequential extension of its second measure.

Example 5.16 schematizes theme C's chord progression, based on the music of the piano. The labels "x1," "x2," and "x3" show the beginnings of three transposed versions of an underlying chord progression. The three progressions divide the octave equally, as shown by the arrows below the examples labeled "T4." Progression x3, which does not actually occur in the music, is shown in brackets.

From G minor to F# major and from B minor to Bb major, the progression is a third flip, labeled by arrows showing the appropriate inversional operation. In the music, the chordal fifths of F# and Bb, shown parenthetically in the example, are displaced by a sixth above the root; this displacement softens the effect of

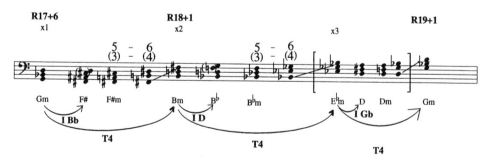

Example 5.16. Symphony no. 6, op. 111/I, R17+6 through R19+1, harmonic analysis

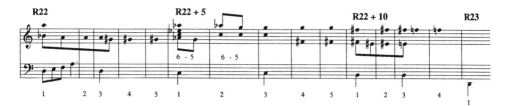

Example 5.17. Symphony no. 6, op. 111/I, R22–R23, motivic development

consecutive parallel perfect fifths, but the example nevertheless shows the progression as a species of third flip. A mode change switches the F♯ and B♭ chords from major to minor, and then a 5–6 motion brings in a six-four chord, labeled by the "5–6" above the staff. Connecting the end of *x1* to the beginning of *x2* is another mode change. Since an E♭ six-four chord does lead to a G-minor chord at R19 and the repeat of theme C, progression *x3* is an ellipsis, represented by the bracketed chord progression.

Of virtually all the development sections that Prokofiev ever wrote, the development of this movement most nearly approaches the classical norm in its dismantling of thematic material and exploration of motivic constituents. To that extent, the development partakes of the spirit and relatively fragmented nature of the exposition.

One passage illustrating this motivic development is given in example 5.17. The first ten measures develop theme A's first measure, shown in the bass clef, while the treble clef sets forth [012], first as (89t) and then as (678). The play of the chromatic upper voice against the bass creates a 6-5 motion in the example's sixth and seventh measures, with C/A♭ moving to C/G. But at the parallel spot five measures later, the bass clef melody breaks the sequence and drops not a whole step but a half step, thus producing a perfect fifth on the downbeat of the eleventh measure. That break in the sequence signals that the B-minor harmony will eventually take on a diminished fifth, showing the influence of variation-form 1.

The example also provides another instance of Prokofiev's mature rhythmic design. The arabic numerals beneath the measures show hypermetric beats. Despite the regularity of a once-repeated five-beat hypermeasure, the first ten measures seem to be struggling against an underlying four-beat model. In particular, the fourth hyperbeat feels as though it was forced between beats 3 and 5 (in a four-bar scheme). But Prokofiev does not rely slavishly upon the effect. Four measures before R23, quadruple hypermeter returns.

The recapitulation is marked by a dramatic change in character, part of whose function is to carefully dissipate the energy accumulated in the development.[33] Like the first movement of the "Classical" Symphony, this movement smoothes over the boundary between the development and the recapitulation using a strategy which urges the listener to reevaluate retrospectively the identity of the formal sections. In the "Classical" Symphony, the recapitulation begins not with the first portion of the first thematic area but instead with its middle portion (in the subtonic), almost as if, in relation to the recapitulation, the development itself were the first part of the first thematic area, albeit greatly expanded. Like the "Classical" Symphony, the Symphony no. 6 enters its recapitulation as though coming upon an event already in progress. Disregarding the development section, the recapitulation orders themes from the exposition in a circular permutation relative to their original order of appearance, beginning with theme B, not theme A. Theme C follows, and theme A then enters to round off the whole movement.

6 Chamber Music

Prokofiev's chamber music, making up a relatively small proportion of his output, contains some of his most inspired work. The chamber works include two string quartets, opp. 50 and 92; the Quintet, op. 39; the Sonata for Two Violins, op. 56; two Sonatas for Violin and Piano, opp. 80 and 94a, the second of which was originally written for flute; the Sonata for Cello, op. 119; the *Overture on Hebrew Themes,* op. 34; and the Sonata for Solo Violin, op. 115. The Sonata for Violin, op. 80, is outstanding and must rank as one of Prokofiev's greatest and most profound compositions.

Most of the chamber music was composed after Prokofiev returned to the Soviet Union in 1935. Only the *Overture on Hebrew Themes,* the String Quartet no. 1, and the Quintet were written prior to that time. The Quintet, one of the most experimental pieces Prokofiev ever wrote, is a non-Soviet piece.

String Quartet no. 1, op. 50

The String Quartet no. 1 was commissioned by the Library of Congress. To prepare himself for composing it, Prokofiev studied Beethoven's quartets.[1] "Before starting work on the quartet I studied Beethoven's quartets, chiefly in railway carriages on my way from one concert to another. In this way I came to understand and greatly admire his quartet technique. Perhaps this explains the some-what 'classical' idiom of the first movement of my quartet. It has, however, two distinctive features: firstly, the Finale is the slow movement and, secondly, the key of B minor is one rarely chosen for quartets. I ended the quartet with a slow movement because the material happened to be the most significant in the whole piece."[2] Of course, ending a work with the "most significant" material is neither necessary nor common practice. More usual in multimovement works of the classical period is to end with material lighter and less demanding and less complex than the material of earlier movements. Even in Prokofiev's own Symphony no. 6, another three-movement work, the most "significant" material occurs in the first two movements. Indeed, the symphony's reputation seems staked more on the first two movements than on the last. At the end of the second movement, the accumulated tension searches for a release, which is then provided by the third movement, an optimistic and playful finale which counterbalances the gravity of the two previous movements.

The formal plan of the String Quartet no. 1 is quite different from that of the Symphony no. 6. In the quartet, the central, second movement is a five-part rondo which fulfills many of the functions of a typical classical finale. In particular, op. 50's rondo, while somewhat long, is light and quick, with clear-cut themes; it also avoids the problems and contrapuntal difficulties presented in a development section. By contrast, the third movement is nearly continuously developmental. From its initial seed, the movement spins out a series of variations which build in complexity.

As Prokofiev indicates, the first movement is in the classical idiom, a fact reflected in part by its sonata form. The first thematic area, in the tonic B minor, confines most of the melodic activity to the upper strings, especially to the first violin. The second thematic area, beginning in m. 30 (R2), is marked by a change in tempo, from *allegro* to *allegro moderato,* and by a more democratic distribution of melodic material among the instruments. At the outset of the tonally discursive second thematic area, a strong hint of F♯ minor, the minor dominant, preserves a vestige of traditional sonata form. The exposition concludes with the closing material beginning in m. 78 (R4). The development extends over mm. 107–183, and in the recapitulation the first thematic area returns in m. 188, the second thematic area returns in m. 209 (now in tonic), and the closing begins in m. 234 (now in tonic).

As is common in sonata-form movements, the opening melody (theme A1) arpeggiates the tonic triad. That arpeggiation occurs here in the first four bars, evident if we consider the theme alone. In m. 3 the tonic arpeggiation is embellished by the subdominant (E minor). In the actual harmonization, a root position C major seventh chord, and not a iv chord, supports the third bar. The C major seventh chord contains an E-minor triad as one of its subsets, so despite the C root, the plagal character of the theme comes through clearly: the straight quarter-note attack rhythm in the third bar proclaims and arpeggiates the E-minor triad.

Subsequent statements of this main theme, particularly those in the development, vary the first two melodic notes, not always beginning on the chordal fifth. By the theme's second bar, however, all of the thematic statements transpose mm. 2–4 with no substantial changes.

The classical idiom to which Prokofiev referred also extends to aspects of voice leading in this movement. While the theme implies a simple harmonization using tonic and subdominant, Prokofiev's treatment is considerably more complex. Example 6.1 shows the basic voice leading over mm. 1–9, measures in which Prokofiev moves from B minor to G♯ minor (A♭ minor), touching on C on the way. The bass is notated an octave lower than it sounds for visual clarity. Over mm. 1–3, the outer voice motion 5–6–5, labeled in the example, lifts B minor up to C, at the same time exposing one of the basic processes of the movement, the transposition T1, here connecting a B root to a C root. C then progresses to its dominant, G, where another 5–6 motion moves G to E♭, the dominant of A♭ minor. Beginning at m. 5, the music seems ready to establish A♭ minor firmly, since the E♭ dominant six-three in m. 5 goes on to cadence on an A♭-minor six-three in m. 6. A♭ minor returns in m. 10 as G♯ minor. The plagal motion in mm. 7–10 affirms A♭'s already established tonic status and derives from the melody over mm. 1–4. A♭ minor's tonic status is short-lived, however, for m. 11 (not shown in the example) returns to C major.

We can, however, develop another aspect of these opening measures. I have

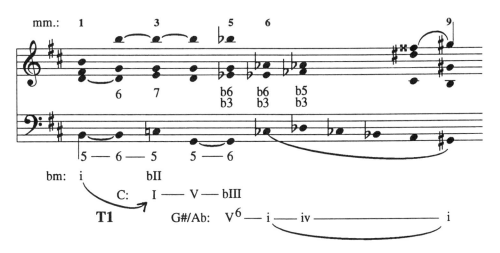

Example 6.1. String Quartet no. 1, op. 50/I, mm. 1–9, harmonic sketch

already referred to the 5−6−5 move which relates B minor and C major and which transposes roots at T1. Over a larger span C can be heard as the middle link in a chain: C from m. 3 rises to D♭ minor in m. 7 (the bass's high point), creating a large-scale form of 3−1 [012], the chromatic trichord; contiguous roots are connected at T1. Example 6.1 showed D♭ as a plagal elaboration in the service of expanding A♭. But several factors tend to feature D♭ rather than subordinate it to A♭. Besides its position as the endlink in the rising chain of half steps connecting B to C to D♭, D♭'s arrival in m. 7 is marked by a textural change: the cello returns for the first time in five measures, the first violin drops out, and the inner voices abandon repeated broken intervals for stepwise scalar patterns. Further, if we hear mm. 1−8 in two-bar groups, then mm. 1, 3, and 7 are all hypermetrically strong, highlighting each increment in 3−1's unfolding.

At the end of the second thematic area (mm. 57−59), a transposed version of 3−1 [012] is presented explicitly. Chord roots ascend chromatically from C (downbeat of m. 57) through D♭ (downbeat of m. 58) to D (downbeat of m. 59). The 3−1 [012] also plays a major role in the development section.

At m. 18 (R1+2), the B-minor melody of the opening returns in varied form to round off the first thematic area. One of the most notable changes since the opening of the movement occurs four measures into the recapitulated melody. In its first appearance (see example 6.1), the third and fourth measures brought in, respectively, a C-major chord (with added seventh) and a G-major chord. The shortened version of theme A1 (beginning at R1+2) substitutes a G♯-minor chord for what before was G major. That substitution is not unprecedented: it transposes the relation between C major, from m. 3, and D♭ minor, from m. 7. But one can also hear the move to G♯ minor as the result of ellipsis: the varied theme accomplishes in two measures what took six measures in the original. The triad pairs C major and D♭ minor and the triad pairs G major and G♯ minor are each a form of 5−22 [01478].[3] In the new, shortened version of the opening theme, C-major and G♯-minor triads stand side by side; together those two chords are a form of 6−20 [014589].[4]

At m. 21 the violin, beginning on E4, states a melody which extends into m. 23. There it overlaps with and is answered by the cello, whose statement extends from m. 23 to m. 25. Each thematic statement is a form of 8−19; the violin's statement comprises (34678teo) and the cello's statement comprises (345789eo). The two forms are not related by an exact pitch inversion but by a pitch-class inversion about E and B ($I^{E/B}$), notes which are prominent in the passage. E is the first note of the violin statement, and B is the first note of the cello statement and the last note of both statements. Notes sounding on the beat within each statement are a form of 5−21, the only pentachordal subset of 6−20 (see the Appendix). In fact, the two forms of 5−21, (478eo) and (78eo3), together create 6–20 (3478e0), the same form of 6–20 that makes up the chord pair C major / G♯ minor from mm. 20–21, so that the harmonic progression of mm. 20–21 prepares the melody of the closing. Each form of 5–21 also contains as subsets two forms of 4–19; the violin's statement contains (4780) and (8e04), the cello's statement (e037) and (78e3).

In contrast to the first thematic area's tonal stability, the second thematic area is much more restless. It does, however, strongly hint at traditional relations, such as the mediant, D major (as in m. 30, R2), and the dominant, F♯ minor (as in mm. 35–37, beginning at R2+5).

The second thematic area is also more democratic and varied in its distribution of melodic material. For example, over the first six measures of R2, the upper strings are paired off against the lower ones; beginning at R2+10 violin and viola are featured; and beginning at R3+9 and continuing until three measures before R4, outer strings (violin 1 and cello) and inner strings (violin 2 and viola) are paired.

Mm. 30–35 (theme B1, beginning at R2) are the beginning of the second thematic area, whose main lyric portion begins in the viola of m. 36 (theme B2). Within these measures, arpeggiated chords descend by whole steps from D (m. 30) through C (mm. 31–32) to B♭ (m. 33) and then return to C in m. 34. Following this, the bass rises through G–G♯–A, a version of 3–1 [012].

To formalize the relation between the whole-tone descent and 3–1 [012] we can simply let "Tn" represent the transposition from one element to the next. When n equals 1, the ascending chromatic trichord is generated; when n equals 10, the descending whole-tone trichord is generated. Both the chordal roots descending by whole steps and the small chromatic set reappear later in the movement.

Beginning in m. 40 (R2+10), a point about midway through the second thematic area, an F-major area briefly intrudes between statements of an F♯-minor key area. We can trace the oscillation between F♯-minor and F major to the first thematic area, where G♯ minor replaced G major (the ellipsis of mm. 20–21), and C major progressed to D♭ minor.[5]

The closing theme, which enters in m. 78 (R4), is firmly rooted in the dominant, F♯. At its beginning, the closing theme is in the major mode, but by m. 95 (R5+2) it moves into the minor mode.[6]

The form of the development section is given in figure 6.1, along with a few comments concerning thematic content, tonal focus, and notable features of the various sections. In the development section Prokofiev utilizes techniques which also appear in the first movements of the Symphony no. 3 and the Symphony no. 6. In op. 50, as in the two symphonies, one of the main activities in the development section is combining and simultaneously stating expository

Theme A1	B minor		m. 107 (R6)	
Theme A1	E minor		m. 113	
Theme B1 variant, C–B♭–A♭			m. 116	C
Theme A1	A minor	C	m. 121	
Theme A1	F♯ minor	C♯	m. 125 (R7)	
Theme B1 variant, D–C–B♭		D	m. 127	D
add closing theme in counterpoint			m. 132	
Closing theme variant, add theme A2 in counterpoint			m. 138	
(theme A2 derives from m. 9 ff.)				
T11 (mm. 138–141) counterpoint inverted			m. 143	
Cadence, extension			m. 147	
Theme B1 variant, T2 (mm. 129–135)			m. 150	E
Theme B2 variant		(C–E♭)	m. 160	
trade upper and lower strings		(C♯–E)	m. 163	
trade upper and lower strings		(F♯–A)	m. 169	
trade upper and lower strings		(G–B♭)	m. 172	
		(G♯–B)	m. 174	

Figure 6.1. String Quartet no. 1, op. 50/1, development, form outline

thematic material. Thus over mm. 107–127, the development tends to preserve the integrity of expository material rather than, for example, separating it into its motivic components and then sequencing that motivic material. However, this development does feature motivic development, especially after m. 132.

M. 116 (R6+9) begins to combine the long, flowing eighth-note motion from the closing of the first thematic area with pitch material deriving from theme B1; in figure 6.1 the result is labeled "theme B1 variant." Beginning in m. 121, statements of the main theme (theme A1) are tied together with pitch-class set 3–1 [012]; the structural set 3–1 [012] is bracketed. In mm. 132–136 the theme B1 variant is combined with material from the closing section of the exposition. And in mm. 138–142 a variant on the closing material is combined with theme A2.

The development section begins traditionally, with a tonic statement of the main theme at m. 107 (R6). At m. 113 a thematic statement in E minor acknowledges the plagal coloration of theme A1. Example 6.2 picks up in m. 113 and shows a 5–6–5 motion pushing E minor up to an F-major chord before moving to C major in m. 116. The 5–6 motion derives from the voice leading discussed in connection with example 6.1. In the passage beginning in m. 116 (R6+9) Prokofiev develops material from mm. 30–33 (the beginning of the second thematic area) by transposing it, accelerating it, and changing the mode of its last chord.

Though mm. 116–120 develop the beginning of the second thematic area,

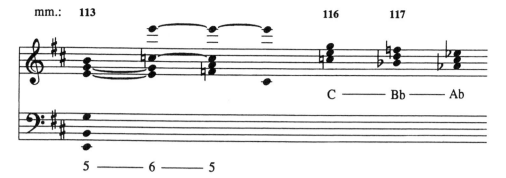

Example 6.2. String Quartet no. 1, op. 50/I, mm. 113–117, harmonic analysis

the wide-ranging arpeggiation and even eighth-note rhythm also recall mm. 21–25. As was discussed earlier, mm. 21–25 feature 4–19 and 8–19. The cello's pitches in m. 118 and m. 120 form 4–19 (4580), making the connection to the earlier passage stronger.

In m. 121 (R6+14) the cello picks up C3 from the end of m. 120 and begins two linked statements of theme A1. The thematic statement beginning in m. 121 is built upon an A-minor triad (with D-minor plagal coloration in m. 123), but instead of beginning on the chordal fifth, E, and exactly transposing the opening theme, the cello begins on its resonant open C string, highlighting that pitch and, as we shall explore presently, initiates a large-scale form of 3–1 [012]. The low C from m. 121 returns in a higher register in m. 123.

One can hear mm. 117–120 interrupting a series of "plagal" statements of theme A1: mm. 107–112 deliver B minor, mm. 113–116 follow with a statement in E minor, mm. 116–120 interrupt, and mm. 121–124 give theme A1 in A minor. In figure 6.1 the tonal areas B minor, E minor, and A minor are italicized to highlight the plagal relations.

But the theme B1 variant of mm. 116–120 initiates a pattern of its own, which interlaces with the statements of theme A1. If we identify a statement of the theme B1 variant by the root of its first arpeggiated triad, then mm. 116–120 give the variant on C, mm. 127–136 give the variant on D, and mm. 150–155 give the variant on E. Each statement is the T2-transpose of the previous one, thus producing a kind of retrograde of the structure analyzed in mm. 30–33, where each statement of the theme B1 variant is the T10–transpose of the previous one. Figure 6.1 shows the tonal succession C–D–E bracketed together on the right-hand side. The successive ascending thematic statements of the theme B1 variant gradually compensate for the local descents within a given statement. Thus, the drop from C to A♭ in mm. 116–120 is eventually compensated for in mm. 150–156, which, at their conclusion, return the music to a tonal focus on C: $(T_2)^3(T_{10})^3 = 0$.

M. 125 (R7) builds its thematic statement around an F#-minor triad (with B-minor coloration in m. 127) and begins on C#, rising chromatically from the previous C. The form of 3–1, (012), is completed in the cello of m. 127, which states and then deliberately repeats the move from C# to D to punctuate that completion. The chromatic line C–C#–D obviously derives from mm. 34–35 and duplicates its root movement.

In m. 127 a transposition of mm. 117–120 begins. Mm. 132–135 repeat mm. 117–120, now combined with the melody of the exposition's closing. M. 137 (R7+12) continues to multiply the contrapuntal threads when it adds a statement of theme A2, exactly transposed from mm. 8–13.

M. 160 begins developing a minor third, a motive from the closing theme, where it appears in original (0–2–3) and inverted (3–1–0) forms. In m. 160, the motive begins on C; it is answered by a form beginning in m. 168 on F#, its tritone-transpose. In figure 6.1, beginning in m. 169, the three forms of this minor third motive are bracketed to show they are tied together by the structural set 3–1 in the form (678).

In m. 179 an F#-major triad is arpeggiated in the first violin; in the following measure a C-minor triad is arpeggiated, reiterating the tritone relation between m. 160 and m. 168. At m. 184, F# returns again, now as the root of an F# six-three chord, the dominant that brings back theme A1 as the recapitulation begins at m. 188. The recapitulation unfolds the themes of the exposition in order and in abbreviated form. As in traditional sonata form, the second thematic area and the closing theme appear transposed at T5 from the exposition.

Sonata no. 1 for Violin and Piano, op. 80/III

The wit and humor so characteristic of much of Prokofiev's music is not so much in evidence in the String Quartet no. 1. Instead, gravity and seriousness, perhaps a result of studying the Beethoven quartets, permeate the work. The Sonata no. 1 for Violin and Piano, op. 80, continues and amplifies the serious vein; no other work of Prokofiev's exceeds its depth and profundity. One suspects Prokofiev was neither competing with other composers, nor publicly displaying compositional technique, nor cleaving to tenets of a modern agenda, nor composing according to Socialist Realism. Relieved of such pressures, he wrote very personal music, which flowed unimpeded from his creative faculties.

The dark color of this sonata is in stark contrast to the other work in the genre, op. 94a (originally written for flute and piano). The Symphony no. 6, composed about the same time (1945–1947) is much closer in spirit to op. 80 than is op. 94a.

The movement is an ABA ternary form: A (m. 1), B (m. 29), A (m. 58). Particularly in the A sections, the movement features virtually no motivic development. Instead, its main developmental strategy is to transpose thematic statements.

Section A states the main theme twice. The melody of section a1 begins from an F triad in m. 8 and returns to an F triad at the end of m. 14. The music of m. 14 then continues on seamlessly, and a cadential extension and transitional material lead to section a2, beginning on an A♭ triad in m. 19. There follows a short transition (mm. 25–31) leading to the section B. The two statements in section A are related at T3, a feature picked up and developed more extensively in section B, where relations at T3 and T6 hint at several octatonic structures.

Example 6.3 shows the melody of section a1. The points of articulation, stemmed in the example, are created by changes in the direction of the melodic line and by durational accent. The melody's first gesture, in mm. 7–8, marks out a major third by moving from C4 to E4 and back. M. 9 reiterates that pitch space by moving upward from C4 to E4 and filling in that interval chromatically. In the second half of m. 9, the melody reverses direction, as though again to fill chromatically the space between E5 and C4. But in that descent, D♮4 moves to C♮4 instead of C♯4 and directs the melody down another half step to the next

Example 6.3. Sonata for Violin and Piano, op. 80/III, mm. 8–15, voice leading and harmonic and set structure

point of articulation, on the downbeat of m. 10. There, metrical and durational accent stress B3. The arrival on B3 not only expands the melodic pitch space but also triggers a change in harmony from E (five-three) to C♯ (six-three). The melody's next point of articulation, and its lower bound, is G♯, intensified and highlighted by its lower neighbor F×.

Mm. 11–13 are a varied repeat of mm. 9–10. But the violin in mm. 11–12 moves through an interval twice as large as it did in mm. 9–10, from G♯3 to E4 rather than from C4 to E4. C♯4 in m. 11 receives metric stress and repetition; C♯4 is shown parenthetically on the analytical staff to indicate its qualified status as a point of articulation. The same C♯ returns on the downbeat of m. 14, where it drives up to arpeggiate an F-major triad and close off the first thematic statement (with a final form of 4–19).

In the analytical staff aligned above the melody, the points of articulation in the melody are extracted, and those occurring in mm. 8–13 and mm. 14–15 are beamed together. Each group beamed together is a form of 4–19. The first group, (8e04), is transformed into the second, (9015), at T1. Taking a somewhat more visceral approach, we can listen for the T1 transformation as a sort of leading tone-tonic gesture which restores tonic. Such a hearing gains support if we take into account root motion in the accompaniment from m. 8 through the first half of m. 10. In that passage, the arpeggiated chords in the piano (shown blocked below the melody in the example) drop a half step from F to E, with the E chord enjoying a minor, then a major, third.

The total pitch-class content of the accompaniment through the passage supports the melodic segmentation in example 6.3. The brackets enclosing the blocked piano chords help us see that, together, the chords are a form of 8–19, the complement of 4–19.[7] Further, 8–19 in the form (45789e01) in fact contains the total pitch-class content of the melodic points of articulation, 7–21 (89e0145).[8]

Within the analytical staff beginning in m. 8, arrows labeled "T8" show how the melody unfolds two descending "major thirds," which together outline an augmented triad, E–C–G♯. These pitch classes adumbrate the pitches in the piano of m. 15, at which point the music is approaching the second statement of the main theme, transposed up a minor third. The T4 arrow signifies the melody's final move from G♯ in m. 13 back to C in m. 15 in the transition leading to the next thematic statement, which begins in m. 19.

A bracket above the staff isolates the T8 arrow divided by a T11 arrow and a T9 arrow. That melodic succession parallels the harmonic root progression, with which it shares the same arrow structure, shown below the staff. The tonic F major yields to an E-minor chord a half step lower. (E's minor mode is eventually transformed to major, creating a form of 4–17 in the process.) After E,

Example 6.4. Sonata for Violin and Piano, op. 80/III, mm. 23–29, harmonic and octatonic structure

the progression moves to C♯ major, from which point it takes advantage of the common tone E♯/F between the triads C♯ major and F major, which facilitates the return to tonic. Regarding E♯–G♯–C♯ as enharmonically equivalent to F–A♭–D♭ produces a 6–5 progression, with a D♭-major six-three chord moving to an F-major triad in root position.

In approaching section B (which begins in m. 29), chordal roots move through a form of 4–28 [0369], a "diminished seventh chord," the first hint of octatonic structure in section B. In example 6.4 I sketch the transition and label the chords which produce this equal division of the octave. From m. 23 to m. 25 the chordal roots together form a complete diminished seventh chord, G–E–B♭–D♭; m. 27 repeats m. 25, thus duplicating the move from B♭ to D♭. From the end of m. 27 to m. 29, where the main theme of section B begins, D♭ descends chromatically through a tritone to G. That tritone relation is recalled, in transposed form, by the triads C and G♭ in mm. 32–33.

Example 6.5 is an analysis of the B section. The main melodic motive throughout this section is a sighing, descending half step. Occurrences of this motive are beamed together above the upper staff. The passage begins with the motive harmonized by the tritone-related triads C and G♭, together making a form of 6–30. The tritone-relation continues the octatonic structure introduced in m. 23 (see example 6.4). While the C and G♭ triads do not project F major, the tonal-interpreting bass does, and it continues to do so by moving to a tonal-interpreting dominant in m. 38. The passing motion in the bass which connects F to C is shown parenthetically, except for the bass D, which enjoys considerable durational emphasis; D is shown outside parentheses but without a stem. The incomplete but implied C-major dominant of m. 38 then progresses to E minor, with which it shares two common tones, and E minor begins the central portion of section B, stretching over mm. 40–53.

These central measures string together forms of the basic half-step motive and expand it by arpeggiating each of its elements. To begin the expanded motive, the piano and violin (which trade roles in m. 43 and again in m. 45, marked on the example) together form a minor triad, and the violin then arpeggiates that triad's dominant. The arpeggiation, labeled "DOMARP," is written out upon its first appearance in the example in a shorthand that does not show

Example 6.5. Sonata for Violin and Piano, op. 80/III, mm. 32–56, analysis of section B

metric setting. Subsequent statements of DOMARP are labeled on the example and represented by their first notes.

Over mm. 40–50, the minor triads depart from and then return to E minor. E minor in m. 50 moves through E♭ minor (creating another version of the sighing motive), and then passing motion returns the music to the tonal-interpreting dominant from which it sprang. The "V" in m. 54 completes the archlike form by returning to "I," supporting the tritone-related triads C and G♭.

The passing motions which sometimes connect the succession of minor triads are shown by slurs in the upper two staves. In example 6.6 I analyze that succession in more detail. Example 6.3 showed how m. 14 returned to F major through a C♯-major triad. That progression involved a common tone (E♯/F) and contrary chromatic motion (G♯/C♯–A/C); the F-major and C♯-major triads together made a form of 5–21. Moving into m. 43 and out of m. 45 involves the "minor" form of the same progression. As is shown in example 6.6, E♭ minor and G minor together make a form of 5–21; so do A♭ minor and E minor. In example 6.5, the sighing motive is brought in twice in mm. 35–38,

Example 6.6. Sonata for Violin and Piano, op. 80/III, mm. 40–50, harmonic and set structure

with the statements a step apart. In example 6.6 I take the transposition scheme but reverse the position of the sighing dyads: "T2" in the example connects Gm/F♯m to Am/A♭m.

Sonata for Flute and Piano, op. 94, Scherzo

On several occasions, Prokofiev sought and received help with his compositions from string players. For example, he worked with the violinist Paul Kochanski on technical details of the Violin Concerto no. 1, and Mstislav Rostropovich helped him in revising the Cello Concerto, op. 58, which became the *Sinfonia Concertante,* op. 125. David Oistrakh suggested that Prokofiev rearrange the Sonata for Flute, op. 94, for violin, a project with which he helped.[9]

Rhythmic vigor, lightness, and quickness place op. 94's scherzo in Prokofiev's toccata line. In the piano's unremitting quarter-note attack point rhythm, op. 94's scherzo resembles the toccata of op. 11 and the scherzo of the Piano Concerto no. 2, two pieces cited by Prokofiev as examples of the toccata line.

Figure 6.2 is a diagram of the form of the second movement of op. 94, a rondo. The opening seven measures of op. 94 expose motives shaping many aspects of the rest of the piece. Three of these motives are the opening chord (B, C, E), the chromatic lines in the outer voices which expand to meet A at the downbeat of m. 7, and the left hand's approach to m. 7.

The key signature and the violin entrance in m. 7, among other clues, suggest an A-minor tonic. The chord in m. 1, however, is tonally ambiguous. It is a "nearly" tonic chord, for it contains the interval C–E, A minor's upper third. The bass B, however, seems like a wrong note, denying to the interval C–E the key-defining support which would have been afforded by A, a more conventional choice for the bass. The chord (B, C, E), however, is a form of [015], a structural set in this movement. The appearance of [015] at the outset of the movement is characteristic.

The influence of [015] appears immediately in the right hand's rising major thirds. In example 6.7a I select the first pair of those thirds, C/E moving to

Section	Measure Numbers	Tonal Area
Introduction	mm. 1–7	A
Section A1		
a1	mm. 7–14	A
a1, slightly varied	mm. 15–19	C
a2	mm. 19–27	A♭ (V/D♭)
cadential extension	mm. 27–34	D♭ (leading tone of D, =C♯)
Section A2		
a1	mm. 34–41	D
a1	mm. 42–46	F (=III/D)
a2	mm. 46–58	A (=V/D)
cadential extension and transition	mm. 58–83	D
Section B		
b1	mm. 83–102	A
b1, slightly varied	mm. 103–122	brings back variation on a2 to return to A
Section A		
a1	mm. 123–130	D
a1, slightly varied	mm. 131–135	F (=III/D)
a2, varied	mm. 136–156	A (=V/D)
transition	mm. 157–161	
Section C		
c1	mm. 162–189	D
c2, octatonic hints	mm. 174–189	A (half cadence in D)
c1	mm. 190–201	D
c2, varied, extended for retransition to section A	mm. 202–227	
Section A	m. 228	

Figure 6.2. Sonata for Flute and Piano, op. 94/II, form outline

D♭/F. In example 6.7b I analyze those thirds in light of the opening chord and show the interwoven, inversionally related forms of [015]: (045) and (015) share the dyad (05). Each pair of chromatically related major thirds in the right hand of mm. 1–6 repeats this structure.

Over the opening six measures, the right hand of the piano rises in unbroken chromatic increments from the opening dyad C/E to the dyad E/G♯ in m. 6, which, as a tonal-interpreting dominant, prepares the entrance on A in m. 7.

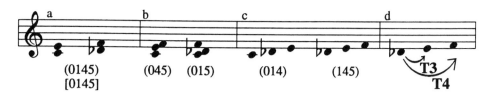

Example 6.7. Sonata for Flute and Piano, op. 94/II, analysis of piano right hand, mm. 1–2

Example 6.8 sketches these measures, showing the chromatic ascent in the right hand. Example 6.8 is an analysis of F3 in m. 1 and m. 3 as a local melodic embellishment of B♭, specifically as a tonal-interpreting dominant of B♭. In m. 3 F receives a lower neighbor, E, before stepping up through G and A to B♭. Piano articulations help clarify the dominant-tonic relation between F and B♭: m. 3 slurs E up to F, and then staccato attacks connect F to B♭. C♯3 in m. 4 is an octave doubling of D♭4, and F♯3 similarly doubles F♯4 in m. 5. B♭2 at the end of m. 6 picks up B♭3 from m. 2 through a change in register. The initial and terminal dyads in the right hand over mm. 1–6 are stemmed, highlighting the augmented triad (048) thus formed. In fact, the lowest notes of the right hand's major thirds chromatically fill in the span from C4 to E4, the pitches of the right hand's first major third. Along with the violin's A in m. 7, the stemmed notes in the treble clef create (8904), a form of 4–19 [0148] sweeping up to the tonic from below.

In contrast to the right hand, which concentrates on traversing chromatic space, the left hand follows a more complex path whose underlying motion is through a chromatic trichord from B in m. 1 through B♭ over mm. 2–6 and finally to A as the violin enters in m. 7. The left hand, in approaching A in m. 7, moves downward to the tonic, compensating the upward melodic motion from G♯ to A.

The brackets in example 6.8 designate two forms of 4–19 [0148] that overlap as the music heads into m. 7. Like the trichordal pairs in example 6.7b and 6.7c, the two forms of 4–19 in the bass clef of example 6.8 share $n - 1$ invariants (where n is the cardinality of the set) and are inversionally related.

Example 6.8. Sonata for Flute and Piano, op. 94/II, mm. 1–7, motivic and set structure

Example 6.7c is an analysis of the chromatically related major thirds similar to that in example 6.7b, but example 6.7c shows interwoven, inversionally related forms of [014]; (014) and (145) share the dyad (14). Example 6.7d is an analysis of (145) from example 6.7c; the arrows "T3" and "T4" show the transpositional relation of (145)'s elements. The three forms of 4–19 discussed in connection with example 6.8, one formed in the right hand, (8904), and two formed in the left hand's approach to m. 7, (5691) and (9t15), interrelate in the same way: T3(5691) = (8904) and T4(5691) = (9t15).

Mm. 7–83 comprise two statements of section A, over mm. 1–34 and mm. 34–83. Mm. 1–34 begin with a tonal focus on A and then move to D♭. D♭ functions enharmonically as C♯ when it leads into the subdominant D, the main tonal area of section A2, beginning in m. 34. The tonal areas of mm. 1–34, A, C, A♭, and D♭, together make (8901), a form of 4–7 [0145], the structural set that occurs in the right hand of mm. 1–6 (see example 6.7).

The tonal areas of section A1 begin as though to arpeggiate the tonic triad: a tonic statement is followed by a mediant statement. But m. 19, rather than moving to the dominant E and completing the tonic arpeggiation, brings in A♭, the dominant of D♭. Progressive harmonic movement in section A1 leads to section A2. Section A2 then carries through on the triadic arpeggiation which was suggested but abandoned by section A1 and, in a circular progression beginning and ending on D, moves through F and A, in mm. 42–46 and mm. 46–58, respectively.

Tonally, section A1 moves from A to D♭ (C♯), whereas section A2 begins and ends on D. Together, these three areas of tonal focus create (912), a form of [015], a structural set familiar from examples 6.7 and 6.8 and appearing as the first chord in the movement. Inversion about A and E (I^{A/E} or T1I), the root and fifth of the tonic triad, transforms (912) into (e04), the first chord of the movement.

Section B, beginning in m. 83, returns to tonic, in the major mode. If one conceives of D♭ at the end of section A1 not as a goal but as part of a subservient motion to D (section A2's tonal focus), then the large-scale tonal motion over mm. 1–122 is i–iv–I, a plagal elaboration of the tonic. That plagal motion is hinted at in the harmonic progression of mm. 7–11, where root motion alternates between A and D.

Section B (beginning with section b1) begins with a melodic arpeggiation and a bass, both of which set forth A major. M. 103, the first measure of section b2, brings in a varied repeat of b1, now in A♭. Then in m. 115 a transition, based on a transformation of the arpeggiation motive from mm. 82–84, projects D♭ in the bass and G♭ in the melody. Like the D♭ in m. 33, m. 122's D♭ functions as C♯ when it moves up to D in m. 123 as section A begins its return. At the same time

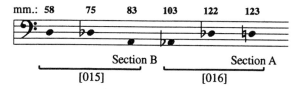

Example 6.9. Sonata for Flute and Piano, op. 94/II, mm. 58–123, set structure of tonal areas

that the bass slides upward, the upper voice G♭ drops to F. The inward chromatic collapse of the outer voices to bring in D minor, along with a2's return, answers the outward chromatic expansion through which the six-measure introduction brought in section a2 in m. 7. The notes G♭, F, D♭, and D make (1256), a form of [0145], a structural set in example 6.8.

In example 6.9 I analyze in more detail than in figure 6.2 the tonal areas from m. 58 (focusing on D) through m. 123. Brackets designate a form of the structural set [015] and a descendant, [016]. Fragmentation transforms [015] into the descendant [016] by placing [01] inside [05] rather than outside it.[10] In example 6.9 both [015] and [016] contain the dyad D♭/D, but [016] slightly stretches A/D♭ to produce A♭/D♭. The total collection (8912) is a form of [0156], a set class descended from the chromatically spaced major thirds in the right hand of the opening (see example 6.8).

Section C contrasts with the energetic sections A and B. Its calm comes from widely spaced intervals, an emphasis on perfect fourths and fifths, a long, less fragmented melodic line, and a move away from the toccata-like surface to a slower, more relaxed harmonic rhythm.

Section C expands upon [0156], descended from the opening structural set [0145] (see example 6.8). Over mm. 162–165 the piano's droning fifth D/A, together with the melodic shifting between F♯ and F♮, creates (2569) (4–17 [0347]), a characteristic set. Together with the durationally accented G♯, the droning fifth creates (892), a form of [016], which is [0156]'s constituent trichord.

Over mm. 173–182 there are hints of octatonic structure which are not rigorously developed. A simple root analysis of the chords produces the progression G dominant ninth to B♭ dominant seventh, with a misspelled flatted fifth (E rather than F♭), to C♯ minor. Leaving out G's major ninth (pitch class 9) produces the octatonic collection (124578te), a form of 8–28.

Example 6.10 is a rhythmic analysis of mm. 1–86; it retains the quarter-note unit of the original written music, but the units are rebarred to show the meter actually felt. The written measure numbers which correspond to the score are shown in the example above the staff. For instance, the music's seventh measure is the third measure in the analysis (which is the first bar of $\frac{3}{2}$ in the example).

Example 6.10. Sonata for Flute and Piano, op. 94/II, mm. 1–86, rhythmic structure

At that point, although the written meter is $\frac{3}{4}$, example 6.10 shows $\frac{3}{2}$ as the operative meter. Below I will use written measure numbers so the reader can compare the analysis and the music.

A note's duration is the same in the music and in the analysis; in the example, groupings, but not durations, are altered to show hypermetric structure. In addition to showing a metric setting different from the one in the written music, the example shows how the rebarred measures themselves are organized on a higher level. The numbers below the measures indicate this higher-level, hypermetric structure. The meter signatures give the "surface" meter. A light double bar indicates some metric change, either in the pulse or in the number of beats per measure. In the following discussion "quadruple" is regarded as a species of "duple."

Beginning at m. 7, the example shows a surface meter of $\frac{3}{2}$ with a larger quadruple grouping. A group of four bars of $\frac{3}{2}$ is followed by two bars of $\frac{3}{2}$ (a four-bar group cut in half) before the onset of m. 19's hemiola. At m. 19 the pulse slows from a half note to a dotted half; at the same time, the surface meter changes from triple to duple (that is, $\frac{3}{2}$ changes to $\frac{12}{4}$). The higher-level quadruple organization persists, however, so the hypermetric structure of mm. 19–33 and mm. 7–14 is the same.

One special feature of Prokofiev's mature compositional style is evident in mm. 19–33. The timespan separating hypermetric downbeats in mm. 19–30 is twelve quarter notes long. However, m. 31 and m. 34 are separated by only nine quarter notes. Thus Prokofiev does not alter the duple hypermetric structure. But by shortening the time separating m. 31's hypermetric downbeat from the following hypermetric downbeat, he marks the return of the opening material (section A2 at m. 34) with a rhythmic acceleration.

Like the first six measures of mm. 7–18, mm. 34–45 are grouped into one quadruple hypermetric bar followed by one duple hypermetric bar. And like the material beginning at m. 19, m. 46 brings a hemiola, changing $\frac{3}{2}$ to $\frac{12}{4}$, while maintaining the higher-level quadruple organization ($4 \times \frac{12}{4}$).

M. 83 is analogous to m. 34 because both measures mark formal junctures. M. 34 brings a return; m. 83 begins a new formal section, marked section B in figure 6.2. In approaching m. 83 and section B, Prokofiev again uses metric acceleration. Unlike in the approach to m. 34, however, the acceleration leading to m. 83 is more gradual and systematic. It begins in m. 62, when by deleting one beat from the measure, Prokofiev changes the meter from $\frac{12}{4}$ to $\frac{9}{4}$. However, mm. 62–67 maintain the duple hypermetric organization already present in the previously operative quadruple hypermeter. In m. 68 the composer deletes another beat from the measure, changing $\frac{9}{4}$ to $\frac{6}{4}$, but then goes on to reorganize the duple hypermeter into triple hypermeter, producing another hemiola, as was also the case at m. 19. Finally, in m. 74 Prokofiev completes the systematic metric acceleration by deleting one more beat from the measure, changing $\frac{6}{4}$ to $\frac{3}{4}$, a meter which persists for a single bar. At m. 74, the written meter is the perceived meter.

M. 75 initiates the transition to section B. The texture alternates between a full, close position chord in both hands of the piano and a two-note interval. This texture creates a half-note pulse in triple meter ($\frac{3}{2}$), thus producing another hemiola by doubling the quarter-note pulse of m. 74's $\frac{3}{4}$. At m. 77, the feeling of suspended forward motion derives in large part from the generously expanded meter, whereby the previous $\frac{3}{2}$ pulse balloons into $\frac{18}{4}$ by tripling the timespan between attack points (from half notes to dotted whole notes). As though compensating for the metric flux in mm. 1–82, section B, beginning at m. 83, settles into a steady $\frac{12}{4}$ meter, which remains unchanged until the return of section A at m. 123.

7 Concertos

T he two violin concertos, opp. 19 and 63, which are separated by more time and compositional experience than the two Sonatas for Violin and Piano, opp. 94a and 80, nevertheless stand in a similar relationship. Op. 19, like op. 94a, is a buoyant, lighthearted piece drawing on a different inspirational fount than op. 63. Similarly, op. 63 and op. 80 are both more serious and weighty than their partners.

Violin Concerto no. 1, op. 19/II

The Violin Concerto no. 1 offers a compendium of violin techniques and effects. The composer was eager to integrate many of these effects into his work and is, I believe, largely successful in so doing. In fact, we have seen that Prokofiev pursued certain aesthetic goals, such as modernism or Socialist Realism, so single-mindedly that the quality of the resulting compositions suffered (to wit, the Symphony no. 2 and, according to Prokofiev, the Symphony no. 7). But the Violin Concerto no. 1 bears up well, despite Prokofiev's eagerness to exploit a wide variety of violin effects. Below I analyze aspects of its second movement scherzo.

The movement is in five parts, if we take A1 and A2 as a unit: A1 (m. 1), A2

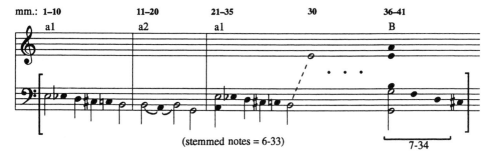

Example 7.1. Violin Concerto no. 1, op. 19/II, mm. 1–41, bass and set structure

(m. 21), B (m. 36), A (m. 57), C (m. 80), and A (m. 120). Example 7.1 is an analysis of the bass over mm. 1–41. The excerpt covers section A and its varied repetition (mm. 1–36) and the beginning of section B (mm. 36–41). The bar-lines divide the excerpt into its constituent parts: a1 (mm. 1–10), a2 (mm. 11–20), a varied repeat of a1 (mm. 21–35), and the first part of section B. The bass in each part spans an interval of the tonal-interpreting E-minor triad, notes of which are open and stemmed in the example. Noteheads are filled in and stemmed when the bass extends at least one and a half measures in the music. The unstemmed, filled-in noteheads extend at most two beats; because of their short duration and the fast tempo, these are analyzed as connectives. Section a1 moves in the bass from E to B; section a2 moves from B to G; and the varied repeat of section a1 moves from E to B. The overall control of the E-minor triad, along with the move from "tonic" to "dominant" that so clearly controls the motion in mm. 1–10 and mm. 21–35, makes the E-minor triad a tonal interpreter.

A transition in mm. 30–36 begins in the bass on the pitch B and ends on G, where it dovetails with the opening of the second main section. In the bass mm. 36–41 move among G, D, and C♯, an ostinato passage which sums up the fore-going bass motion. Taken together, all of the pitch classes of mm. 36–41 create a form of 7–34, (124579e). Of the form's four distinct hexachordal subsets, 6–33 is represented twice, and one of the forms of 6–33, (79e124), duplicates the pitch-class set formed by the stemmed notes in the bass line. Mm. 36–41 are therefore a kind of summary of the preceding music.

Now let us focus on some melodic features of mm. 1–10. Throughout this passage two octads govern two distinct realms of the music. The octad 8–23 governs the large-scale structure, while the octatonic collection 8–28 governs the detail.

The violin melody over mm. 1–10 comprises an octatonic collection, expressed as alternating whole and half steps. The whole steps are traversed (and filled in) in the two-sixteenths-plus-eighth motive, with statements of the

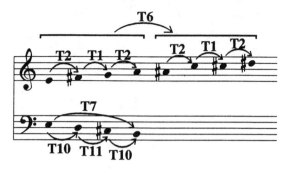

Example 7.2. Violin Concerto no. 1, op. 19/II, mm. 3–9, analysis of set structure in violin melody and bass

motive separated by half steps. The eight degrees of symmetry of 8–28 (four transpositions and four inversions produce complete invariance) inhibit the music's orientation to a referential pitch class.[1] But within the context of the bass line, one can hear a tonal-interpreting motion from tonic to dominant, thus situating the melody within an E-minor tonal focus.

The whole steps constitutive of the violin's part over mm. 1–10 are highlighted by Prokofiev's bow marking and slurring, so they are an easily perceivable feature of the musical surface. Example 7.2 gives the violin line in a nonrhythmic setting; the arrows marked "T2" show the whole steps. The arrangement of pitches in the treble clef in the ordering whole step, half step, whole step is a nearly paradigmatic realization of the so-called 2–1–2 form of the octatonic scale except that in the written music in m. 3, the final dyad occurs as D♯–C♯, in reverse order from what example 7.2 shows.

In section a2, beginning in m. 11, whole steps are again arrayed prominently, but the order is different than in section a1. Beginning at m. 11, forms of 5–20 [01378] twice succeed one another at T10 [= (T10)²]; from m. 11 to m. 19 the passage moves at T8 [= (T10)²]. The first form of 5–20 is (459e0), an "F major seventh chord over B bass" or the "F chord." The "F chord," (459e0), passes down through an "E♭" chord, (2379t), in m. 14 to a "D♭ chord," (01578), in m. 19. The motion is interrupted once when m. 16 returns to (459e0).

From m. 11 to m. 19 the bass moves from B to G. These two pitch classes return in reversed order in mm. 40–45 (and in varied repetition in mm. 50–55), again in the bass. Example 7.3 schematizes mm. 40–54, a portion of section B, and provides an analysis of those measures according to the model of mm. 11–19.

In examples 7.2 and 7.3 inverse transpositional relations are also brought into play. In example 7.2, the treble clef is analyzed in two disjunct tetrachords; the succession of pitch-class transpositions within each tetrachord is 2–1–2. The bass tetrachord inverts each transposition to produce the succession 10–11–10.

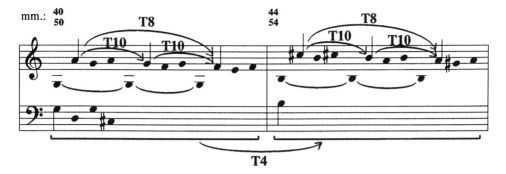

Example 7.3. Violin Concerto no. 1, op. 19/II, mm. 40–54, sequential structure

In example 7.3, a barline separates transpositionally related passages. Within a passage, T8 moves the treble clef melody from its beginning to its end. With the inverse-related transposition T4, shown below the lower staff, mm. 40–43 (and mm. 50–53) are then transposed into mm. 44–45 (and mm. 54–55).

In example 7.4 I propose a larger-scale structure for mm. 1–10, one which engages the bass and the melody. These measures comprise two phrases; the first phrase cadences on D in m. 5 and the second phrase cadences on B in m. 9. The cadential points of articulation D and B, while marked clearly by the violin flourishes, lie outside the melody's form of the octatonic collection (see example 7.2); the cadential points are integrated in example 7.4a. Each of the two phrases comprises two similar subphrases. In the example I extract points of articulation at beginnings and endings of phrases. Phrase beginnings are represented by the last pitch of the chromatic trichord which begins the larger phrase; phrase endings are represented by the last pitch of the chromatic trichord which ends the larger phrase. In m. 3, the first phrase moves from F♯5 to C♯6. M. 4 begins much like m. 3 but moves from F♯5 to C6, at which point the violin abandons the two-sixteenths-plus-eighth rhythmic motive in favor of straight eighth notes and ascends from C through C♯ toward the first melodic

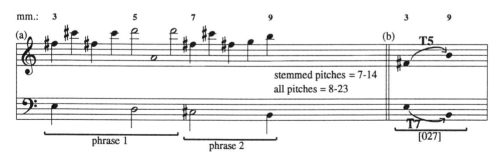

Example 7.4. Violin Concerto no. 1, op. 19/II, mm. 3–9, set structure

cadence on D. The example therefore shows F♯, C♯, F♯, C, and D as the main melodic notes of mm. 1–6, supported by E, then D, in the bass.

The second phrase begins in m. 7, where the violin moves from F♯5 to C♯6 in m. 8. M. 8 begins like m. 7, but because the second phrase begins a beat later than the first, only six notes of the second subphrase in m. 8 are played before the phrase passes up from G to B for the second cadence in m. 9. The example shows F♯, C♯, F♯, and B supported by C♯ and then B in the bass. The set formed by the stemmed pitches in the example—that is, the main melodic pitches along with the main bass pitches—is 7–14, a subset of 8–23. Two gestures occur over mm. 5–6: the flute descends from A6 to D4, and the violin twice races up from A4 to D6. Both gestures emphasize the compound fourth A4/D6. So example 7.4a includes A as a main pitch (D is already included as part of 7–14). The set formed by the addition of the pitch A is 8–23. Confirming the propriety of asserting 8–23, section a returns in m. 21; there the low strings explicitly set forth the pitch A as the bass harmonic support.

Example 7.4b is a further distillation of example 7.4a, showing only the first and last melody and bass note. The arrows point out an inversional relation: as the melody ascends a perfect fourth from beginning to end, the bass descends a perfect fourth. The melody and bass invert into one another about B, the dominant. E and B go on to govern the registral extremes as mm. 11–20 get under way. The low strings and bassoon play B3 while the violin solo plays E6.

The large-scale structuring power of 6–33, discussed earlier in connection with example 7.1, extends as well to 8–23. The 6–33 is also a subset of 8–23, where, in fact, it is represented maximally, occurring four times.[2]

Mm. 34–36 constitute a four-voiced transitional passage. The melody chromatically traverses a perfect fourth from D5 in m. 34 to A4 in m. 36. However, the arrow structure of example 7.2's bass tetrachord is reproduced by regarding upbeats as passing tones. In that case, $T_{10}(T_{11}(T_{10}(D))) = A$. The perfect fourth making up the melodic span of each voice-leading strand is reflected in the characteristic quartal spacing of the treble chords. Indeed, the upper voice motion from D5 down to A4 "unfolds" quite clearly the vertical fourth A4/D5 in the chord of m. 34.

The perfect fourth and its generated transformations T_5 and T_7 affect this movement in several ways. The basic harmony of section a2 (beginning in m. 11) is 5–20. Example 7.5 displays this harmony and then shows it untangled. Example 7.5b separates 5–20 into two components, both of which are forms of 3–4. These two components relate at T_5, as the arrow shows. In the example the embedded form of 3–9 is pulled out and spaced in stacked perfect fifths. Another instance of a prominent perfect fourth occurs in mm. 5–6, which celebrate the cadence in m. 5; the violin and flute at that point present a perfect fourth.[3]

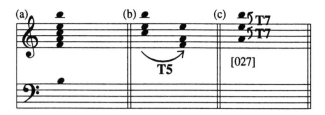

Example 7.5. Violin Concerto no. 1, op. 19/II, m. 11, harmonic structure

Now let us return to the interval A–D, which is reiterated by the violin in mm. 5–6. At that early point in the piece, the "tonic" E still resonates in the ear—after all, the bass has played E right up until the middle of m. 4, where it steps down to D. Consequently, there is a strong sense in which (249) colors the opening six measures.

The violin solo in m. 10, analyzed in example 7.6a, next presents the same pitch-class set, (249), in a spacing that features perfect fifths. The stacked perfect fifths in the violin solo at the end of section a1 (m. 10) then appear in transposed form embedded within 5–20 at the beginning of section a2. Section C, beginning at m. 80, also features (249) in the stacked perfect fifths of the horns. These fifths are shown as open noteheads in example 7.6b.

We are thus brought back to mm. 34–36. There, forms of [027] are conspicuous components of forms of 4–22, the set class of each complete four-note chord. Further, (249), familiar from m. 10, is both the very first form of [027] heard in m. 34 and, in m. 36, a subset 7–34, toward which the passage aims.

Piano Concerto no. 3, op. 26

Prokofiev's Piano Concerto no. 3, op. 26, is one of his best-known works, as well as the most famous of the five piano concertos. The work was completed at St. Brevin-les-Pins when Konstantin Balmont, the concerto's dedicatee, lived nearby. Balmont even wrote a poem in response to the concerto.[4]

Following its successful premiere in Chicago in 1921, the concerto increased

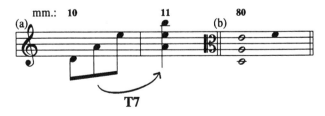

Example 7.6. Violin Concerto no. 1, op. 19/II, mm. 10–11 and m. 80, the pitch-class set (249)

in popularity. Prokofiev responded to and encouraged its popularity by often performing it during his concert tours. For instance, in his tour of the Soviet Union in 1927 he performed it in Moscow to an admittedly partisan crowd. Prokofiev reports: "At the end the hall shouted its head off. I don't think I ever got such a reception anywhere. I am called out over and over again."[5]

The composition of the work occupied Prokofiev intermittently over the years 1917–1921. Characteristically, he was reluctant to discard any of his compositional productions, and much of the concerto began as a different work in a different genre, which Prokofiev started but did not complete. Prokofiev describes how thematic material for the Piano Concerto no. 3 accumulated:

> In 1916–17 I had tried several times to return to the Third Concerto. I wrote a beginning for it (two themes) and two variations on the theme of the second movement. At about the same time I contemplated writing a 'white quartet,' i.e. an absolutely diatonic string quartet that could be played only on the white keys of the piano. . . . However, I found the task too difficult, I was afraid it would prove too monotonous, and now in 1921 I decided to split up the material: . . . the first and second themes of the finale went into the finale of the Third Concerto. Thus when I began working on the latter I already had the entire thematic material apart from the subordinate theme of the first movement and the third theme of the finale.[6]

In a romantic scripting of the compositional process, the composer is more or less at the mercy of mysterious creative powers. Therefore, one might expect the Concerto no. 3 to fight its way through the composer's imaginative faculty, struggling on its way to the page. But the Concerto no. 3 seems to owe a bigger debt to craft and thematic thrift than a romantic would be comfortable with. After amassing the proper number and types of themes, all that remained for Prokofiev was some sewing together, some musical development, and some repairs.

However unsatisfactory romantics might find this type of compositional method, Prokofiev's plainly practical approach served him well elsewhere, most notably in composing for film. Whatever role inspiration may have played for Prokofiev, either it was ever present or in certain situations Prokofiev's compositional craft was sufficient in its stead. For instance, while working with Prokofiev on the film *Alexander Nevsky,* Sergei Eisenstein reported on Prokofiev's highly controlled working habits. "[Prokofiev says:] 'At twelve noon you'll have the music.' We are coming out of the small projection room. And although it's now midnight, I'm completely calm. At exactly 11:55 A.M., a small dark blue car will drive through the studio gates. Sergei Prokofiev will get out of it. In his hands will be the next musical number for *Alexander Nevsky*. We look at a new piece of film at night. In the morning a new piece of music will be ready for it. Prokofiev works like a clock. This clock isn't fast and it isn't slow."[7]

The Concerto no. 3 does not show some of the bad features that might result from a too-cerebral approach. The music is rhythmically forceful without being predictable. And, as we have seen, Prokofiev was concerned that purely white-key music is not sustainable; it must be relieved, presumably by some sort of chromaticism. The first and the last movements of the Concerto no. 3 begin with white-key themes, though neither remains white-key.

The second movement, too, provides an effective contrast to the white-key features of the outer movements. The second movement also displays the inventiveness and creativity which in a romantic view might be lacking were the work devoid of inspiration. Variations I, II, IV, and V preserve the theme more or less intact and offer reharmonizations and different contexts, ranging from the meditative variation I to the energetic, rhythmically driving variations II and V. At the midpoint stands variation III, notable for its subtly hidden connections to the Tema.

In the second movement we observe the interplay of characteristic diatonic and non-tonal collections.[8] One constellation of diatonic collections features perfect fifths and fourths; its members can be generated by a T5-cycle. These set classes include 4−23 [0257], its subset 3−9 [027], and its superset 5−35 [02459]. A second constellation comprises non-tonal collections, all of which are supersets of the augmented triad 3−12 [048]. These supersets include 4−19 [0148] and two of 4−19's supersets, 5−21 [01458] and 5−22 [01478].

The form of the Tema is a rounded binary (in aba' form) in E minor. Part 1 extends over mm. 1−4 (a), concluding with a half cadence on B; part 2 begins with a motion to the dominant over mm. 5−12 (b), and mm. 13−17 (a') are a varied reprise of mm. 1−4. Example 7.7 reproduces aspects of the Tema. Motive *i* is labeled in the first measure. Motive *i* is a stepwise descent, expressed as a form of 4-2 [0124] in its first appearance in m. 1. As can be seen clearly in example 7.8, the first four notes in m. 2 transpose motive *i* down a whole step (or a pitch-class transposition at T10). Motive *i* is also stretched when m. 2 extends it by one note to bring in B4 on beat 3; the resulting motive is labeled "motive i+" in example 7.8. Motive *i,* and the downward transposition by T10, occur throughout the movement.

Part 1 of the Tema occupies four measures; it reaches its goal at m. 3, beat 3, a half cadential chord over the tonal-interpreting dominant B. Here, the B chord is minor, not an unusual choice for Prokofiev.[9] From m. 3, beat 3 to the end of m. 4, a stepwise descent in the bass aims at returning to the E-minor tonic. Though E arrives on the last beat of m. 4, it functions as a tonal-interpreting dominant of A, not as a tonic, and it leads directly to part 2.

Example 7.7. Piano Concerto no. 3, op. 26/II, Tema, mm. 1–17, melodic analysis

Section b of the Tema derives from part 1 by a development of motive *i*. Below the music in example 7.7, part of motive *i* is bracketed: m. 1's last three eighth notes, which descend chromatically from E5. To begin part 2, m. 5 takes this small chromatic motive, along with the upward leap of a perfect fourth with which the theme begins, and transposes it up a perfect fourth. As though correcting a too-low A5 in m. 5, m. 7 boosts the melody up one more step from A5 to B5. Mm. 7–8 then take mm. 5–6 as a basic model and transpose them up one step. Part 2 concludes in m. 12 with a traditional half cadence on the dominant B, now a major triad instead of a minor one. A varied reprise of section a rounds off the form by closing down to the tonic.

In example 7.8 the stemmed notes in mm. 1–3 form the underlying melodic

Example 7.8. Piano Concerto no. 3, op. 26/II, Tema, mm. 1–11, motivic analysis

structure. This structure begins on the tonic E, rises to F#, and then descends stepwise to arrive at the dominant B. The minor-scale pentachord which is beamed together and labeled "MPENT" can be understood as a diatonic form of motive $i+$, that form of motive i which in m. 2 is extended to five notes. MPENT is then exactly transposed at T_5, shown below the staff of mm. 3–4, when the stepwise bass begins in m. 3, precisely when MPENT in the melody is completed. After that bass statement, there are inverted major-scale forms of the original minor pentachord; these are labeled "INV." Above the bass staff, beginning in m. 8, a beam shows a slightly altered form of MPENT in the bass. This larger-scale form of MPENT is a nearly exact, ordered pitch-class repetition of MPENT from section a, except for the alteration of C# to C♮.

Beginning in m. 9 and extending to m. 12, one can hear a circle-of-fifths progression, E–A–D–G–C–F–B, labeled below the bottom staff. Bass "roots" in mm. 5–9 spell out the pitch succession A–B–A (shown parenthetically), thus reproducing at T_5 the melodic succession E–F#–E, formed on the odd beats of m. 1 to the downbeat of m. 2 (also shown parenthetically).

The bass motion of part 1 gives a clue to another melodic structure. Through to the beginning of m. 3, ascending perfect fourths and fifths in the bass create a form of 4–23, (9e24). The bass of part 2, beginning with m. 5, features forms of 4–23 as well. The eighth- and sixteenth-note scalar fragments each span a perfect fifth; an example is the A to E leading into m. 6. In fact, three overlapping forms of 4–23 are formed as the bass works its way to its goal, a B dominant triad in m. 12. Mm. 5–10 yield (469e), m. 10 to the downbeat of m. 11 yields (2479), and m. 11 (including its upbeat) to m. 12's downbeat yields (0257). Each successive form of 4–23 is the T_{10}-transpose of the previous one. As was mentioned earlier, the T_{10} transposition can be heard to derive from the same process that connects the two forms of motive i in mm. 1–2.

A structure related to [0257] occurs in the melody, shown in the analytical staff of example 7.7. The set 3–9 [027] in the form (46e), a descendant of [0257], is formed in mm. 1–4 by the first and last notes and the melodic peaks. Agogic accent stresses further the pitches E5 in m. 1 and B4 in mm. 3–4. Parallelism highlights the close relation between F#5 in m. 1 and E5 in m. 2, since m. 2, beats 1–2, transposes m. 1, beats 3–4, down a step, returning F# to the E from which it departed.

Mm. 5–7, beginning part 2, are a variation of mm. 1–4. Stemmed and beamed together in the analytical staff of example 7.7 are each of two forms of [027], one over mm. 1–4 and the other over mm. 5–7. I have already mentioned the upward transposition by a perfect fourth between the incipits of m. 1 and of m. 4. The arrow labeled "T_5" indicates that the transpositional relations between points of articulation in each passage reinforces the move toward the subdominant. Taken together, the two forms of 3–9 [027], (46e) and (9e4), create (469e), a form of 4–23 [0257] that is identical to the form of 4–23 in the bass of mm. 5–10 (discussed earlier).[10]

As is typical of a rounded binary, section b expresses the dominant. In the Tema, the bass arrives at the dominant B in m. 12, at the end of section b. Over mm. 7–12, the melody traverses the interval from B5 down to D#5, an interval of the dominant triad, but does so in a nontraditional fashion. In example 7.7 I show this melodic motion by stemming and beaming together three versions of a motive labeled "x." In any of its guises, the motive descends through two descending whole steps, as shown in *x1* by the two T10 arrows. The succession *x1–x2–x3* reflects the internal structure of any one of the motives, as is shown by the T10 arrows below the analytical staff. Further, the headnotes of *x1, x2,* and *x3* are precisely the ordered form of *x1* itself.

The whole-tone structure shown by the T10 arrows in example 7.7, which begin from B5, is not unprecedented. B5 in m. 7 is, in fact, supported harmonically by (9e15), a form of 4–24 [0248], a superset of [048] (and a subset of the whole-tone scale). That harmony is shown in filled-in noteheads in example 7.7.

Two less prominent, but nevertheless characteristic, structures occur in m. 6 and in mm. 9–10. Both collections are supersets of [048] and [0148], and both collections are formed from non-diatonic chord progressions. The progression in m. 6, from beat 2 to beat 3 in the right hand, is a G#-minor triad moving to an E-minor triad; together they create a form of 5–21 [01458]. M. 10 and m. 11 both contain the progression F# minor to F major, a third flip; together the two chords create a form of 5–22 [01478].

In contrast to the previous two variations, variation III obscures the theme and enters with pronounced forcefulness. Abetting its generally aggressive demeanor is the piano's syncopated two-voiced triplet figuration playing against the spare but insistent orchestral bass. Also, the rounded binary form is gone, now replaced by the form given in figure 7.1.

The form given in figure 7.1 comprises a series of episodes which alternately vary motive *i* and vary mm. 5–6 and mm. 9–12 of the Tema's part 2. Especially in its first measures, variation III deftly conceals its source in part 1 of the Tema by radically transforming motive *i*. In example 7.9 I take the piano's first measure in the third variation, preserving the original beaming and using dotted lines to mark off a succession of triads. The right hand plays one stream of arpeggiated triads while the left hand plays another. Each hand plays a total of four chords. In an analytical staff the root succession of the triads is beamed together, and each strand is labeled. Like motive *i,* each strand is a form of 4–2, but now inverted from (2346) in m. 1 of the Tema. All the triads are minor ones except for the last, which is augmented and formed from both hands together.

a1 (one measure pattern)	mm. 1–2	T4
extension	mm. 3–4	(based on motive *i*)
a2	mm. 5–6	T3 (C–Eb)
extension	mm. 7–9	(based on m. 7)
b1	mm. 10–11	(based on mm. 5–6)
b1	mm. 12–13	
a2	m. 14	T3
a1	m. 15	
a3	m. 16	T8
a4	m. 17	T9
b2	mm. 18–26	(based on mm. 9–12)
	[mm. 18–21 and mm. 22–26 (with cadence)]	
a1	mm. 26–27	T4
extended cadence	mm. 28–32	

Figure 7.1. Piano Concerto no. 3, op. 26/II, variation III, form outline

For those augmented triads the analytical staff shows Ab and C as "roots" because of their prominent position at a bend in the contour.

The change in chord quality from minor, in the first through the third chords, to augmented, in the last chord, coincides with the change from a half step to a whole step between successive chordal roots. If we regard the third-to-last eighth note attack in example 7.9 as an appoggiatura, occupying rhythmically the slots belonging to Ab and C on an underlying level, then statements of section a also preserve motive *i*'s even attack rhythm.

As is indicated in example 7.9, minor triads related at T4 produce a form of

Example 7.9. Piano Concerto no. 3, op. 26/II, variation III, m. 1, set structure

5–21. In m. 6 of the Tema, the progression of G♯ minor to E minor helps prepare the T4 relation between example 7.9's staves. The set formed by minor triads separated by a half step is 6z19. For instance, C minor and B minor together make 6z19, which is a superset of 5–21 and 5–22 (I shall develop the connection to 5–22 later). In example 7.9 maximum intersection under transposition between each form of 5–21 (the minor triad pairs C/E, B/E♭, and B♭/D) and each form of 6z19 (the minor triad pairs C/B, B/B♭, E/E♭, and E♭/D) occurs at transposition levels deriving from the structure of 5–21. For instance, (e0347) produces four invariants with (e02367) at T0, T3, T7, T8, and T11.

The material labeled "a1" through "a4" in figure 7.1 occurs as "a1" in its most pervasive form and is especially prominent at the beginning and ending of the movement. The right arrow on the analytical staff of example 7.9 indicates the T4 relation between the right- and left-hand streams of triads. Figure 7.1's third column charts how that relation changes with the various presentations of a1, a2, a3, and a4. As indicated below the analytical staff in example 7.9, the two streams traverse a form of [048], a set class to reappear in section b1.

Each statement of section a comprises the same stream of triads in the left hand, except for section a4, which departs somewhat from the established pattern. Against the virtually fixed left-hand pattern, the right hand plays transposed forms of its original pattern. The changing relation of the right-hand pattern to the left accounts for the four variants of section a.

In example 7.10 I survey the four different relations of the right to the left hand in sections a1, a2, a3, and a4. I begin by taking the root of the left hand's first chord, C, and, for comparison, go on to show the corresponding root of the right hand's first chord. For the sake of convenience, these roots are displayed as real pitches, and the right hand's roots are entered in order of appearance; sections are given below the staff.[11] The arrows T4, T3, T−4, and T−3 show the inversional symmetry about C(4). The bracket shows that all the pitches in the example form 5–22 [01478]. As a subset of 6z19, 5–22's presence

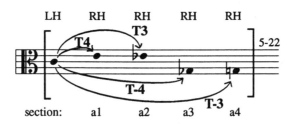

Example 7.10. Piano Concerto no. 3, op. 26/II, variation III, harmonic relations in sections a1, a2, a3, and a4

a. melodic structure

b. transformation

Example 7.11. Piano Concerto no. 3, op. 26/II, variation III, R65 through R65+1

has already been felt in the pairs of chromatically descending minor triads ana-lyzed in connection with example 7.9.

The orchestra of section b1 plays an emphatic melodic statement based on mm. 5–6 of the Tema. Example 7.11a shows the relevant portion of mm. 5–6 from the Tema, in which the clarinet line has been dropped an octave and the bass line raised an octave in order to fit conveniently on one staff. Like motive *i,* the upper strand begins with two consecutive descending half steps, but motive *i* then descends a whole step; the clarinet in m. 6 descends a minor third. In example 7.11a, however, the clarinet's variant is labeled "motive i'," and its structure is shown precisely, that is, $T_{11} - T_{11} - T_9$.

Example 7.11b shows how variation III transforms mm. 5–6. The variation combines example 7.11a's two voice-leading components into a single strand. Also, the ascending eighth-note run targeting the barline is a form of MPENT, while example 7.11a's bass is a form of INV (see example 7.8). More interesting is the treatment of motive *i'.* Figure 7.2 shows a comparison of motive *i'* and its transformation in variation III. Both forms of the motive proceed by two equal, contiguous increments and one larger one. When $x = 11$ (see 1a in the figure), the transpositions move from T_{11} to T_{11} to T_9; when $x = 8$ the transpositions

(1) $(x)(x)(x - 2)$
    (a) $11–11–9$ $(x = 11)$
    (b) $8–8–6$ $(x = 8)$
(2) $R[(x)(x)(x-2)] = (x-2)(x)(x)$
    (a) $9–11–11$ $(x = 11)$
    (b) $6–8–8$ $(x = 8)$

Figure 7.2. Piano Concerto no. 3, op. 26/II, motive *i'* and its transformation in variation III

A1: mm. 1–41

B: mm. 42–82

A2: mm. 83–146

C

    c1 (a): lyric theme, C#: mm. 147–169

    c2 (b): chromatic piano entrance: mm. 170–199

    c1 (a): lyric theme

        E: mm. 200–209 (200–207/208–209 [transition]: 8 + 2)

        C: mm. 210–231 (210–217/217–231: 8 + 15)

        F#: mm. 232–244 (232–235/236–243/244 [transition]: 4 + 8 + 1)

        B♭: mm. 245–256 (245–248/249–256: 4 + 8)

        C#: mm. 257–274 (257–264/264–274: 8 + 11)

A3: mm. 275–419

Figure 7.3. Piano Concerto no. 3, op. 26/III, form outline

move from T8 to T8 to T6. The second form of the motive (2) retrogrades the first. At 2b we can see the result when $x = 8$.[12] Further, transformed motive i' embeds an augmented triad, one that is familiar from section a1 and is also embedded in the harmony of m. 11 in the Tema.

The last movement is a five-part rondo, diagrammed in figure 7.3. The following discussion centers on aspects of section C.

Example 7.12 gives the lyric theme to a portion of section C (section c1: mm. 147–158, beginning at R110), along with an analytical staff aligned below. In the analytical staff I pull out triadic outlines of C# chords. In figure 7.3 theme of section c1 is transposed over mm. 200–274; the roots of analogous chords label

Example 7.12. Piano Concerto no. 3, op. 26/III, mm. 147–158, set structure of melody

Example 7.13. Piano Concerto no. 3, op. 26/III, mm. 170–180, melodic analysis

the transpositional levels. In example 7.12, C♯-major triads are beamed together below the staff, and C♯-minor triads are beamed together above the staff. Together the two triads form (1458) (4–17), which itself can be analyzed as a pair of major thirds, C♯/E♯ and E/G♯, separated by a minor third: T3(15) = (48).

Example 7.13 is an analysis of the piano's theme for section c2, beginning in m. 170 (R114). The bracket above the upper staff marks a double neighbor motion around B4; the neighbor notes A♯4 and C5 are each approached through an ascending chromatic line. Hence the large-scale chromatic neighbor motion embellishing B5 is itself diminuted by smaller-scale chromatic lines.

Beginning in m. 176 a chromatic line descends from B4 to G4 and then slides up to A♭4 before descending to E4. The lower staff charts the two intervals traversed and shows how they express a form of 4–17 (478e). A T3 arrow and a T9 arrow show 4–17's construction from two major thirds. If the A♭ on the lower staff is regarded as enharmonically equivalent to G♯, then an E major/minor chord underlies mm. 170–199. T3 interrelates C♯ major/minor, underlying mm. 147–169, and E major/minor, underlying mm. 170–199, just as it relates the constituent "major thirds" within each form of 4–17 [0347].

Returning to example 7.13, we see that following the descent from B4 to E4 under the second bracket (m. 176), the line continues to descend chromatically, with one shift in register which occurs under the third bracket, until it returns to its starting point, B4. In the lower staff an arrow marks E♭4's shift upward to E♭5.

The top staff in example 7.14 gives part of the solo piano's right hand, and the middle staff gives the melody for section c1 when it returns in m. 200. The

Example 7.14. Piano Concerto no. 3, op. 26/III, mm. 200–206, harmonic and set structure

lower staff shows underlying harmonies. The solo piano's right-hand harmonization of the melody reflects both the stepwise chromaticism of section c2 and the T_3 relation expressed within 4–17. The piano right hand in even-numbered measures features parallel triads. Mm. 200 and 202 feature major triads; m. 204 gives the minor triad version. In root motion these even-numbered measures move by T_9 from beginning to end, expressing a relation deriving from the structure of 4–17 (see example 7.13). In fact, the letter names below the middle staff (E, G, E) reflect the motion through T_3 (from E to G) and T_9 (from G back to E), which governs the entire seven measures. The specific relation between E and G is first expressed between m. 200 and m. 202, as shown by the T_3 arrow. Mm. 203–205 provide stepwise harmonic passing motion which connects G in m. 202 to E in m. 206.

In m. 206, durational accent partitions the six triads into the chord pairs C♯ major / E major and D major / F major. Each pair of chords clearly expresses the T_3 relation. On the other hand, T_1, which transposes C♯/E into D/F, is an elaboration of the chromatic upper neighbor motion in m. 200.

The form diagram in figure 7.3 provides extra detail on some aspects of the phrase structure in c1's reprise over mm. 200–274. Figure 7.3 shows five thematic statements, none of which are identical. Let us begin by noting that a transposition by T_9 connects the first statement, focused on E, to the last, focused on C♯ (the original tonal focus of mm. 147–169). Thus the process so prevalent in examples 7.13 and 7.14 above also influences c1's reprise.

While none of the five thematic statements are identical, there are some resemblances. For mm. 210–274, the second through the fifth thematic statements, there is an archlike symmetry. Two long phrases (mm. 210–231 and mm. 257–274) enclose two smaller phrases (mm. 232–244 and mm. 245–256). The long phrases, spanning twenty-two and eighteen measures respectively, both have a one-measure overlap between their two subphrases. Measures where the overlaps occur are italicized on the example.

Mm. 232–244 and mm. 245–256 have different tonal foci, and mm. 232–244 conclude with a single transitional measure, which is absent in mm. 245–256. But the small phrases do exhibit similarities. Both mm. 232–244 and mm. 245–256 begin with a four-measure phrase which attempts to continue but is cut off in the fifth measure when the theme begins again, as though the first four measures need correcting.

As is evident from the varied mix of phrase and subphrase lengths, overlaps, and transitions, the phrase structure of section C is strikingly mature in its malleability and unpredictability. The squareness and regularity that we observed in the *Scythian Suite,* op. 20, is absent. In its place is a proselike free verse by a composer who is comfortable and confident.

The last of Prokofiev's five piano concertos was written before his return to the Soviet Union. Its genesis resembles in some ways that of the Third Concerto.

> In 1932 I wrote the Fifth Piano Concerto. . . . Since [the composition of the Fourth Concerto] my conception of this form had changed somewhat . . . and finally I had accumulated a good number of vigorous major themes in my notebook. I had not intended the concerto to be difficult and at first had even contemplated calling it "Music for Piano and Orchestra." . . . But in the end it turned out to be complicated. . . . What was the explanation? I searched for a "new simplicity" only to discover that this new simplicity, with its novel forms and, chiefly, new tonal structure, was not understood. The fact that here and there my efforts to write simply were not successful is beside the point. I did not give up, hoping that the bulk of my music would in time prove to be quite simple when the ear grew accustomed to the new melodies, that is, when these melodies became the accepted idiom.[13]

On the one hand Prokofiev describes the nonromantic process of composing a piece after a sufficient number of themes have accumulated. But on the other hand, this composition seems to have taken on its own character, insisting on becoming a complex concerto for piano, despite the composer's original intentions to keep the work simple and to title it "Music for Piano and Orchestra" rather than "Concerto." Also of special interest in this passage is Prokofiev's hope that in time this work and others would eventually prove to be simple and be accepted by the public. Zhdanov articulated and rejected precisely this argument at the musicians' conference which preceded the Decree of 1948.

In this movement, as in op. 19/II, different structural sets govern different realms of the music. One constellation of structural sets is generated by the T_5-cycle and includes 4-23 and its complement $8-23$, and $5-35$ and its complement $7-35$.[14] The set $4-23$ dominates local harmonic structure; the set $8-23$ dominates large-scale melodic structure. The other constellation of structural sets is built around $7-21$ and its superset $8-19$.

Figure 7.4 is an outline of the ternary form of the movement. Section A's graceful, unhurried melody eloquently represents Prokofiev's lyric line. The emphasis on sets generated by T_5-cycles reaches back to works such as op. 9/1, where that type of set was a central factor in defining the presence of the lyric line (see Chapter 2).

Section A is a single period comprising two long phrases. The first phrase runs over mm. $5-15$ and moves from the opening B♭ tonal focus to a half

A	
introduction	mm. 1–4
phrase 1	mm. 5–15
transition	mm. 16–17
phrase 2	mm. 18–29
B	
b1	mm. 30–46
b2	mm. 47–57
transition	mm. 58–63
b2	mm. 64–75
b2	mm. 76–83
transition	mm. 84–90 (T11 of mm. 58–63)
b3 retransition	mm. 91–107 (hints of A in melodic contour)
A	
phrase 1	mm. 108–117
coda	mm. 118–122

Figure 7.4. Piano Concerto no. 5, op. 55/IV, form outline

cadence on C. The second phrase begins from an E♭ tonal focus and closes as the movement began, on B♭. A four-measure introduction precedes the first phrase, and a three-measure transition separates the first phrase from the second.

The extended length of the first phrase, eleven bars in a slow duple meter, is largely the result of weak downbeat arrivals. The music of section A consistently prevents structural accent from coordinating with metric accent, thus disarming some of the force of downbeats and enabling the melody to maintain forward momentum and slide past potential natural cadence points. At the movement's beginning the weak-beat F's played by the flutes in m. 2 and m. 3 draw our attention to upbeats, thus preparing an important aspect of the rhythmic structure of the melody when it gets under way beginning in m. 5.

In the melody, the primary strategy for weakening downbeat arrivals involves the rhythmic motive 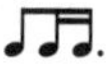. The energy of the sixteenth notes added to the eighth note can weaken and subvert the downbeat arrival by driving the melody on past the downbeat, as in m. 6, m. 10, m. 11, and m. 14. But in a different metric position the same rhythmic motive may also forcefully accelerate toward the barline, only to brake and sustain through the ensuing downbeat, as in mm. 7–8 and mm. 8–9.

The first phrase closes in m. 15, but in a wonderfully understated way. M. 15 finally delivers the downbeat arrival denied in the previous measures, but offers it as unobtrusively as possible. At the downbeat of m. 15 the orchestra and the melody drop out and leave the piano left hand playing alone on the downbeat; the piano sounds a single interval implying a first inversion C-major triad, a relatively weak close for the phrase.

The rhythmic forward flow of this phrase is achieved even though the phrase comprises three quadruple hypermeasures. In some contexts such hypermetric regularity could impede the musical inertia. The conclusion of the first hypermeasure comes in m. 8, where it is marked by D5 tied across the barline (an event which recalls D5 restruck across the barline in mm. 5–6). The second hypermeasure, beginning in m. 9, activates the upper register, which will be picked up and explored more fully by the second phrase. The third hypermeasure, beginning in m. 13, moves toward the half cadence on C by arpeggiating C's dominant, the G-major triad in m. 13. B♮ in m. 13 and E♮ in m. 14 explicitly defeat the two-flat signature, further setting off the third hypermeasure. Mm. 11–15 descend stepwise from E♭6 (a note elaborated by the E♭-minor arpeggiation) through D6 (a note elaborated by the G-major arpeggiation), finally cadencing on C. E♭6 and D6 both arrive on written downbeats and on hypermetric beat 3 and beat 1, respectively. M. 15 is the understated measure discussed above and contains no substantial melodic motion. Instead, the melody comes to C on the last beat of m. 14 (not on the downbeat of m. 15), a final reminder of the rhythmic-metric interaction so characteristic of this phrase. A passage in the winds fills the rest of the hypermeasure, and it leads to E♭ in m. 17. M. 17 is a prefix to the hypermeasure which begins in m. 18.[15]

Example 7.15 is an analysis of some aspects of section A (mm. 4–29). The following remarks center on the first phrase (mm. 1–15), treated in more detail in the example than the second phrase is. The first phrase contains several small fragments, labeled "a" through "e" in the example. Through m. 10, fragments *a, b,* and *c* rise to stemmed main notes, and each is immediately repeated and slightly varied. Fragments *d* and *e* are not repeated; they are set off from fragments *a–c* in other ways as well. Fragments *a, b,* and *c* combine to ascend slowly through an arpeggiated B♭ major triad whose components are stemmed below and beamed together. Fragments *d* and *e* respond by descending stepwise from E♭ in m. 11 through D in m. 13 to C in m. 14. Chromatic contrast also pairs fragments *d* and *e*: fragment *d* adds flats to those provided by the signature, while fragment *e* subtracts them.

At m. 11 the music changes harmony and abandons the repeated motivic cells in the melody. Beamed together over mm. 11–12 in example 7.15 are the elements of the E♭-minor triad arpeggiated on the beat. The arpeggiation motif continues into m. 13, when a C pedal arrives, over which the melody arpeggiates a G-major triad, dominant of C, to lead to the C cadence in m. 14. The notes of the G-major arpeggiation are also beamed together. The main melodic pitches

Example 7.15. Piano Concerto no. 5, op. 55/IV, mm. 4–29, harmonic and motivic structure

of mm. 1–29, those which are stemmed upward in example 7.15, form 8–23, whose complement is 4–23 [0257].

The structural set 4–23 [0257] is characteristic in the movement. It is the only harmonic set class played in the first twelve measures. Mm. 1–8 first present 4–23 in the form (57to) with B♭ in the bass. M. 9 presents (7902) with G in the bass; m. 10 gives the same harmony as m. 9, but the bass changes to C. And in mm. 11–12 the music moves outside the prevailing B♭ collection: the harmony becomes (358t) while the bass leaps down to F. Mm. 13–14 are supported by a change in bass (F2 to C3) and a change in set class (4–23 to 4–20). The 4–23 can be heard in the open noteheads of the bass over mm. 5–15. In fact, this melodic form of 4–23 is identical to the original harmonic form of 4–23 in m. 5 (57to). The set 4–23 is also formed in the open noteheads of the bass in the second phrase, mm. 17–29; that form is (to35), transposed at T5 from (57to) and reflecting the constructive process T5.

The insistence on D5 in m. 5 and D5's return in m. 13 suggest reading E♭5, expanded by the arpeggiated E♭-minor harmony over mm. 11–12, as a suffix type of upper neighbor to m. 5's D5. Still, E♭ is expanded by the melodic arpeggiation and enjoys a certain amount of stability, even though it steers between the opening B♭ and the C cadence. The three tonal foci of the melody, B♭ and C at the beginning and at the end and E♭ in the middle, together form (to3) ([025]), a trichordal descendant of 4–23. The pitch classes (to3) are also contained in the harmonic form of 4–23 in m. 5.

Providing a slight counter to the tonal feeling imparted by the ic5-rich sets 4−23 and 8−23 is a non-tonal component. For instance, in op. 19/II we noticed an interesting interaction between 8−23 and 8−28. I have already discussed the roles of 4−23 and 8−23. Example 7.15 shows the elements of each of four tonal interpreters beamed together with downward stems. A B♭ triad underlies mm. 5−10, an E♭-minor triad underlies mm. 11−12, a G triad underlies mm. 13−14, and a C triad underlies mm. 14−15 (the C triad occurs explicitly and in complete form on the last eighth of m. 15). The underlying tonal-interpreting triads B♭ major, E♭ minor, G major, and C major form two overlapping non-tonal sets characteristic of Prokofiev's music. B♭, E♭ minor, and G together form 7−21 (te23567), a set which dominated the analysis of op. 39/IV. And the E♭ minor, G, and C triads form 8−19 (te023467), a close relative of 7−21 (see the Appendix).

Imagining the C-major triad in m. 15 as our goal, we can hear E♭6, which begins the stepwise close, as an inflected chordal third, suggesting the influence of 4−17 (0347) at the end of the phrase. While 4−17 is not a prominent surface feature of this passage (though it often is in other passages in Prokofiev's music), it does recur analogously at the end of the period: D♭−C−B♭ in the melody of mm. 25−28 descends toward a harmonic close on a B♭-major triad in m. 29.

Two remarks need to be made about the relation of the first theme to the beginning of the second theme (mm. 30−33). First, taken together, all the pitches of mm. 30−33 are a form of set class 9−7, which is one of only two nine-note supersets of 8−23.[16] In spite of the contrasting character of the second theme, suggesting minor keys rather than major ones and featuring frantic, soaring arpeggios rather than a leisurely, gently turning melody, the superset relation does provide a link to the first. Second, B♭ major, the cadential chord of the first theme (m. 29), and B minor, the opening harmony of section B, relate via the third flip. The mediant of both chords, D, is an I-center exchanging B♭ and F♯, and B and F.

In example 7.16 underlying harmonic and melodic motion has been analyzed for the central portion of section B, mm. 47−84. These measures are dense and highly chromatic. To explain them, the analysis concentrates on phrase beginnings, phrase goals, and features of sharp contrast, such as the chromatic inflection of enduring notes.

Despite the complexity of this passage, the main melodic motive of section b2 is rather simple and straightforward; it is based on an ascending five-note scale. It appears in both melody and bass, and it concludes in two different ways. In the first version, after ascending through a perfect fifth, it continues stepwise through the octave, as is the case in the bass of mm. 47−51, where the notes are

Example 7.16. Piano Concerto no. 5, op. 55/IV, mm. 47–84, harmonic sketch

stemmed and beamed together. In the second version, after completing five notes, the motive leaps directly up to the octave, as in the melody of mm. 47–52, stemmed and beamed together in the treble staff of the example.

In figure 7.4, three statements of section b2, the central portion of section B, are bracketed together; each statement is slightly different. Mm. 47–63 contain the complete form of section b2, comprising three parts. The complete form of section b2 begins with a statement of the main melodic motive; then it continues to a third flip, an event highlighted by thick and widely spaced piano

sonorities; and to conclude, the phrase funnels into a complex transitional passage (which is not analyzed in the example).[17] The second and third statements
of section b2 are incomplete: the second statement of b2 (mm. 64–75) omits
the transitional passage and the last statement of b2 (mm. 76–89) omits the
third flip.

A 5–6 motion, considerably embellished, is the main voice-leading strategy
for negotiating changes in tonal focus through this section.[18] The 5–6 motions
are shown below the grand staff in example 7.16. The "(5)" in the example indicates that the fifth above the bass is implied and not literal. Thus in mm. 47–48,
when one might expect G to be sounding in the chord, it is not. Only on the
second beat of m. 49 does the C dominant seventh appear in complete form
(but in "second inversion").

Quotation marks around the number 5, as in m. 70, mean that the 5–6
motion begins from a six-three chord rather than from a five-three chord.

As is evident on the example, 5–6 motions occur twice within each of the
first two statements of section b2. In the first statement of section b2, the C
chord in m. 47 leads to an A♭ six-three chord in m. 51. A♭ six-three in m. 51 connects to G minor via a chromatic move which combines an incomplete
common-tone diminished seventh chord, created when C/E♭/A♭ slips down to
B/D/A♭, with the bass tonal-interpreting dominant gesture D–F♯; D–F♯ is
beamed together on the example. The G-minor chord in m. 53, the goal of the
D dominant, then moves to an E♭-major chord through a 5–6 motion. E♭ six-
three then leads to E minor via a third flip, a progression placing special
emphasis on the chromatic change from E♭/B♭ to E/B. E2 sounds prominently
in the bass of m. 57, and B6 sounds in the melody of the same measure, where
it responds to B♭ in m. 52 and in m. 55.

The first two statements of section b2 sequence downward at T11: m. 47
begins by focusing on C, and m. 64 begins by focusing on B. Continuing the pattern into the third statement would bring in B♭, and indeed, B♭ does enter
according to sequence at m. 75. But following that arrival on B♭, the bass continues to slide downward, and the third statement of section b2 comes in on G
in m. 77. Given its starting point, however, this third statement proceeds
according to the sequence until mm. 83–84, which lead D minor to a B♭-minor
chord. The B♭-minor chord, recalling the "correct" B♭-minor chord of m. 75,
begins a retransition based on the transitional material of mm. 30–46 and mm.
58–63.

The progression D minor to B♭ minor in mm. 83–84 is, in fact, an "inverted"
form of the 5–6 motion which has so predominated. Example 7.17 is an
analysis of the combination of C major and A♭ major, the two triads involved

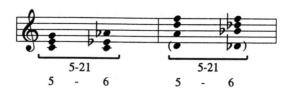

Example 7.17. Piano Concerto no. 5, op. 55/IV, generating forms of 5–21 [01458] from 5–6 motions

in the 5–6 motion over mm. 47–51, as a form of 5–21. The two triads hold C in common while the interval E/G expands in chromatic motion contrary to Eb/Ab. Similarly, D minor to Bb minor, the chord progression in mm. 83–84 which delivers the expected successor to m. 64's B minor, is also a form of 5–21 (an I-related form). The two triads hold F in common while A/D contracts in chromatic motion contrary to Bb/Db.

8 Vocal Music

Prokofiev's works for voice are not as generally familiar as are, for example, his piano sonatas or his symphonies. Yet, even leaving aside operas and cantatas, he produced numerous works for voice, including nine sets of original songs for solo voice and piano; two settings of Russian folk songs for voice and piano, one of which is for tenor-bass duet and piano; "The Ugly Duckling," an extended setting of the Hans Christian Andersen fairy tale; two collections of music from his other compositions, arranged for voice and piano; and one collection of mass songs for voice and piano.

Over two periods, 1914–1922 and 1935–1945, Prokofiev averaged nearly one work for voice and piano per year. His literary sources for these works were, on the whole, of high quality, and he set texts by such formidable poets as Konstantin Balmont, Anna Akhmatova, and Alexander Pushkin. Both his wives were, in one way or another, closely involved with his songs. His first wife, Lina Llubera, a singer, premiered op. 36, the Balmont songs, as well as op. 73, the Pushkin songs; his second wife, Mira Mendelson, supplied the text for the verse of the fifth song of op. 79.[1]

Of the songs that Prokofiev composed, we shall examine selections from opp. 27, 36, and 73. Opp. 27/1 and 36/1 belong to that large category of Prokofiev's compositions which occupy moderate positions on a scale from traditional to innovative. Of the three collections, op. 36 is the most innovative, perhaps because of the inspiration provided by the texts of Balmont, whose poetry found extremely modern expression once before in the cantata *Seven, They Are Seven*, op. 30. Op. 73, as we shall see, is much more traditional than the other three collections.

The selected works all have texts originally written in Russian; op. 36 was translated into French by the composer.

The Akhmatova Songs, op. 27/1

The songs of op. 27 have been favorably received from the time of their first appearance. Harlow Robinson singles out the songs of op. 27, saying of them that "perhaps they are [Prokofiev's] most successful song cycle."[2] Israel Nestyev, in his first biography, is also impressed. He remarks: "The sober strength and exalted humanity of Prokofiev's lyricism made themselves most strongly felt in five songs written to verses by Anna Akhmatova in five days during November 1916."[3] Though a tremendously popular poet, Akhmatova was in continual conflict with the Soviet government.[4] Nevertheless, op. 27 was able, for the most part, to retain Nestyev's admiration even in the rewritten second biography, a work in which in many other cases the author reversed positions set forth in the first biography. Considerably expanding his original commentary, Nestyev generally praises the collection and its "warm tender lyricism." But op. 27 did not pass Nestyev's revised judgment completely unharmed. His expanded commentary takes an apparently unfounded and gratuitous swipe at the music, undoubtedly motivated by the poet's official disfavor. He comments: "Thus, despite Prokofiev's tendency toward bright, sunny, and human lyricism, this music to Akhmatova's poetry is permeated with the morbid characteristics of decadent art."[5] This remark is especially ironic with respect to the cycle's first song, whose lyricism is most evident in its first nineteen measures. Whatever "bright, sunny" impression is made by the music is surely matched by the text: the title of the poem comes from its first line, "Sun filled the room."[6]

Judith Hemschemeyer's translation of the poem appears below. The poem describes an instance of remembering, an event which passes quickly in the real time of everyday life. In Akhmatova's interpretation, the event expands to fill the entire poem. But there is a double movement, for the poem itself is an act of reflection, the memory of a memory.

Sun filled the room
With a yellow, transparent haze.

I woke up and remembered:
Darling, it's your nameday.
Because of this even the snowy
Distances beyond the windows are warm,
Because of this even I, insomniac that I am,
Have slept like a communicant.[7]

To begin analyzing the memory, the poet reconstructs and retraces the events from just waking up to remembering the friend's nameday, then backtracks to the sleep which preceded consciousness. The moment of remembering, like the sunlight waking the sleeper, bursts upon the lyric subject's consciousness, filling it. As we learn in the second half of the poem, the sunlight also possesses the power to transform "the snowy distances beyond the windows," distances which are sleep's territory, a smooth expanse of white.

Prokofiev's setting emphasizes a misfit between narrative and historical chronology. Narrative chronology begins at the beginning of the poem, but historical chronology begins in line 5 or, in the song, halfway through, at m. 20. Hence the first half of the song flows from sleeping to waking, the second half from waking to sleeping. At the same time, Prokofiev's setting analogizes two of the poem's central themes, memory and transformation.

Op. 27/1 is a binary form AB (mm. 1–19; mm. 20–38). Mm. 1–19 set the poem's first four lines; mm. 20–38 set the last four lines. Section A is vigorous and outgoing, corresponding to the sunlight and the joyful occasion of the nameday. By comparison, section B is more introspective and reserved, corresponding to the stillness of the insomniac's rare deep sleep. The two halves of the music are not unrelated, however, and in the discussion I will show parallels between the two sections which make section B a kind of variation of section A.

Within section A there are two smaller sections, mm. 1–9 and mm. 10–19. Mm. 1–9 are "chordal": verticalizing the repeating figures in the right hand produces triads with added notes; in the piano left hand and the voice, where most of the melodic material occurs, lines move through arpeggiated chords and emphasize the intervals of thirds and fourths. Mm. 10–19 are more "scalar": beginning in m. 10, contrasting scalar passages and stepwise melodic motion become more prominent. Subtler textural changes divide mm. 1–9 and mm. 10–19. A silent piano left hand and a single harmony in the piano right hand set mm. 1–5 apart. A thickened texture, created by the now-active piano left hand, and measure-to-measure chord progression accelerate the forward movement of mm. 6–9. A change in piano figuration from a repeated two-measure harmonic pattern to widely spaced harmonies separates mm. 10–13 from mm. 14–19.

Harmonic stasis, tonal interpreters, metric and registral accent, and directed stepwise motion all interact to create tonal focus. Throughout the song tonal areas find expression in the bass, in large part due to tonal-interpreting perfect fifths formed between the bass and an upper voice. Mm. 1–5 center on E, while mm. 6–9 move from C to A. Through mm. 1–5 the shimmering piano part oscillates between the metrically accented open fifth E/B and the A/F♯, which is placed on offbeats. The vocal reiteration of E and B also helps to center these measures on E.

M. 6 thickens the texture by activating a new register and adding a bass. M. 6 also shifts the tonal emphasis from E by introducing a C tonal interpreter. F♯ carries over from mm. 1–5 into m. 6 and forms a relation with C, which becomes more explicit in mm. 13–14, mm. 18–19, and again in mm. 32–35. M. 6 emphasizes F♯ in two ways. F♯ is the sole element foreign to a C-major tonality, and the staccato articulation on C and F♯ on the last two beats of the measure sets the tritone C5/F♯5 into relief against the legato background.

M. 10 changes the texture again, now introducing parallel scalar runs in the piano. After a one-measure rest in m. 9, the voice enters on G in m. 10, in unison with the piano left hand. Eliminating the octave shift in the left hand from m. 9 to m. 10 reveals that m. 10 continues the stepwise bass descent and carries it through from G in m. 10 to F♯ in m. 11. Mm. 12–13 repeat on downbeats the G–to–F♯ progression. M. 14 breaks this pattern and brings in a C tonal interpreter, highlighted registrally by the piano extremes from E6 to C4 and by the vocal fifth from G down to C. F♮ in m. 14 also conspicuously neutralizes F♯, which has been present in every measure of the piece thus far.

The tonal interpreters E (m. 1), C (m. 6), A (m. 9), and F♯ (m. 11 and m. 13) outline an F♯ half-diminished seventh chord, whose downward arpeggiation is completed in m. 13. Mm. 14–15 bring in a tonal-interpreting C major seventh chord. As though recapitulating this progression, mm. 18–19, which close the piece's first half, alternate between a C-major seventh chord and an F♯ half-diminished seventh chord.

Section A contains internal cadences, the most emphatic one at m. 8 and a weaker one at m. 5. Section B, on the other hand, is more continuous and seamless, partly owing to the reiterated accompaniment pattern which endures unchanged over mm. 20–33. It begins by stating a referential home sonority in m. 20 (revoiced from the end of m. 19) to emphasize the tonal center E rather than C. Mm. 20–25, parallel to mm. 1–5 in section A, project E by highlighting the fifth E/B.

The parallelism between the two halves of the form continues. In mm. 5–6 the music moves from an E center to a C center. Mm. 25–28 elaborate that gesture by filling it in stepwise: the music passes down from a bass E in m. 25, through D in mm. 26–27, and on to C in m. 28.[8]

M. 28 freezes in the piano a pedal bass C2 and, above that, E3 and F♯4. The voice fixes E5 and E4. Against these fixed notes, the piano's mobile voices move in parallel tenths from A3/C5 to B♭3/D♭5 in m. 32.

Op. 27/1 relies upon two general types of diatonic sets. The first features perfect fourths and fifths and forms a constellation about 4−23. Of these sets, 3−9, 9−9, 4−23, and 8−23 can be generated either by a T5 or a T7 cycle. The second type of set, which features triads, forms a constellation about 3−11. This constellation includes 4−14 and 4−22. Section A introduces both types of sets. Fifth-based sets—in particular, forms of 4−23—dominate mm. 1−5; m. 6 begins introducing triad-based sets.

Example 8.1 shows forms of 3−7, 3−9, and 4−23 saturating the opening five measures of the vocal line. In the upper staff in example 8.1 the vocal line of mm. 3−8 is reproduced; some noncontiguous pitches are extracted from it in the analytical staff aligned below. Set class 3−7 on the analytical staff is formed on the downbeats of mm. 3−5 as the melody rises from B through C♯ to E. Then m. 6 initiates a form of 4−23 as the vocal line descends from E to D to B and finally to A. Forms of 3−7 and 3−9 are shown in brackets on the upper staff. The 4−23 in the voice is thoroughly prepared by the piano: it occurs as the prominent piano accompaniment, E−F♯−A−B (469e). Its realization as the repeating, alternating intervals of a fifth and a third portrays the shimmering light as it infuses the narrator's room. The union of all the pitches in the piano and the voice in mm. 1−6 is 9−9, the complement of 3−9, a fifth-based trichord.

Mm. 20−28 elaborate the collection (469e). As mentioned earlier, mm. 20−28 parallel mm. 1−6, where (469e) constitutes the piano accompaniment. Just as the harmony over D arrives in m. 26 and lasts for two measures, so F♯ is understood as a main note in force for the same two measures, embellished by a skip down to D. Reinforcing the reading of F♯ as the main vocal pitch of mm. 26−27 is the motion in outer-voice tenths (10−10) from m. 26 to m. 28. F♯/D in m. 26 drops to E/C in m. 28. In the melody F♯ and E, together with the downbeats of mm. 21−25, form 4−23 (469e), precisely the same pitches as in mm.

Example 8.1. Op. 27/1, mm. 3−8, melodic analysis

1–5, except that here the pitches are sung by the voice rather than played by the piano.

The vocal E which arrives in m. 28 carries through for seven measures. Mm. 34–36 disturb the vocal stasis by stepping up to G and then arpeggiating downward through a C dominant seventh chord before coming to rest on C. The vocal move from m. 26 to the end of the song—from E to C—recapitulates again the progression first heard over mm. 5–6 and again over mm. 25–28.

As we have seen, the pitch set (A4, B4, E5, F#5), a form of 4–23 [0257] deriving from mm. 1–5, is one of the features of the voice in mm. 21–28. A second feature contributing to section B's developmental character is the outer voice E/C, which in section B, as in section A, follows the appearance of (9e46).

Moving at the rate of one bass note per measure beginning with m. 6, the bass sinks from C4 through B3 to A3, with each bass note supporting an added-ninth chord. C and A each support a form of 4–22, the major triad with a filled-in lower third; B supports a form of 4–14, a minor triad with filled-in lower third. Forms of 4–22 recur throughout the song, as on the downbeats of m. 11 and m. 13 and in mm. 22–23 and mm. 26–28, where they are embedded.[9]

We can now explore how these pitch-class relations interpret the text. In mm. 10–11 the narrator is still waking up. Only in mm. 12–13 does she (let us assume that Akhmatova is narrating) remember it is the friend's nameday. M. 14 celebrates that remembrance with unique figuration in the piano and with F#'s displacement by F♮. Mm. 14–15 remember E and B from mm. 1–5; the piano places them as the locally highest pitches, with E6 being the highest pitch in the piece thus far. The pitch B6 enters as an even higher melodic pitch in mm. 18–19, concluding this section. But before section A concludes, it remembers all the pitches from the piano of mm. 1–5: A and F# enter again in m. 16, and along with E and B they complete the music's memory of mm. 1–5.

The interval C/G occurs on the downbeat of m. 6 and of m. 14. In both cases, G displaces an earlier G#. In m. 4, the voice introduces G#, which can be heard to extend by implication through m. 5, there being nothing to contradict it. In m. 6, G5, registrally accented, sets the Russian word which means "shines." M. 6 gathers together a textural change, a harmonic change, and a chromatic displacement to mark the text at this point and to emphasize the radiance of knowledge, as the room continues to fill with sunlight. We can imagine m. 6 portraying the actual moment when the lyric subject recalls that the day is the friend's nameday. In mm. 10–19 she reports that memory to the friend. Specifically, m. 14 remembers the high G from m. 6 as well as the fifth C/G. G's final prominent appearance is at the end of the song where the piano is drawn into G5's high register.

Memory is depicted in another way. Mm. 14–19 begin and end with two forms of the same set, 6z25: mm. 14−15 bring in (e02457), and mm. 18−19 bring in (69047e). The piano figuration in mm. 14−15 highlights the arrival of 6z25. Each hand spans a wide range, contrasting with the confined scalework of mm. 10−13. Mm. 14−15 also introduce a four-note pattern in which the right hand twice descends and then ascends while the left hand alternately descends and ascends. These non-synchronous contours contrast with the parallel motion of mm. 10−13. Mm. 16−17 return to the parallel ascending scalar passagework of mm. 10−13 and introduce F♯ and A, two elements foreign to 6z25 (e02457). The union of these new tones with 6z25 forms 8−23 (45679e02), the abstract complement of 4−23, the set presented by the piano of mm. 1−5. Section A closes with a second form of 6z25, played in a high register in mm. 18−19.

The two forms of 6z25 are related about the inversional centers C/B and F/F♯. The two sets hold invariant and display prominently a tonal-interpreting C-major triad, considerably enhancing the aural similarity of the two passages. The effect of this inversion on pitch-class content is to hold five pitch classes invariant and to exchange F for F♯. As I noted earlier, F♯ is replaced in mm. 14−15 and restored in mm. 16−19. Excepting mm. 8−9, mm. 14−15, the white-key measures, are the only measures in section A which do not contain F♯. Like F and F♯, the elements of the other, tritone-related I-center, C/B, are also realized concretely, occurring as registral extremes.

The 6z25 also unites three prominent set classes from mm. 1−9. In its subset structure (e02457) contains 4−23 (0257), 4−14 (9e04), and 4−22 (0247). The presence of all three basic tetrachords from mm. 1−9, where the tetrachords are presented separately, is yet another way mm. 14−19 express recovered memory.

In example 8.2 we can see how mm. 20−28 apply inversional balance in voice

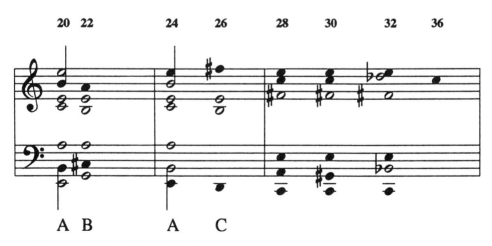

Example 8.2. Op. 27/1, mm. 20−36, harmonic structure

leading. Three chords are labeled. Chord A (e047) is revoiced from the end of section A in m. 19, a change that brings the arpeggiated E-minor triad to prominence in the left hand and colors the entire sonority more darkly. Opposed stems isolate B4–E5 in the treble clef and E2/B2 in the bass clef. B4 and B2 are inner components, E5 and E2 outer components. In moving from chord A to chord B, the inner components balance: filled-in noteheads show that B4–A4 balances B2–C♯3. In moving from chord A to chord C the outer components balance: filled-in noteheads show that E5–F♯5 balances E2–D2.

In m. 20 the bass line, beginning from E in chord A, begins a downward drive toward m. 28. M. 20 revoices m. 19's C-major seventh chord to emphasize the E-minor tonal-interpreting subset; m. 28 revoices m. 19's F♯ half-diminished seventh chord. Incremental changes in m. 28's chord then lead to the chord of m. 32. M. 28 is also a target of the voice, which seizes E and does not relinquish it until m. 34. The voice does eventually conclude on C in m. 36. Beginning in m. 28 the piano gives octave support to E, holding on to E for the remainder of the song, as well as holding on to C until m. 36. In addition to the piano left hand holding on to C2 and E3 and the piano right hand holding on to F♯4, the voice moves between E4 and E5. Over mm. 29–32, the other voices slowly move to complete an F♯-major triad whose third and fifth arrive in m. 32 and are enharmonically spelled as B♭ and D♭ rather than as A♯ and C♯.

As example 8.2 shows, the chord in m. 32 can be divided into two components, represented by filled-in noteheads and open noteheads. The filled-in noteheads represent an incomplete C-major triad; the open noteheads represent a misspelled F♯-major chord.

Thus, m. 32 transforms the tritone C/F♯ in a new way. In its first appearance C/F♯ was expressed in the bass from m. 6 to m. 11. C/F♯ was then realized as the root succession in mm. 18–19. Now mm. 32–35 express C/F♯ as C/E in the outer voices, an incomplete C-major triad sounding simultaneously with F♯/B♭/D♭ in the inner voices, a misspelled F♯-major triad.

Over mm. 29–38 the tempo slackens to portray the gradual fall into sleep. Mm. 36–38 finally settle on E, the tonal focus from which the song began. By moving from C to E over mm. 35–38, the music reverses the awakening which occurred over mm. 1–6 and returns the lyric subject to sleep.

The Balmont Songs, op. 36/2

Prokofiev and his first wife, Lina Llubera, translated Balmont's Russian poem into French and set it to music. My translation of the French version of Balmont's poem appears below. The translation is keyed to figure 8.1, which outlines the song's form. The musical material of section I recurs in sections II and

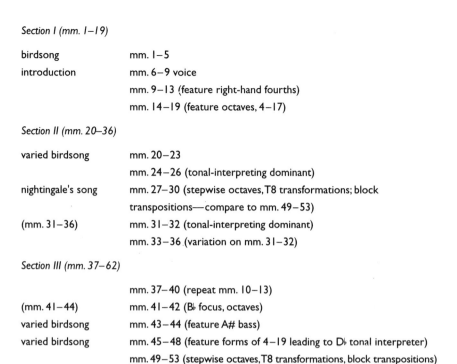

Figure 8.1. Balmont songs, op. 36/2, form outline

III but in reordered and varied form and along with new material, so that the structure of the piece is loosely strophic and tripartite.

Section I (mm. 1–19):

My story begins with the swallow
    [and] completes itself with the nightingale.
Look, the swallows return!
They wish to tell us spring arrives.
When the spring storm comes,
    quickly, wash yourself with milk to be white, to be white,
    to be sure to please the beautiful maidens.

Section II (mm. 20–36):

Take care with the swallow's nest and see that you do not destroy it.
If not, your nose, covered with blemishes, will be the joke of every hussy.

Listen to the song of the nightingale,
    listen well to the magic song.

However, be wary of its beautiful trills:
> they are malicious, they are of the devil,
> as well as of an infinite sorrow.
Be careful, friend, listen to me well.

Section III (mm. 37–62):

> Happy shall be your reward,
> > if you find in that song a divine note.
> Do you know that in these love songs hides the inconstancy of a cuckoo?

> Do not follow his vile example,
> > cherish love and be faithful.
> Take up the nightingale's song,
> > which attains the highest peaks.

> Singing thus, you come near to God,
> > to the sky and to the stars.

I wish to focus my remarks on the opening four-measure birdsong, shown and analyzed in example 8.3, and its relation to the three poetic subjects: the swallows, the nightingale, and the narrator.

The birdsong enjoys a peculiarly ambiguous identity and, as we shall see, plays a paradoxical role in the narrative. It is saturated with fourths, one of which, E♭4–A♭4 in m. 1, is especially noticeable for disrupting the E-minor triadic arpeggiation otherwise so clearly projected over the first five and a half beats. Having been so clearly marked in m. 1, the pitch classes 3 and 8 are easy to hear coming back in m. 9 as D♯5–G♯5, where the dyad depicts musically the return of the swallows as well as their constancy ("Regarde, les hirondelles reviennent!"). The voice in m. 11 gives special emphasis to D♯5–G♯5 when it soars up to G♯5 and the eighth-note motion gives way to quarter notes and finally to a half note at the end of m. 11.

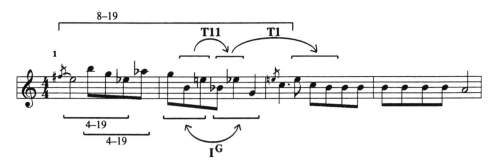

Example 8.3. Op. 36/2, mm. 1–4, the birdsong, melodic analysis

The birdsong is also associated with the song of the nightingale. We hear the distinctive sinuous curve of mm. 1–4 repeated in mm. 20–21, 43–44, 48–49, and 59–62. Heard as the swallow's song, the repetitions depict constancy. But within the context of the traditionally beautiful nightingale's song, the repetitions, by virtue of their insistence, aim to seduce us. In narrative chronology, we first look at the birds, then we listen to the birds, then we appropriate their song, being led gradually from passive outside observer to involved participant. The changing poetic perspective becomes a metaphor for a gradual seduction.

The birdsong is, however, the exclusive property of birds. Besides its prominent introductory role, where it is textually independent, the birdsong counterpoints but never sets the vocal melody. By avoiding vocal utterance and remaining solely in the piano's realm, the birdsong sets up a tension, which the narrator, beginning in m. 31 (section II), turns into an antagonism.

Beginning in section II (mm. 20–36) the narrator exhorts us to listen carefully to the nightingale's song and at the same time warns against the seductive power of its superficial beauty ("prends garde à ses beaux trilles, ils sont malins, ils sont du diable"). The imperatives "écoute le chant du rossignol" and "écoute moi bien" bound the pertinent strophe; we are commanded to ignore the nightingale. The blunt, rhythmically monotonous ascending scale that sets the warning syllabically contrasts strongly with the gentle turns of the birdsong. A rhetorically effective and alluring musical setting for the line would deliver the warning more convincingly than the one used. But as the music tells us, the poetic narrator can only aspire to the beauty of the nightingale's song, desiring to appropriate it but warning against it at the same time.

The narrator does, however, acknowledge a rich reward for the one who can listen deeply—without being seduced ("sois fidèle")—and take up the nightingale's song ("Entonne le chant du rossignol"). One can hardly avoid reading in this an epigrammatic critical spur: the poem invites us, challenges us, to read past the surface and to make a close analysis of the song which uncovers its true underlying structure. Might we then find a secret hidden in the birdsong?

The two most important structural sets in this piece are 4–17 and 4–19. The discussion here concentrates on the structure of the first four measures, the birdsong, and shows its influence upon the structure of the song as a whole.

The four-bar birdsong not only begins the piece but articulates the beginning of section II and closes the piece. It also occurs within section III, dominating mm. 43–44 and m. 48. In its first appearance in mm. 1–4, it is unaccompanied for its first two bars, then harmonized in mm. 3–4.

The birdsong gravitates toward an E tonal center, staked out above all by E5, held for two beats, and its subsequent ascent to B5. The first three pitches, discounting the grace note F♯, arpeggiate an E-minor triad. G, the minor third, recurs on the downbeat of m. 2 and, on the last beat of m. 2, as the lowest note of the melody. B4, a "dominant," is attacked repeatedly over mm. 4–5, further reinforcing the E-centricity.

Example 8.3 reproduces the birdsong and highlights its saturation with 4–19, a set class frequently encountered in Prokofiev's music. Brackets show two overlapping forms of 4–19, and angle brackets show that the melody up to the downbeat of m. 3 forms 8–19, its complement. Three other, noncontiguous forms of 4–19 can be extracted from example 8.3's melody; they are (4780), (0348), and (8e04). Each of these forms of 4–19 embeds the augmented triad Ab5–E5–C5. Ab5 is part of the "disrupting" dyad Eb5–Ab5; E is the tonal center; C5 receives an agogic accent on the downbeat of m. 3. The augmented triad Ab–C–E features the pitch-class transformation T8: T8(Ab) = E, T8(E) = C, T8(C) = (Ab). The three forms of 4–19 are also interrelated by the T8 transformation: T8(4780) = (0348), T8(0348) = (8e04), T8(8e04) = (4780).

Embedded within the melody in example 8.3 are two forms of 4–17 [0347]. One is an E major / minor chord, the other is a C major / minor chord. Their presence in the opening adumbrates 4–17's explicit dominance of mm. 9–19, mm. 27–30, and mm. 49–53.

The five pitches of m. 1 (E, B, G, Eb, Ab) and the chord at the downbeat of m. 3 (A, Db, F, C, E) are each a form of 5–21. The two collections invert about E (pitch class 4), the single pitch held invariant between the two forms and the tonal center of these opening measures.

M. 2 exhibits an inversional relation which is registrally exact. G5 and G4 frame that measure. Their priority is clear: G4 is the lowest note of this melody, and the pitch class G is the minor third of the E-minor triad whose arpeggiation opened the piece. Brackets and the double-headed arrow show the ordered pitch-inversional relation of the two sets.

The melody moves from m. 1 to m. 2 through Ab and G (pitch classes 7 and 8), the "major/minor third" of the E chord. Pitch class 8 reappears in the voice of m. 5. The piano in m. 6 then drops G♯ to G, reproducing the pitch-class succession across the barline from m. 1 to m. 2. The G octave in m. 6 is given extra emphasis by the registral accent. The introduction finally leads into m. 9, beginning the main body of the piece. At that point the voice and piano converge on the quadrupled, metrically accented G♯. The piece, in various ways, goes on to play out 4–17's characteristic major/minor third as a conflict. The "chromatic" oscillation between pitch classes 7 and 8 also recalls the arrow structure above the staff in example 8.3, which shows the oscillation by half step of B/E and Bb/Eb.

In m. 4 the cadential melodic A is harmonized by a D-major triad, a passing chord connecting E in the opening four bars, to C in m. 7. One can locate the

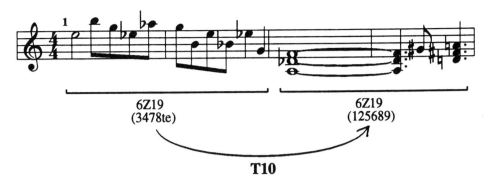

Example 8.4. Op. 36/2, mm. 1–4, the birdsong, forms of 6z19 [013478]

move to D beginning in m. 3, where the harmonic event on the downbeat creates a natural, textural segmentation. In fact, a tonal-interpreting "dominant" to "tonic" gesture leads the bass A of m. 3 to the bass D of m. 4. Reinforcing the whole-step descent, from an E center to a D center, is a set transformation. The melody of mm. 1–2, excluding the F♯ grace note, forms 6z19 and is transformed at T10 into mm. 3–4, as is shown in example 8.4.

The introduction reaches its goal in m. 7 with the music's arrival on a C chord. M. 8 then leads into section I, which begins in m. 9 on a G♯ chord. Thus the introduction traverses a descending major third from E to C in two whole-step increments; the process derives from the structural set 4–19.

In example 8.5 I return to the opening melody and extract the series of ascending fourths saturating the texture of m. 1, beat 4, through m. 3, beat 1. In the example these fourths are separated into an upper and a lower strand, with each strand beamed together. Each strand is a form of the structural set 4–19. Within the upper form, arrows show the T8 gestures taking A♭ through E to C.

E♭/A♭, bracketed in example 8.5, disrupts the E-minor arpeggiation from m. 1, beat 1, through m. 2, beat 2. In mm. 10ff. the same dyad recurs, spelled as D♯/G♯ and, along with the regularly repeated B♯4–B4, forms the structural set 4–17, a G♯ "major/minor" chord. M. 14, marked by a change of texture, returns to the opening tonal area through the E major/minor chord, laid out in the piano accompaniment.

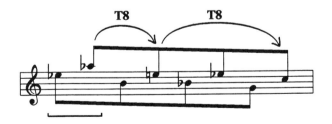

Example 8.5. Op. 36/2, mm. 1–4, the birdsong, structure of ascending fourths

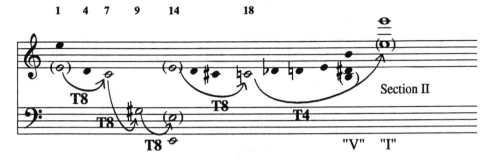

Example 8.6. Op. 36/2, mm. 1–9, symmetrical tonal structure based on T4–T8 transformations

Example 8.6 develops one possible reading of section I (mm. 1–19). I take as constructive the T4–T8 process deriving from the structural set 4–19, understanding G♯, part of the dyad D♯5–G♯5 (and its earlier manifestation as E♭5–A♭5), as a controlling sonority over mm. 10–12 which is succeeded by E in m. 14. Notes indicated parenthetically shift actual pitches into a register convenient for showing the successive T8 transpositions. One feature aiding this hearing is set-class equivalence: both the G♯ (mm. 9–12) and E (mm. 14–16) tonal interpreters occur within forms of 4–17. Further, as over mm. 1–7, E in m. 14 leads to C in m. 18, passing through D on the way.

According to this reading, section I descends through even divisions of the octave, thus realizing successive T8 transpositions. Upon reaching C in m. 18 the piano right hand abandons the B octave, and the line reverses direction and ascends a major third, picking up E again at the onset of section II (m. 20). Example 8.6 shows in quotation marks the V–I harmonic progression linking the end of section I to section II. Within the symmetrical tonal scheme of example 8.6, the importance of such conventional cadential movement is downplayed.

There is, however, a second reading for mm. 1–19. Whereas mm. 10–12 are read as essentially G♯-centered in example 8.6, one may well hear these measures as under the control of B. The apparently incomplete C♯7 of m. 10 is an appoggiatura chord in which the dyad C♯4–E♯4 embellishes B3–D♯4; the inner voice B4, like the bass B2, is a pedal. B is prominent for other reasons: B triads occur in mm. 10–11, the pitch B is the lowest in the piano part and is prominently stated on the downbeat of m. 12, and the voice outlines a B triad over mm. 10–11, only briefly ascending to G♯ in m. 12. In this new reading, G♯ becomes auxiliary (either an added sixth to the B chord or an upper neighbor to F♯) rather than structural, and the B♯/B♮ dyad that we previously regarded as a major/minor third of a G♯ chord is a chromatic inflection of the dominant, B; the dyad is thus perhaps more properly spelled C–B.

Example 8.7. Op. 36/2, mm. 1–19, tonal structure based on the tonic-dominant relation

Example 8.6 also gives very little emphasis to the B♭ chord of m. 13. That chord actually carries more structural weight than example 8.6 shows, because it concludes mm. 9–13; m. 14 brings a change of texture and a new subsection.[10]

Example 8.7 is a reinterpretation of example 8.6's points of articulation. Here, C in m. 7, rather than skipping to G♯, passes down to B in m. 10. A parenthetical arrow remains on example 8.7 to show the articulating role played by mm. 6–7, measures which round off the introduction without completely arresting forward momentum; mm. 8–9 lean into the primary melodic material.[11]

To indicate that B♭ in m. 13 delineates a subsection, it is now an open notehead. E in m. 14 and C in m. 18 both retain their open noteheads, while the dominant B in m. 19 gains one. Now we can hear the points of articulation revolving around the tonic and the dominant. Specifically, B of the E–B axis acquires embellishment through chromatic upper and lower neighbors, an interpretation that also imparts extra resonance to C in m. 7 since it foreshadows C in m. 18.

Example 8.7 shows a much more traditional reading than does example 8.6 by giving a higher value to tonic-dominant relations, around which each section can now be heard to revolve. Example 8.6 is not misguided or "wrong"; example 8.7 is not meant to replace it. Rather, the two examples show the music from different perspectives.

In example 8.6 the perfect fourth E♭–A♭ (D♯–G♯) from the birdsong contributes G♯ as the controlling sonority over mm. 10–12, and the augmented triads embedded in it generate T4–T8 transpositions among the points of articulation. In example 8.8, in contrast, we see the major points of articulation over the entire song, portrayed in open noteheads. A characteristic descent by two whole steps is labeled "a." In all cases but one, motive *a* is a segment of a line descending from E through C to B. Sections I and II articulate virtually identical areas, focusing on B and E. Section I also moves to C and B♭, chromatic neighbors to B. Section II moves to G (m. 33) between statements of B in m. 31 and

Section I

Section II

Section III

Example 8.8. Op. 36/2, tonal and motivic structure

m. 37. Section III veers off from sections I and II most strikingly when B♭ and E♭ replace B and E. This modulation departs from B in m. 37 and returns to B, via motive *a'*, in m. 53. E in m. 55 initiates a form of motive *a*, descending through D in m. 57.[12]

M. 59 (*Meno mosso*) telescopes several gestures, thereby accelerating the pace of events as the piece moves toward the final cadence. B, the target of the descent from E, arrives in m. 59 simultaneously with the fifth A-E below, a fifth which begins the drive to the end of the piece. Example 8.8 therefore shows m. 59 expressing two superposed points of articulation, one concluding a gesture, one initiating a gesture.

The material closing section II over mm. 33–36 renews the competition between G and G♯ (pitch classes 7 and 8) by positioning G prominently in the outer voices. An on-beat G octave begins this passage in m. 31. In mm. 34–35 G is then kept alive, metrically and registrally accented in the left hand, and the voice settles on G in m. 35. Three tenuto Gs lead into m. 36, where the a tempo marking pairs G with E♭ in a version of the oscillating dyad from mm. 9ff. That dyad returns to its original sixteenth-note speed in the second half of m. 36. E♭–G is, of course, the wrong dyad, and section III begins by correcting it to D♯–G♯ and restoring G♯ at the same time. G♯ is not again explicitly challenged until the end of the piece, mm. 57–60. Strong-beat statements in the piano and voice of mm. 57–58 give G♯ in the upper voice, but the voice's last pitch, the whole note in m. 60, seems to decide finally in favor of G♮. The piano in the song's last two measures remains neutral: the last two sounds we hear are B3 and a low E octave.

Where m. 13's arrival on B♭ is quickly left and then subsequently "corrected" to B in m. 19, mm. 40 ff. revel in the B♭ arrival. B♭'s chromatic encirclement in the piano part of mm. 41–42 transposes and places in the foreground the neighboring motion around B that occurred in section I, shown in example 8.8. B♭ persists in the bass through mm. 43–44, where it is spelled A♯, and on into m. 45, at which point T5 takes it to E♭ in m. 46. Open noteheads on example 8.8 help portray the emphasis on E/B over mm. 1–37. Over mm. 40–49 E♭/B♭ emerges, and then E/B returns in m. 53 and persists to the end of the song. Thus E/B to E♭/B♭ to E/B reproduces on a large scale the progression marked in example 8.3 by "T11" and "T1."

As promised by the text there is, indeed, a reward for reading the structure of the birdsong closely. The T4–T8 transformations which derive from 4–19 in the birdsong control motive *a* in example 8.8, as well as example 8.6's analysis of mm. 1–19. The 4–17 from the birdsong is a prominent feature of mm. 14 ff. (and related passages), and the conflict introduced by (478e)'s major/minor third continues throughout the song. Finally, the "semitonal" conflict between pitch classes 7 and 8 is transferred to the succession E/B to E♭/B♭ to E/B first in the birdsong and then in the points of articulation over the entire song.

The Pushkin Songs, op. 73/2

Seven, They Are Seven, op. 30, and the Pushkin songs, op. 73, were both composed in direct response to political events in Russia. *Seven, They Are Seven,* begun in 1917, came immediately after the "Classical" Symphony and in strong contrast to it. In its modernism it belongs with works such as the *Scythian Suite,* Symphony no. 2, and the Quintet. Prokofiev says of op. 30 that in it he felt "the desire to create something huge, something cosmic. . . . I too had been subconsciously affected by the revolutionary events that had shaken Russia to its foundations, and now all this clamoured for expression."[13] Though Prokofiev was in St. Petersburg during the February Revolution and may well have been profoundly shaken, concerns for his career moved him to more consequential action. Later in 1917 he asked for and received permission from Anatole Lunacharsky to leave the country. Prokofiev did not return permanently until nearly twenty years later.

Op. 73's political motivation was the Pushkin centennial, a thoroughly benign force compared to the 1917 Revolution. Even within the context of Prokofiev's art-song output, the Pushkin songs are tame: they are much more conventional than either op. 27 or op. 36. Harlow Robinson attributes their retreat from modernism to "the reactionary turn Soviet culture was taking by the late 1930s."[14] He goes on: "Conventional in structure and sentimental in their melodies, the songs are much less interesting than his early 'prosaic,' Mussorgskian songs to poems by Akhmatova and Balmont. . . . Where the early songs were spare, angular, and stark, the Pushkin songs . . . were surprisingly sweet and cloying."[15]

Nestyev has little to say of the op. 73 songs in his first biography, but in his second he seems to be influenced by precisely the reactionary turn which Robinson points out. Where Robinson is disappointed in op. 73 for what he perceives as undue restraint on the composer's part, Nestyev discerns distracting complexity and a capricious modernist influence. Indeed, Nestyev seems to stop just short of accusing Prokofiev of Formalism, a position virtually impossible to square with Robinson's. "The songs of Op. 73 lack the simplicity and naturalness of vocal melody which characterizes the classical examples of Russian lyricism. . . . Complicated harmonies and an abundance of shifting tonalities make certain passages (especially in the middle sections of the second and third songs) difficult to understand."[16]

Regardless of how one judges op. 73, the structures in it are familiar, even in the second song and in its middle section. Let us turn now to an analysis of some of the aspects of op. 73/2.

Figure 8.2 displays the ternary form of the song. Section A projects G major through the repeated tonal-interpreting $\hat{5}-\hat{1}$ bass motion and through the vocal arpeggiation of a G-major triad. In mm. 1–8 the $\hat{5}-\hat{1}$ bass motion is embedded within a complete arpeggiation of a G-major triad.

A considerably restrained modern line is responsible for the special attention

Section	Measure Numbers	Tonal Focus	Form
A	mm. 1–16	G	a1
	mm. 17–32	A♭	a2
	mm. 33–48	G	a1
	mm. 49–60	embellishment of E♭	a3
B	mm. 61–76	A♭–E♭	b1
		A♭	
	mm. 77–86	A–E	b2
A	mm. 87–102	A♭	
	m. 103	embellishment of E	a3

Figure 8.2. Pushkin songs, op. 73/2, form outline

accorded to added-note chords, careful voicing, and sonority in general. For instance, the G tonic triad of m. 1 is embedded in a chord with added seventh and thirteenth, voiced to highlight the interval of a sixth in the left hand. The sixth duplicates the voice's incipit at a different pitch level.

The chromaticism in m. 1, brought on by the move to A♯, briefly creates on beat 2 a form of 5−26, a pentachordal superset of 4−19 and 3−12. The 3−12, a prominent subset of 4−19, occurs in m. 16 as an altered E♭ dominant chord which leads into m. 17's A♭ tonal area. The 4−19, mostly a feature of harmonic color in m. 1, gains considerably more independence over mm. 49−60, as we shall see below. If one hears A♯ as B♭, then m. 1 hints at a mode change from G major to G minor and therefore suggests the set class 4−17 [0347].

A varied restatement of mm. 1−16 occurs in mm. 17−32, now transposed up a half step to A♭. Though mm. 25−32 depart the furthest from mm. 1−16, similarities remain. For instance, mm. 25−28 feature chromatic shifting between A♭−D♭−F and A♭−C♭−F♭; together these two chords form 5−32 (458e1). The 5−32 is a pentachordal superset of 4−17 (1458). The 4−17 is the major-minor chord within which back-and-forth shifting from major to minor strongly colors these measures. Its distinctive major-minor thirds F and F♭ are registrally accented here, just as B and A♯ (B♭) were in m. 1, and they are metrically accented as well.

The 4−19 plays a big role in mm. 49−60. Whereas the E♭ augmented triad of m. 16 is an altered dominant which yields immediately to A♭ in the following measure, the E♭ augmented triad in m. 48 is expanded over mm. 49−60 before bringing in A♭ in m. 61. The strategy for expanding the E♭ chord efficiently multiplies the number of distinct forms of 4−19 which are heard: a minimum number of notes produces a maximum number of forms of 4−19. Within mm. 49−52 is a form of 6−20, (2367te), which contains three prominent forms of 4−19, all of which contain the E♭ augmented chord: (7te3), (e237), and (367e).[17] The 6−20 also contains a form of 4−17, (367t).

In section B, both 4−19 and 4−17 play important roles in structuring the chord progression. In example 8.9, stems, beams, and arrows are used to analyze mm. 61−68, the first phrase of section B. Beginning and ending the progression are two tonal-interpreting anchors, labeled "I" and "V." Expanding the A♭ tonality is an arpeggiation of an A♭-minor triad in the bass of mm. 61−64. The progression from A♭ major in m. 60 to B minor, enharmonically C♭ minor, is especially striking and throws into relief the collection (8e03), a form of the structural set 4−17 formed by A♭ major plus A♭ minor.

The B minor triad of mm. 62−63 then surprisingly progresses in m. 64 to E♭ minor, a rather distant tonal center. If we read B minor as C♭ minor, then the progression C♭ minor to E♭ minor is related to A major to C♭ minor since the

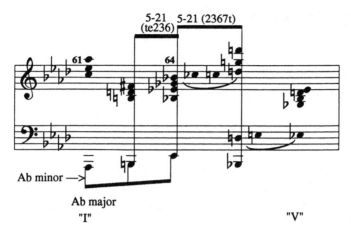

Example 8.9. Op. 73/2, mm. 61–68, harmonic and set structure

root of each target chord neutralizes the third of the initial chord. C♭ neutralizes C in moving from A♭ major to C♭ minor, and E♭ neutralizes E♭ in moving from C♭ minor to E♭ minor. Because they alter chordal thirds, these progressions also hint at two forms of 4–17, those being A♭ major/minor, (8e03), and B major/minor, (e236). The G-minor six-three chord in m. 66 continues, by variation, the pattern of neutralizing the third of the previous chord, for G, its root, displaces E♭ minor's G♭.

Taken together, the two chords B minor and E♭ minor form (te236), 5–21, labeled in the example. E♭ minor then combines with G minor in m. 66 to form (2367t), another form of 5–21 overlapping with (te236). The two forms of 5–21 share 4–19 (236t) and are related at T4, a constructive process in the augmented triad which is a characteristic subset of both 5–21 and 4–19.

A common-tone progression leads G minor to an altered B♭-dominant chord and finally to an E♭ major seventh chord which concludes the phrase in m. 68. The mode change from E♭ minor, capping the bass arpeggiation in m. 64, to E♭ major, at the end of the phrase in m. 68, creates another form of 4–17, (367t).

The Gambler, *op. 24*

Beginning with *The Giant* in 1900, a very ambitious project for a nine-year-old, and concluding with the massive *War and Peace*, which absorbed his attention from 1941 until 1952, Prokofiev never ceased trying to compose opera; in all he composed eight.[18] To understand his strong attraction to opera, it is useful to recall his respect for Diaghilev's artistic judgment, as when Diaghilev rejected Prokofiev's score for the ballet *Ala and Lolly*, an assessment with which Prokofiev quickly agreed. But when Diaghilev proclaimed the death of opera—and ballet's ascendance—Prokofiev was deaf; he was actively engaged in composing opera all his life.[19]

Unfortunately, Prokofiev's operas seemed always to encounter formidable obstacles to their staging. *The Flaming Angel* was never produced in Prokofiev's lifetime, and *War and Peace* came to completion only after many revisions and with great difficulties.[20] *The Gambler,* too, had a long and difficult journey from Prokofiev's pen to the stage. He began it in 1915 and completed it in 1917. While arrangements had been made for the work's premiere in 1917, including rehearsal, the premiere did not take place until twelve years later, in 1929.[21]

Dostoevsky's work satisfied Prokofiev on many points. First and foremost, he felt that the compact plot was well suited to an operatic adaptation. He was also drawn to Dostoevsky's prose and sought to preserve as much as possible the natural rhythms of the spoken dialogue. To achieve that end and to permit the libretto to guide the musical setting, Prokofiev discarded the idea of opera as a staged spectacle which focused on the performers rather than the plot and which comprised a series of discrete pieces. Instead, Prokofiev turned to a more seamless and through-composed style, though he still incorporated specific musical themes and associated them with specific characters and events. The resulting work stands as one of Prokofiev's best operas, along with *Love for Three Oranges* and *War and Peace.*

The following discussion centers on act III. I return to earlier material when necessary to interpret the music.

The General hopes to marry Blanche, a woman of questionable character, more interested in worldly than spiritual things, who has nevertheless captured the General's heart. The General's bad finances, however, complicate the romance. He owes a considerable sum of money to the Marquis, and before he can marry Blanche, he must clear his debts.

The Marquis is an unctuous, ingratiating man, friendly when it suits his needs. During act III the Marquis is very friendly to the General. In another character or in other circumstances, the Marquis's magnanimity toward the General might be a sign of kindness or warmheartedness, but these are qualities which the Marquis does not possess. The Marquis realizes that he may be able to help secure funds for the General; solving the General's problem solves his own. Thus his behavior toward the General is, in fact, completely consistent with his character.

The General is counting on a sizable inheritance from Grandmother to clear his debts; she is an extremely wealthy woman whose home is in Moscow. At the beginning of the opera, the General, Blanche, and the Marquis speculate about Grandmother's bad health. The Marquis, never reserved about issues concerning money, hopefully offers that she might be dead. The General, naturally, is especially eager to follow the Marquis in believing in her imminent, if not actual, demise. But at the end of act II Grandmother shows up at Roulettenburg, surprising everyone. The General, Blanche, and the Marquis are notably disheartened by Grandmother's conspicuous well-being; Pauline, the General's young daughter-in-law, and Alexis, a young man in love with Pauline, on the other hand, are delighted. Grandmother further dampens the General's hopes by engaging in a spectacularly healthy and wild bout of gambling. Act III centers on the General's deteriorating psychological state and growing distress brought on by Grandmother's gambling. Powerless to stop her from squandering his inheritance-to-be, which he regards as already his, and unable to confront his impotence—a feeling that he never experienced in a military capacity—the General is left literally speechless (or songless) time and again.

As a means of paying off debt, the inheritance has an uncomplicated economic value. But the General knows in his heart that the inheritance has more significance as a means of securing Blanche's love, for Blanche's attachment to him does not depend exclusively on reciprocated affections.

Act III begins with the General bemoaning his difficult situation; he directs his ire toward Grandmother and frets about his future with Blanche. The Marquis, when he enters, commiserates with the General but also injects a measure of rationality and calm to counterbalance the General's hysteria. Blanche then comes upon the scene and proceeds to berate the General for his impotence and then to suggest a solution to the problem—a solution, she makes clear, that she is not morally constrained to provide.

The General attempts to enlist Alexis's aid to rescue Grandmother and to steer her away from the gaming tables before she squanders her fortune completely. Alexis does not blindly carry out the order. As is his unfailing habit when dealing with the unexpected, the General is rendered incapable of carrying on a dialogue with Alexis. Conversational exchange remains out of the General's reach, so, resorting to military monologue, he commands Alexis to leave Grandmother. He hopes that losing Alexis will be a blow sufficiently severe to distract Grandmother from the gaming tables. The Marquis, a shrewd judge of human nature and, unlike the General, never at a loss for words, intercedes. Slightly modifying the General's plan, he entreats Alexis to stay with Grandmother and use his influence to guide her and curtail but not extinguish her gambling. Eager for any help from Alexis, the General becomes ever more emphatic and hysterical, attaching to the Marquis's suggestion a desperate plea.

One of the gamblers, Prince Nilsky, provides a narration which mediates between Grandmother's activities in the gaming room and the scene with the General, the Marquis, and Alexis. Nilsky interrupts their conversation with his account of Grandmother's losses. At this point, Blanche, preferring a more secure relationship than the one she is about to embark upon, gives up on the General and goes off with Nilsky. Alexis, alone, reflects on what has just transpired. He concludes in his soliloquy that only his feelings for Pauline justify his association with individuals such as the General, the Marquis, and Blanche. His thoughts turn to Pauline completely. Pauline enters and Alexis tells her that he foresees a bad outcome; she must be careful.

Finally, Grandmother enters and relates the extent of her losses to Alexis and Pauline. Grandmother retires. The General follows Grandmother and attempts to gain an audience with her. Her servant Potapitch steadfastly denies the General audience, and the act closes with the General losing control of the situation and himself, wordlessly screaming in frustration.[22]

THE ORCHESTRAL PRELUDE

The orchestral prelude to act III is familiar; the music occurred before in act II, at R174. By act III, the music of the prelude has acquired a special significance. To understand its meaning, we must trace some of the opera's themes. At the end of act I, Alexis, prodded and, indeed, commanded by Pauline, had insulted a German Baron of high social stature. The General appropriately took personal responsibility for Alexis's action and sought to rectify the situation by apologizing to the Baron on Alexis's behalf and without Alexis's knowledge. As a further step, the General planned to expel Alexis from Roulettenburg at once. This sort of comprehensive plan, conceived in a vacuum and without any second-party counsel, betrays the General's military background at the same time that it highlights his social ineptness.

Alexis is furious about the General's unsolicited intervention and regards it as a dire personal insult. To regain his honor, Alexis challenges the General to a duel and vows to chastise the Baron for accepting from the General an apology by proxy rather than an apology directly from Alexis. These events lead into the music of R174.

At R174 the General reacts to Alexis's show of dignity in a revealing manner. Evidently losing control of a situation that he previously assumed to be fully in hand, the General can only stammer, alternately pleading for Alexis to calm himself and threatening to have him arrested. (Reacting to Grandmother's gambling, the General later threatens her with arrest, another of his typically unilateral approaches to a problem. The threat of Grandmother's arrest, like the threat of Alexis's arrest, is an idle one.)

As act III again confirms, the General is incapable of effectively improvising. The music of R174 by itself becomes a metaphor for the General's inability to direct the course of events. R174's reappearance in the orchestral prelude to act III sets the stage for the ensuing dramatic action.

The orchestral prelude proceeds in a manner characteristic of Prokofiev. The tune in mm. 1–2 (R293 = m. 1) is repeated and slightly varied over mm. 3–4 and more drastically varied in m. 5. On strong beats from m. 1 to m. 2, the melody passes down from C to B to A, traversing a minor third and bringing T9 into play. Dynamic accent, the tenuto direction on C, B, and A, and metric accent clearly mark out this descent. Mm. 1–4 return at R294, transposed up a perfect fourth.

The tune of the first four bars is nearly devoid of chromaticism and recalls Moisson-Franckhauser's observation that Prokofiev has a "certain predilection for simple tonalities, often C major." M. 5 abruptly upsets the established white-key context, virtually without preparation. Similar disruption occurs one measure before R295. Nevertheless, T9 motions persist in m. 5, taking Ab/C to F/A.

In example 8.10 this interrupting passage is studied by abstracting the melody of m. 5, thrice-repeated in that measure. I analyze the melody of m. 5 as an accelerated, reharmonized, and compound version of the melody of mm. 1–2. Like the melody in mm. 1–2, the upper strand begins on C and passes through B to A. The lower strand begins on Ab and passes through G to F. The two passing notes are shown parenthetically on the example.

In example 8.10a the melodic strands are separated: each strand spans a minor third, beamed together in the example. A major third separates the strands, shown by the arrows labeled "T4" and "T8." Example 8.10b presents a different view: the beginning and ending dyads, each spanning a major third, are isolated. These two dyads are separated by a minor third, shown by the arrows labeled "T3" and "T9."

F, Ab, A, and C are the pitches making up the initial and terminal points of the melody. Together they form 4–17, a structural set in the movement. Example 8.10 shows the internal processes generating the collection, and seeing them positions us to apprehend connections to other passages with different pitch-class collections which are driven by the same processes. For example, though m. 5 disrupts the continuity of mm. 1–4, it does not introduce unprecedented material. The melodies of both passages are driven by the same transpositional process, a downward transposition of a minor third.

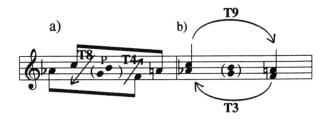

Example 8.10. *The Gambler,* op. 24, act III, m. 5, melodic analysis

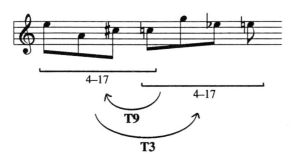

Example 8.11. *The Gambler,* op. 24, act III, R294+4, set structure

One measure before R295, the continuity of the previous four measures, which begin at R294, is interrupted. The first four measures of R294 transpose the first four measures of R293. But the next measure, while parallel in function to m. 5, is not its transposition; nevertheless, its pitch structure is related. Example 8.11 is an analysis of the set structure of the melody of R294+4. The brackets below the staff isolate by order the first four pitches and, with one overlap, the next four pitches. Each bracket contains a form of 4−17. From example 8.10 we are familiar with the role of T3 in the internal structure of these forms of 4−17; the arrows in example 8.11 show that the two forms themselves relate at either T3 or T9, depending on which set is chosen as referential. T3 − T9 relates the major thirds of 4−17, as in example 8.10b, just as it relates the two forms of 4−17 in example 8.11.

THE GENERAL'S SOLILOQUY: R297−R312

Following the orchestral prelude is the General's soliloquy, in which he considers Grandmother's destructive gambling, his unfortunate distance from her and consequent lack of direct control, and her closeness to Alexis, who is in the General's opinion a young fool in whom Grandmother's affection is pathetically misplaced. A form of 4−17, the structural set established by the prelude, provides the repetitive, blustery accompaniment for the General's plaint. From R298+1 to R300, 4−17, in the form (0347), appears, virtually unadorned, as an ostinato. Like the General's character, the accompaniment is inflexible and, after a time, unimaginative. Through its association with the music of R174, 4−17 transmits the dramatic action's ever-increasing immunity to the General's wishes.

Forms of 4−17 also occur at the beginning and at the end of R303, which concludes with the dramatic *Generalpause.* The two forms relate at T−4, a dynamic process derived from example 8.10a.

At the soliloquy's conclusion at R310, the General mocks Grandmother's reaction to his attempts at reasoning with her. With a sort of masochistic relish,

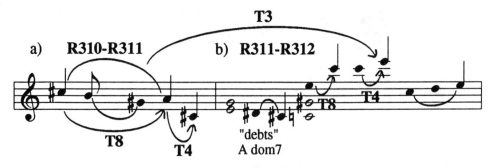

Example 8.12. *The Gambler*, op. 24, act III, R310 through R311 and R311 through R312, transpositional structure

he repeats Grandmother's stinging words, originally addressed to the General as though to a child: "Not a penny, not a penny for you." The General has evidently been thinking, remembering, and burning from these words, which closed act II. The melody in which he mocks Grandmother, analyzed in example 8.12a, is taken from the orchestral doubling beginning at R310. This is a clever dramatic ploy on the part of Prokofiev. As the act unfolds, the music (which was originally Grandmother's) becomes associated with the General's financial difficulties; we can call this the General's debt music. As long as Grandmother is alive—as long as her theme can be heard—the General's troubles remain.

Like the melodic strands in example 8.10, the music in example 8.12a passes through a third. But example 8.12a differs in several respects. Its passing note, B, is embellished (now by G♯); its initial and terminal notes, C♯ and A, are not. The line, via octave transfer, returns to its starting point, C♯. And the melody of example 8.12a spans a major third, not a minor one, so the dynamic process involved is T4, deriving from the harmonic structure shown in example 8.10a.

The music of R311 is sketched in example 8.12b. The vocal line cadences on an embellished A "dominant seventh" chord, setting the word "debts." There follows a solo instrumental echo, during which the General contemplates his problem and seeks its solution. Like the General when he says, "And my debts?" the echoing instrument ponders a problem. In fact, the music in example 8.12b actually is an echo—a transposed and retrograded version of example 8.12a in which passing and neighbor notes are eliminated. By recalling and retracing example 8.12a's melody, the music in example 8.12b becomes a powerful metaphor for memory.

The arrow connecting examples 8.12a and 8.12b shows the process T3 again. The pitch classes articulating each gesture are stemmed upward. These upward-stemmed pitch classes, C♯, A, C, and E, form the structural set 4–17.[23]

Blanche's love for the General is contingent upon his inheriting Grand-mother's fortune. But the General refuses to confront the fact that Blanche ranks worldly matters—and money, in particular—above spiritual ones. In contrast, the General's love for Blanche is unconditional, even though he knows that gaining Blanche's commitment to marriage also necessarily entails overcoming his bad financial situation. As the General's psychological state deteriorates, he elevates Blanche to symbolic status. As he begins to realize, she represents an ideal state, one in which his personal and financial difficulties—encompassing essentially all of his spiritual and material concerns—are resolved. But, little by little, even the General himself begins to suspect that his ideal might be unat-tainable. Blanche's symbolism increases for the General in direct proportion to the desperateness of his situation and dramatically amplifies the urgency with which he pursues his inheritance.

Parts of the voice, the orchestral melody, and the accompaniment beginning at R312+3 are shown in example 8.13. The music depicts the love between the General and Blanche. It is deliberately paced and languid, contrasting with much of the other music in the act (and the opera), which is often ostinato-like or very rapidly changing. The voice in R312 has a clear tune, familiar in some degree from the orchestral prelude. The prelude featured descent through a minor third, a descending half step followed by a descending whole step; the voice of R312 collapses the prelude's melody and makes it chromatic but preserves strong-beat arrivals. In the bass staff in the example the elements of the descent are beamed together.

The orchestral melody of R312 spans the perverse dissonance of an aug-mented octave, from B6 down to B♭5, beamed together above the staff. At the melody's conclusion, a 9–8 "suspension" of F♯–to–E maintains forward drive, and it is imitated by the bass (where F♯–to–E creates a 7–8 suspension). The

Example 8.13. *The Gambler,* op. 24, act III, R312+4, set and harmonic structure

conspicuous dissonances, both melodic and harmonic, are as characteristic of the motive as are its measured rhythm and tunefulness. The distorted quality imparted to the tune by the dissonances portrays the asymmetry of the love between the General and Blanche and also suggests the General's pitiable consciousness of that love's true nature.

The orchestral melody in example 8.13 highlights minor thirds. Beamed together and labeled are two forms of the structural set 4−17. The arrow labeled "T3" shows the pitch-class transposition of (478e) into (7te2). The transposition by T3 recalls both examples 8.10 and 8.11.

Near the end of the act, Grandmother is exhausted from her gaming but unrepentant. She seeks refuge in her room, leaving her valet outside as a guard. The General, completely desperate at this point, attempts to gain an audience with Grandmother, but he is denied that audience by the valet. Being rebuffed by a valet completes the General's psychological deterioration. The episode throws into high relief his impotence on virtually every front, and the General himself realizes his hopeless situation. Forgetting about the valet momentarily, he slumps down, self-absorbed, and concludes the act as he began it, with a monological complaint. He starts by bemoaning his loss of Blanche, addressing her as though she were present. This music, taken as it appears in R423, is shown in example 8.14. The music is now associated with the General's mental sickness.

Example 8.14 is an analysis of D♭ as an upper neighbor to C♭, and B♭ as a skip embellishing D♭. C♭'s metric placement and agogic accent reinforce D♭'s auxiliary function. Brackets at the end of example 8.14 mark off three forms of the structural set 4−17. Each verticality is a major third, and arrows moving from left to right label motion by T9. Example 8.14, then, is another manifestation of the processes in example 8.10b. Example 8.14 shows 4−17's final appearance in

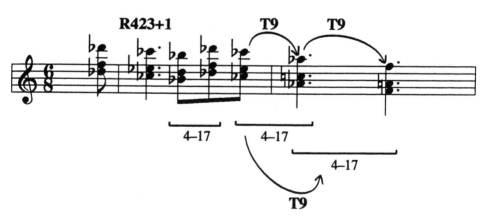

Example 8.14. *The Gambler,* op. 24, act III, R423+1 through R423+2, set structure

act III. Its meaning has been enriched and transformed: from being a sign of the General's ineffectualness, at the act's beginning, it has become a sign of his mental breakdown, at the act's conclusion.

Alexis's earlier prediction of a bad outcome comes true for the General, who is overwhelmed by the way things have turned out. By the end of the act, he comprehends clearly his rapidly deteriorating future and his powerlessness to influence events. This realization renders him totally speechless, able only to moan. Ironically the moan, though tragic, is richer in meaning than any of his vacuous, pompous speeches.

Some Thoughts in Closing

(musical staff lines)

Assumptions about the structure of music are unfounded, I think, if they do not begin with the musical surface. My analyses have been generated with surface in mind, and I have worked from there toward larger-scale structure and "deeper" structure. In general, the motivic structures ("structural sets") which are given on the surface of the music are easy to apprehend, and they are richly informative about the content of the work. In this view, I follow Italo Calvino's Mr. Palomar, who reminds us not to underestimate the richness of a surface: "It is only after you have come to know the surface of things . . . that you can venture to seek what is underneath. But the surface of things is inexhaustible."[1]

The deeper structures virtually always reflect aspects of the surface, which themselves may be traditional and tonal or otherwise. While one may want to decide in some unequivocal way whether Prokofiev is a traditional composer or a modernist, I would suggest that the question is irrelevant. The argument that Prokofiev is a traditional composer and that his music is essentially identical to traditionally tonal music augments neither the sophistication of traditional tonality nor the distinctiveness of Prokofiev's music, nor does it advance our comprehension and analysis of traditional tonality. Arguing that Prokofiev is essentially a modernist—and that modernism is a positive attribute—is tacitly to adopt the romantic point of view and give a high valuation to genius and novelty. If Prokofiev's position in the twentieth century can be viewed positively in romantic terms, his rescuers need to concentrate on the unique interaction of tonality with Prokofiev's individualism and craft. Otherwise, romantics may be obliged to ignore Prokofiev's works in favor of other, more novel products from more radical and innovative composers. Rather than choose sides, I have showed how the play between the familiar and expected, on the one hand, and the surprising and unaccountable, on the other, projects that sound which is Prokofiev's.[2]

Whatever role Prokofiev's nationalism may have played in his music, it must at least have driven him to return to the country of his birth. One's homeland and source of upbringing and custom naturally exert a powerful force, but it is hard to comprehend why anyone would choose to return to the Soviet Union of Stalin's purges. Did Prokofiev feel compelled to return because he was committed to being a Soviet composer? He certainly attempted to incorporate ideological concerns into his music. After his return to the Soviet Union he sought to write music that, in style and content, was guided by the tenets of new simplicity and Socialist Realism.[3]

But Prokofiev failed to gain much official approval for his politically motivated music. For example, even before Stalin's terror Prokofiev composed the ballet *Le Pas d'acier,* a work whose goal it was to present, in Robinson's words, "the joy of communal industrial labor," a topic apparently worthy of official sanction and encouragement.[4] But when Prokofiev visited the USSR in 1929 and proposed that the Bolshoi Theater produce it, "the cultural bureaucrats . . . attack[ed] him and his ballet with vicious hostility, barely able to conceal their pleasure at teaching him a lesson in Soviet reality."[5] Even the later opera *Story of a Real Man* did not succeed in impressing the officials.[6] While Prokofiev may have wanted to develop as a Soviet composer, it would appear that he was happier and his music was better when he was not worrying about how it might conform to an ideology.

Finally, how might one view Prokofiev as a twentieth-century composer? He is widely admired, but he has not had the clear and profound impact on subsequent composers that, for example, Schoenberg has had; he has spawned no clear-cut isms (such as impressionism, or expressionism, or serialism, or primitivism). We have already seen how placing Prokofiev in a nationalist category is at least somewhat problematic: a large portion of his compositional career was spent outside his homeland, and that portion spent inside the Soviet Union was not unequivocally successful.

Because Prokofiev had traditional leanings and was not an iconoclastic, radically inventive composer, his music may not have actively engaged subsequent composers in the same way as Schoenberg's or Stravinsky's. Like the bad fit of wrong note into a traditional context, Prokofiev's traditional temperament makes him an awkward fit into a century with both an ever-accelerating rate of change in virtually all areas of human endeavor and an obsession with innovation. Prokofiev, though not a radical innovator, was a skilled craftsman and a fluent and prolific composer endowed with great artistry. These assessments, which stand up to analysis, challenge precisely the Romanticism whose legacy exerted such a profound influence on the composer himself.

Appendix: Some Pertinent Set and Set-Class Relations

I. Some Aspects of Sets Related to 4−19

8−19 [01245689] contains its abstract complement 4−19 [0148] eight times, the maximum representation of any tetrachord in any octachord. While five octachords contain a tetrachordal subset eight times, only in the case of 8−19 is that tetrachord the abstract complement. By this measure, 4−19 and 8−19 are especially closely bound.

There are five distinct pentachordal supersets of 4−19. These are listed below in figure A.1. All of these pentachords, with the exception of 5−13 [01248], contain 4−19 as a subset twice; 5−13 contains 4−19 once.

5z17 and 5z37 are z-related pentachords; they share the interval vector <212320>.

II. Triadic-Flip Chords

The "major-minor" chord 4−17 [0347] is formed by the union of fifth-flip-related triads. For example, an A-minor triad (904) and an A-major triad (914) are related by IA/E (= T1I). The union of an A-minor triad with an A-major triad, (9014), is a form of [0347].

5−22 [01478] is formed by the union of third-flip-related triads. For example, an A-minor triad (904) and an Ab-major triad (803) are related by IC/C (= T0I). The union of an A-minor triad with an Ab-major triad, (89034), is a form of [01478].

III. 3−11 in the Subset Structures of 6−20, 5−21, and 6z19

6−20 [014589] contains the subset 3−11 [037] six times. For example, the pitch-class set (014589), or (C, C♯, E/Fb, F, Ab, A), contains the following major and minor triads: (904), (A, C, E) = A minor; (580), (F, Ab, C) = F minor; (590), (F, A, C) = F major; (148), (Db, Fb, Ab) = Db minor; (914), (A, C♯, E) = A major; (158), (Db, F, Ab) = Db major. The spacing by major thirds of the three major-minor chords Db, F, and A reflects the augmented triads in the subset structure of 6−20—specifically, (048) and (159). Three pairings of these triadic subsets produce 6−20: (904)/(158) = A minor / Db major; (580)/(914) = F minor / A major; (148)/(590) = Db minor / F major.

6−20, with six degrees of symmetry, contains a single pentachordal subset; that subset is 5−21, represented in 6−20 six times.[1]

5−13 [01248]	4−19 (1x)
5z17 [01348]	4−19 (2x)
5−21 [01458]	4−19 (2x)
5−22 [01478]	4−19 (2x)
5z37 [03458]	4−19 (2x)

Figure A.1. Pentachordal supersets of 4−19 [0148]

5–21 [01458] contains the subset 3–11 [037] three times. For example, the pitch-class set (01458), or (C, C♯, E, F, A♭), contains the following major or minor triads: (580), (F, A♭, C) = F minor; (148), (D♭, F♭, A♭) = D♭ minor; (158), (D♭, F, A♭) = D♭ major.

6z19 [013478] contains the subset 3–11 [037] four times. For example, the pitch-class set (013478) contains the following major and minor triads: (037), (C, E♭, G) = C minor; (803), (A♭, C, E♭) = A♭ major; (047), (C, E, G) = C major; (148), (D♭, F♭, A♭) = D♭ minor. (037)/(047) represents the fifth-flip tetrachord, or the major-minor chord (4–17 [0347]), while (047)/(148) represents the fifth-flip pentachord (5–22 [01478]).

IV. The Fragmentation Approach

Fragmentation offers a convenient conceptualization of some of these relations. To begin, imagine that one is given a major triad and a minor triad. These triads can be arranged in several different ways relative to one another. If they are arranged to overlap at their roots and fifths, a form of 4–17 [0347] results. If they share a chordal third, a form of 5–22 [01458] results. (Compare to the discussion of triadic-flip chords.)

If the chords are spaced with the root of the major triad a major third below that of the minor triad, 4–20 [0158] results. If they are spaced with the root of the minor triad a major third below that of the major triad, 6–20 [014589] results.

If they are spaced with the root of the major triad a semitone below the root of the minor triad, 5–22 [01458] results (compare to the discussion of triadic-flip chords). If they are spaced with the root of the minor triad a semitone below the root of the major triad, 6z19 [013478] results.

V. Some K/Kh Relations Involving 4–19/8–19

Figure A.2 is a K/Kh table pertinent to 4–19.[2] The table shows relations for 4–19/8–19, for 4–19's five pentachordal supersets and their complements, and for three hexachords, 6–20 and the z-pair 6z19/6z44. Figure A.2's derivation can be followed in figure A.3, which gives specific information on the number of times a subset is represented in its superset.

		5–13/7–13	5z17/7z17	5–21/7–21	5–22/7–22	5z37/7z37
5–13/7–13	Kh					
5z17/7z17	Kh					
5–21/7–21	Kh					
5–22/7–22	Kh					
5z37/7z37	Kh					
6z19/z44	Kh	no relation	K (6z19 and 6z44)	Kh (6z19 and 6z44)	Kh (6z19 and 6z44)	K (6z19 and 6z44)
6–20	Kh	no relation	no relation	Kh	no relation	no relation

Figure A.2. K/Kh table for some sets related to 4–19/8–19

Superset	8–19	7–13	5–13		4–19/8–19	
Subset	7–13 (1x)	4–19 (2x)	4–19 (1x)		5–13/7–13 Kh	
Superset	8–19	7–21	5–21		4–19/8–19	
Subset	7–21 (2x)	4–19 (7x)	4–19 (2x)		5–21/7–21 Kh	
Superset	8–19	7–22	5–22		4–19/8–19	
Subset	7–22	4–19 (4x)	4–19 (2x)		5–22/7–22 Kh	
Superset	8–19	7z17	5z17		4–19/8–19	
Subset	7z17 (1x)	4–19 (4x)	4–19 (2x)		5z17/7z17 Kh	
Superset	8–19	7z37	5z37		4–19/8–19	
Subset	7z37 (1x)	4–19 (4x)	4–19 (2x)		5z37/7z37 Kh	
Superset	8–19	6–20			4–19/8–19	
Subset	6–20 (1x)	4–19 (6x)			6–20 Kh	
Superset	8–19	8–19	6z19	6z44	4–19/8–19	4–19/8–19
Subset	6z19 (3x)	6z44 (3x)	4–19 (3x)	4–19 (3x)	6z19 Kh	6z44 Kh
Superset	7–13	7–13	6z19	6z44	5–13/7–13	
Subset	6z19 (0x)	6z44 (0x)	5–13 (0x)	5–13 (0x)	6z19/6z44 no relation	
Superset	7–13	6–20			5–13/7–13	
Subset	6–20 (0x)	5–13 (0x)			6–20 no relation	
Superset	7z17	7z17	6z19	6z44	5z17/7z17	5z17/7z17
Subset	6z19 (0x)	6z44 (2x)	5z17 (1x)	5z17 (0x)	6z19 K	6z44 K
Superset	7z17	6–20			5z17/7z17	
Subset	6–20 (0x)	5z17 (0x)			6–20 no relation	
Superset	7–21	7–21	6z19	6z44	5–21/7–21	5–21/7–21
Subset	6z19 (1x)	6z44 (1x)	5–21 (1x)	5–21 (1x)	6z19 Kh	6z44 Kh

(*Continued on next page*)

Figure A.3. Detailed subset relations for some sets related to 4–19/8–19

Superset	7–21	6–20			5–21/7–21	
Subset	6–20 (1x)	5–21 (6x)			6–20	
					Kh	
Superset	7–22	7–22	6z19	6z44	5–22/7–22	5–22/7–22
Subset	6z19 (2x)	6z44 (2x)	5–22 (1x)	5–22 (1x)	6z19	6z44
					Kh	Kh
Superset	7–22	6–20			5–22/7–22	
Subset	6–20 (0x)	5–22 (0x)			6–20	
					no relation	
Superset	7z37	7z37	6z19	6z44	5z37/7z37	5z37/7z37
Subset	6z19 (2x)	6z44 (0x)	5z37 (0x)	5z37 (1x)	6z19	6z44
					K	K
Superset	7z37	6–20			5z37/7z37	
Subset	6–20 (0x)	5z37 (0x)			6–20	
					no relation	

Figure A.3. (*continued*)

Several features of the tables deserve comment. 4–19/8–19 is in the relation Kh to all the sets shown on Figure A.2. 5–21/7–21 is in the relation Kh to all three hexachords shown on the table. 7–21 contains 4–19 seven times, the uniquely maximum representation of any tetrachord in any heptachord.

Notes

1: Approaching the Music

1 Woody Allen has even continued Prokofiev's film music career by proxy, using his music to score the movie *Love and Death*.

2 Sources on Russian history include James Billington, *The Icon and the Axe: An Interpretive History of Russian Culture* (1966; reprint, New York: Vintage Books, 1970); Edward J. Brown, *The Proletarian Episode in Russian Literature, 1928–32* (New York: Octagon Books, 1971); and Nicholas V. Riasanovsky, *A History of Russia*, 4th ed. (New York: Oxford University Press, 1984). Aspects of Russian music are discussed in Malcolm Brown, ed., *Slavonic and Western Music: Essays for Gerald Abraham* (Ann Arbor, Mich.: UMI Research Press; Oxford: Oxford University Press, 1985); and Gordon D. McQuere, ed., *Russian Theoretical Thought in Music* (Ann Arbor, Mich.: UMI Research Press, 1983).

3 Israel Nestyev's first biography, *Sergei Prokofiev: His Musical Life*, translated by Rose Prokofieva (New York: Alfred A. Knopf, 1946), was published in English; censors deemed the book ideologically defective, and it was not published in Russian. Nestyev's second biography, *Prokofiev*, translated by Florence Jonas (Stanford, Calif.: Stanford University Press, 1960), was originally published in Russian (Moscow: Gosudarstvennoe Muzikalnoe Izdaltelstvo, 1957) in an expanded and ideologically repaired version. I will refer to the two biographies as "first biography (1946)" and "second biography (1957)."

4 Felix Salzer has analyzed the beginning of Prokofiev's Piano Sonata no. 8 in his book *Structural Hearing*, 2 vols. (1952; reprint, New York: Dover Publications, 1962). More recent is Richard Bass's article "Prokofiev's Technique of Chromatic Displacement," *Music Analysis* 7/2 (1988): 197–214.

5 Nestyev, first biography (1946), p. 120.

6 Nestyev, second biography (1957), p. 231.

7 Victor Seroff, *Sergei Prokofiev: A Soviet Tragedy* (New York: Taplinger Publishing Co., 1969), p. 266.

8 Lawrence Hanson and Elisabeth Hanson, *Prokofiev: A Biography in Three Movements* (New York: Random House, 1964). Also available is Claude Samuel, *Prokofiev*, translated by Miriam John (New York: Grossman, 1971).

9 See Harlow Robinson, *Sergei Prokofiev* (New York: Paragon House, 1987); and David Gutman, *Prokofiev* (London: Alderman, 1988).

10 Nestyev, second biography (1957), p. 224

11 Jonathan D. Kramer, *Listen to the Music: A Self-Guided Tour Through the Orchestral Repertoire* (New York: Schirmer Books, 1988), p. 518.

12 "La musique de Prokofiev est toujours très tonale, avec une certain prédilection pour les tonalités simples, souvent ut majeur, ce qui n'est pas sans surprendre si l'on pense a l'attrait de la musique modale en Russe.

"Par un jeu subtil d'altérations accidentelles (vvodnyi ton) il développe une sorte d'échelle diatonique élargie qui ne s'apparente absolument pas à l'échelle chromatique traditionelle, puisqu'elle conserve sa fonction tonale. Tous les sons de l'échelle diatonique simple peuvent être altérés sans pour outant déterminer de modulation, la tonalité de base subsiste" (Suzanne Moisson-Franckhauser, *Sergei Prokofiev et les courants esthetiques de son temps, 1891–1953* [Paris: Publications orientalistes de France, 1974], pp. 306–307, my translation).

13 I also note in her comments the reference to "C major" as a kind of preferred tonality in Prokofiev's music. Prokofiev himself once attempted to write a "white" string quartet that was entirely white-key, based on the C-major collection.

14 Robert Wason, *Figured Bass Theory from Albrechtsberger to Schenker and Schoenberg* (Ann Arbor, Mich.: UMI Research Press, 1984), p. 59.

15 When Moisson-Franckhauser mentions "Prokofiev's predilection for simple tonalities, often C major," she seems to be referring in another way to Prokofiev's white-key melodies.

16 The essay is in Sergei Prokofiev, *Autobiography, Articles, Reminiscences,* translated by Rose Prokofieva (London: Central Books, 1960), pp. 115–116.

17 Sergei Prokofiev, *Autobiography,* in his *Soviet Diary 1927 and Other Writings,* translated and edited by Oleg Prokofiev (London: Faber and Faber, 1991), p. 232.

18 See Robinson, *Prokofiev,* p. 77; and *Prokofiev by Prokofiev,* translated by Guy Daniels (London: MacDonald General Books, 1979), p. 132.

19 Prokofiev, *Autobiography,* in *Soviet Diary 1927,* p. 277.

20 This is precisely the sort of evidence pounced on by Nestyev, in his second biography (1957), who sees in Prokofiev's remarks confirmation of the decadent influence of the West. Nestyev finds in the Symphony no. 2 and the Quintet, op. 39, "the most striking examples of the effect of formalistic influences" (p. 241). The root of the problem, according to Nestyev, is that "Prokofiev nevertheless felt the pressure of the aesthetically overrefined taste of the bourgeois West" (p. 241).

21 Robinson, *Prokofiev,* pp. 188–189. Nestyev, in the second biography (1957), also cites the letter, p. 212.

22 Robinson, *Prokofiev,* pp. 72–73.

23 From the ballet Prokofiev made the concert piece *Scythian Suite.*

24 Interpreting facts such as these is one of the most important forces driving the Nestyev and Seroff biographies. Where Nestyev perceives decadent, bourgeois influence, Seroff perceives freedom. Where Nestyev perceives a healthy and nurturing artistic environment, Seroff perceives shackles.

25 See *Testimony: The Memoirs of Dmitri Shostakovich,* related to and edited by Solomon Volkov; translated by Antonina W. Bouis (New York: Harper and Row, 1979).

26 For a time, Zhdanov was party chief in Leningrad, where he replaced Sergei Kirov following Kirov's assassination. See, for instance, Alexander Werth, *Musical Uproar in Moscow* (Westport, Conn.: Greenwood Press, 1973), p. 36; or Robert Conquest, *The Great Terror* (New York: Oxford University Press, 1990), p. 47.

27 Boris Schwarz, *Music and Musical Life in Soviet Russia, 1917–1981* (Bloomington: Indiana University Press, 1972), p. 114.

28 It is only fair to Russian Formalism that we separate it from Zhdanov's political, polemical term Formalism. Zhdanov's Formalism lacks the intellectual grounding of Russian Formalism; he applies the term to music he does not like. Russian Formalism—a term not embraced by the critics so indicated (see Stephen Bann and John E. Bowlt, eds., *Russian Formalism* [Edinburgh: Scottish Academic Press, 1973], p. 10)—generally focuses not on the "story" of a work, which could be told in many different ways, but on its literary and constructed qualities. See Bann and Bowlt, eds., *Russian Formalism,* for reproductions of some of the seminal essays written by Tzvetan Todorov, Viktor Shklovsky, Roman Jakobson, and Boris Eikhenbaum, among others. For an introduction to and overview of Russian Formalism, see also Raman Selden, *A Reader's Guide to Contemporary Literary Theory,* 2nd ed., (Lexington: University Press of Kentucky, 1989), chapter 1.

29 See, for example, Vaughn James, "Socialist Realism," in his *Soviet Socialist Realism: Origins and Theory* (New York: St. Martin's Press, 1973).

30 "Sie soll klar und einfach sein, aber nicht in Schablone verfallen. Die Einfachheit darf nicht die alte Einfachheit, sondern muss eine neue sein" (*Sergej Prokofjew: Dokumente, Briefe, Erinnerungen,* compiled, edited, and annotated by S. I. Schlifstein; German translation by Felix Loesch [Moscow: Staatlichen Musikverlag, 1961], p. 200, my translation).

31 Werth, *Musical Uproar,* p. 80.

32 Ibid., p. 80.

33 Ibid., pp. 80–81.

34 Ibid., p. 81.

35 Schwarz says: "Unquestionably, the Symphony-Concerto [op. 125] is the high point of Prokofiev's last creative years" (Schwarz, *Music and Musical Life,* p. 237). Robinson comments that the "*Sinfonia Concertante* [op. 125] is an enormously appealing and powerful composition, and one of Prokofiev's crowning achievements in the concerto form" (Robinson, *Prokofiev,* p. 489).

36 "After a closed performance at the Composer's Union in late December 1951, he insistently asked his colleagues "But isn't it too simple?"" (Robinson, *Prokofiev,* p. 490). See also Dmitri Kabalewsky, "Sergej Prokofjew," in Prokofiev, *Sergej Prokofjew: Dokumente, Briefe, Erinnerungen,* p. 400: "Ist die Musik auch nicht zu einfach?"

37 Nestyev, in the second biography (1957), cites a letter from Prokofiev to Asafiev in which Prokofiev expresses his feelings about some of Stravinsky's "neoclassical" works. Prokofiev says: "For although I love Bach and find nothing wrong in composing according to his principles, I don't think one should write stylized imitations of him. For this reason I find the Concerto less valuable than *The Wedding* or *The Rite of Spring,* since, generally speaking, everything which is imitative, like *Pulcinella* or my own *Classical Symphony,* has less value" (Nestyev, second biography [1957], p. 203).

38 On Romanticism and music see, for example, Arnold Whittall, *Romantic Music: A Concise History from Schubert to Sibelius* (London: Thames and Hudson, 1987); or Leon Plantinga, *Romantic Music: A History of Musical Style in Nineteenth-Century Europe* (New York: W. W. Norton, 1984); or Leonard Meyer's chapter "Romanticism" in his book *Style and Music: Theory, History, and Ideology* (Philadelphia: University of Pennsylvania Press, 1989), pp. 163–217.

39 Goethe, from his *Poetry and Truth,* excerpted in Eugen Weber, ed., *The Western Tradition,* (Boston: D. C. Heath, 1959), p. 533.

40 Voltaire, cited in Peter le Huray and James Day, eds., *Music and Aesthetics in the Eighteenth and Early Nineteenth Centuries,* abridged ed. (Cambridge: Cambridge University Press, 1981), p. 86.

41 Judith Shklar, *After Utopia: The Decline of Political Faith* (Princeton, N.J.: Princeton University Press, 1957), p. 42.

42 Kant is by no means an unqualified romantic, however. By seeking truth first in philosophy rather than in art and by putting the race ahead of the individual, Kant shows Enlightenment characteristics. Shklar points out that "to Kant, as to all the philosophers, progress meant the advancement of the race as a whole, not the happiness or perfection of the individual. This, to romanticism, was a meaningless abstraction" (Shklar, *After Utopia,* p. 68). Lewis Rowell articulates some aspects of Kant's equivocal position: "Kant in his *Critique of Judgment* (1790), writes under the influence of the eighteenth-century *Affektenlehre* and cannot be regarded as a representative of the Romantic movement; but certain ideas in the following passage suggest characteristic themes in the Romantic aesthetic—the intensity of music, its indeterminacy, and the universality of its communication by means of sensation" (Lewis Rowell, *Thinking About Music* [Amherst: University of Massachesetts Press, 1983], p. 124.) For the purposes of my argument, unequivocally deciding Kant's position as either essentially Enlightenment or essentially romantic is beside the point. Despite his Enlightenment allegiances, Kant, with his turn inward, provides Romanticism with a grounding for its high valuation of the individual.

43 Hans-Georg Gadamer, *Truth and Method* (New York: Crossroad, 1975), translated by Sheed and Ward, Ltd.; edited by Garrett Barden and John Cumming, p. 50. In this passage, Gadamer is discussing the relation of taste to works of art and works of genius in Kant's philosophy.

44 Carl Dahlhaus, *Between Romanticism and Modernism: Four Studies in the Music of the Later Nineteenth Century,* translated by Mary Whittall (Berkeley: University of California Press, 1980), pp. 97–98.

45 Liah Greenfeld, *Nationalism: Five Roads to Modernity* (Cambridge: Harvard University Press, 1992), p. 15.

46 Ibid., p. 16.

47 Ibid., p. 265.

48 Ibid., p. 223.

49 At the 1948 conference, Zhdanov referred repeatedly to this venerated tradition. There can be little doubt that in a country so self-conscious about its world-

historical significance, its nineteenth-century musical tradition served as a model for its twentieth-century descendants. The Balakirev Circle refused to follow a Western model of musical training, offering in its place training of the individual. Glinka developed a distinctively Russian sound, whose success is attributed to his acquaintance with folk materials. Such a tradition is, understandably, extremely attractive to the Soviet mentality.

50 The Balakirev Circle consisted of Cesar Cui, Modest Musorgsky, Alexander Borodin, and Nikolai Rimsky-Korsakov, led by Mili Balakirev.

51 See also Robert C. Ridenour, *Nationalism, Modernism, and Personal Rivalry in Nineteenth-Century Russian Music* (Ann Arbor, Mich.: UMI Press, 1981).

52 Ibid., pp. 77–78.

53 For an account of the Balakirev Circle's struggle against the Conservatory, see Ridenour, *Nationalism, Modernism.*

54 Nikolai Rimsky-Korsakov, *My Musical Life,* translated by Judah A. Joffe (1923; reprint, London: Faber and Faber, 1989), p. 117.

55 Ibid., chapters 10 and 12.

56 Ibid., p. 116.

57 Ibid., pp. 20–21.

58 At the same time, we must recognize that composers writing tonal pieces now come to grips with and comment upon music history since 1900 in their works. The slow movement of George Rochberg's Third Quartet may remind us of Beethoven, but our perception of the work certainly depends in large part on knowing that Rochberg did not always write this way. One cannot divorce the idea of tonal composition from the historical context in which it occurs.

59 Antoine de Saint-Exupéry, *The Little Prince,* translated by Katherine Woods (New York: Harcourt, Brace and World, 1943), p. 3.

60 In discussing orchestration classes taught by Rimsky-Korsakov in 1906–1908, Prokofiev remarked: "I must admit that in two years I learned nothing in those classes" (Prokofiev, *Autobiography,* in *Soviet Diary 1927,* p. 237). Stravinsky's relationship with Rimsky-Korsakov was entirely different. Eric Walter White describes some aspects of it: "There is no doubt that Rimsky-Korsakov had become a sort of father figure in Stravinsky's life since his own father's death in 1902, and he deeply and sincerely mourned him. On returning to Ustilug, he composed *a Funeral Dirge,* and this was performed in St. Petersburg at the first Belaiev concert of the autumn season, which was entirely dedicated to Rimsky-Korsakov's memory. Unfortunately the score of this work was lost in the Russian Revolution; but if Stravinsky's memory could be trusted, it was the best of his works before *The Firebird*" (Eric Walter White, *Stravinsky: The Composer and His Works,* 2nd ed. [Berkeley: University of California Press, 1979], p. 30).

61 I cite just a few examples here: Joseph Straus, in "The Problem of Prolongation in Post-Tonal Music," *Journal of Music Theory* 31 (1987): 1–21, considers the issue from a Schenkerian perspective. Richard Taruskin and Allen Forte, in letters to the editor in *Music Analysis* 5 (1986), pp. 313–337, debate the nature of tonality in

Stravinsky's *Le Sacre du Printemps*. James Baker, in *The Music of Alexander Scriabin* (New Haven: Yale University Press, 1983), Paul Wilson, in *The Music of Bela Bartok* (New Haven: Yale University Press, 1992), and Richard Parks, in *The Music of Claude Debussy* (New Haven: Yale University Press, 1989), confront tonality in non-traditional contexts. David Lewin, in "Klumpenhouwer Networks and Some Iso-graphies That Involve Them," *Music Theory Spectrum* 12/1 (Spring 1990): 83–120, suggests an approach to music that can show hierarchy, an integral feature of Schenkerian analysis, without resorting to a notion of prolongation. Issues related to the interface of tonal (or traditional) and non-tonal aspects in some musics are explored by Allen Forte in "New Approaches to the Linear Analysis of Music," *Journal of the American Musicological Society* 41 (1988): 315–348, and in "Musorgsky as Modernist," *Music Analysis* 9 (1990): 3–46.

62 One notable exception is Richard Bass, "Prokofiev's Technique of Chromatic Displacement," *Music Analysis* 7/2 (1988): 197–214.

63 In the Piano Sonata no. 5, last movement, a D# and a B are added to the caden-tial C-major triad; at the end of the Piano Sonata no. 6's first movement, B♭ is added to the final (incomplete) A-major triad.

64 I follow Leonard Ratner, in *Classic Music: Expression, Form, and Style* (New York: Schirmer Books, 1980), in taking the term "type" to designate a completely worked out "topic." March, gavotte, and waltz are "types." "*Characteristic figures . . .* formed a rich legacy for classic composers. . . . They [figures] are designated here as *topics*—subjects for musical discourse. Topics appear as fully worked-out pieces, i.e., *types,* or as figures and progressions within a piece, i.e., *styles.* The distinction between types and styles is flexible; minuets and marches represent complete types of composition, but they also furnish styles for other pieces" (p. 9).

65 See, for example, William Austin, "Prokofiev's Fifth Symphony," *Music Review* 17 (1956): 205–220.

66 Salzer, *Structural Hearing,* vol. 1, p. 205. For a discussion of Salzer's modification of Schenkerian theory, see Jonathan Dunsby and Arnold Whittall, *Music Analysis in Theory and Practice* (New York: Yale University Press, 1988), part II, chapter 5.

67 In general I follow John Rahn, *Basic Atonal Theory* (New York: Schirmer Books, 1980), in nomenclature. However, in the present book, unless otherwise noted, square brackets enclose prime forms and indicate what Rahn would call a Tn/TnI-type. A prime form (or Tn/TnI-type) is a particular representative of the set class based on either transpositional (Tn) or inversional (TnI) equivalence. I name a Tn/TnI-type both by its prime form and by Forte's set name, or both, so that "[0347]" and "4–17" refer to the same set class. I will explicitly note when brackets indicate a Tn-type only, that is, an equivalence class based on transposi-tional equivalence only.

Parentheses will be used to enclose particular pitch-class sets. For example, the Tn/TnI-type [0148] is not inversionally symmetrical. Hence, a particular pitch-class set which is a realization of the Tn/TnI-type [0148] may be a member either of the Tn equivalence class [0148] or the Tn equivalence class [0348], but not both.

The set (236t) is a member of the Tn equivalence class [0148] (as well as a member of the Tn/TnI equivalence class [0148]), whereas (256t) is a member of the Tn equivalence class [0348] (as well as a member of the Tn/TnI equivalence class [0148]).

68 Here I follow Rahn's distinction between different Tn-types within the same Tn/TnI-type. See chapter 4 of his *Basic Atonal Theory*.

69 One could also represent it as $T_{11}(T_1(x))$ in its complete form, patterned on a broad hearing of E♭ – E – E♭ over mm. 1 – 5.

2: Constancy and Change

1 Sergei Prokofiev, *Autobiography,* in his *Soviet Diary 1927 and Other Writings,* translated and edited by Oleg Prokofiev (Boston: Northeastern University Press, 1992), pp. 248 – 249. This is also discussed in Israel Nestyev, *Sergei Prokofiev: His Musical Life,* translated by Rose Prokofieva (New York: Alfred A. Knopf, 1946), pp. 68 – 75. I refer to this book henceforth as Nestyev's first biography (1946).

2 Harlow Robinson, *Sergei Prokofiev* (New York: Paragon House, 1987), p. 144.

3 Lewis Rowell identifies exoticism as a distinctly romantic value; see Lewis Rowell, *Thinking About Music* (Amherst: University of Massachusetts Press, 1983), p. 118.

4 Prokofiev, *Autobiography,* in *Soviet Diary 1927,* p. 264.

5 On the Ballets Russes see, for example, Nancy Van Norman Baer, comp., *The Art of Enchantment: Diaghilev's Ballets Russes, 1909–1929* (San Francisco: Fine Arts Museums, 1988). The essays in that book touch on many aspects of the Ballets Russes; see especially Dale Harris's essay, "Diaghilev's Ballets Russes and the Vogue for Orientalism," in which Harris discusses the tremendous force exerted by the Ballets Russes on the world of fashion.

6 Prokofiev, *Autobiography,* in *Soviet Diary 1927,* p. 264. In the *Autobiography,* Prokofiev goes on to say: "No wonder the black lift attendant in the hotel touched my sleeve and remarked with some awe, 'Steel muscles . . .' He evidently thought I was a boxer" (p. 264).

7 There is no shortfall of exemplary lyric pieces. As we shall see in Chapter 8, Nestyev, among others, recognized the lyric line in the Ahkmatova songs, op. 27.

8 Alexander Werth, *Musical Uproar in Moscow* (1949; reprint, Westport, Conn.: Greenwood Press, 1973), p. 78.

9 Ibid., p. 72.

10 To be fair to Rimsky-Korsakov, his view of the Balakirev Circle's aesthetics, as well as his own, changed over time and underwent some self-motivated revision. See, for example, Nikolai Rimsky-Korsakov, *My Musical Life,* translated by Judah A. Joffe (1923; reprint, London: Faber and Faber, 1979), chapters 20 and 22.

11 Prokofiev, *Autobiography,* in *Soviet Diary 1927,* p. 244.

12 Such inversional balance is a common feature in Prokofiev's music. For a discussion of inversional balance in Schoenberg's music see David Lewin, "Inversional Balance as an Organizing Force in Schoenberg's Music and Thought," *Perspectives of New Music* 6/2 (Spring–Summer 1968): 1–21.

13 I follow the system of registral designation suggested by the Acoustical Society of America. C4 designates middle C; G#4 represents the pitch an augmented fifth above middle C. Higher octaves are represented by higher integers, so D5 represents the pitch lying a major ninth above middle C (that is, an octave plus a major second above middle C). Similarly, lower integers represent lower octaves; C2 designates the pitch lying two octaves below middle C.

14 I follow John Rahn, *Basic Atonal Theory* (New York: Schirmer Books, 1980), in nomenclature. The "ip" stands for pitch interval and indicates the number of semitones separating two pitches. Context will clarify whether the pitch interval measures magnitude only (the "unordered" pitch interval) or both magnitude and direction (the "ordered" pitch interval). See chapter 2 of *Basic Atonal Theory*.

15 The lower case letters "t" and "e" always stand for the pitch-class integers 10 (*ten*) and 11 (*eleven*), respectively. When showing transposition, I will always use the uppercase letter "T" to avoid confusing it with the pitch-class integer symbol "t."

16 Complementation is a general concept embracing two subconcepts, literal complementation and abstract complementation. In literal complementation, given some universe of elements U and the subset A of U, Ā (read "A-bar") is the collection of all elements in U which are not contained in A. If A and Ā are each a member of an equivalence class, /A/ and /Ā/ respectively, then any member of /A/ and any member of /Ā/ are abstract complements of one another, even if they share some elements. For example, given the universe of chromatic pitch classes, (0257) and (89te1346) are literal complements. Five tetrachordal subsets of (89te1346) have the same Tn/TnI-type as (0257) and thus belong to the same equivalence class. These five pitch-class sets, (469e), (68e1), (8t13), (e146), and (1368), are abstract complements of (89te1346).

17 *The American Heritage Dictionary,* 2nd college ed. (1982).

18 The melodic voice analyzed in example 2.3 (and also moving between B♭4 and D5) emerges as the descant in mm. 2–3. In m. 1 and m. 4, however, the strand to which B♭5 belongs is projected above the one participating in the voice exchange.

19 Prokofiev was very fond of this sort of mode change, and we shall find in his music frequent use of the so-called major-minor chord (4–17 [0347]). See the Appendix.

20 This terminology is from Douglass Green, *Form in Tonal Music: An Introduction to Analysis,* 2nd ed. (Fort Worth, Tex.: Holt, Rinehart, and Winston, 1979).

21 "I found myself acquiring a taste for Haydn and Mozart, which later found expression in the 'Classical' Symphony" (Prokofiev, *Autobiography,* in *Soviet Diary 1927,* p. 242).

22 William Rothstein, in *Phrase Rhythm in Tonal Music* (New York: Schirmer Books, 1989), pp. 34–36, analyzes such an instance in Haydn's Quartet in F major, op. 77, at the beginning of the first movement.

23 By this I mean that when the grouping structure is "in-phase" with hypermetric structure, a four-bar hypermeter will contain a cadence in the last measure, a metrically weak measure. I borrow the term "in-phase" from Fred Lerdahl and Ray

Jackendoff, *A Generative Theory of Tonal Music* (Cambridge: MIT Press, 1983), pp. 32–33.

24 I borrow the term "compound melody" from Allen Forte and Steven E. Gilbert, *Introduction to Schenkerian Analysis* (New York: W. W. Norton, 1982). The concept of compound melody is introduced in chapter 3. It refers to a single-line melody outlining more than one voice-leading strand.

25 Riemann, for example, did explicitly recognize the possibility of two simultaneous harmonic functions, but the two did not share equal stature. "It is possible to comprehend two kinds of clang-representation at the same time. However, one clang is always more prominent, and the presence of the other appears as a disturbance of the primary clang, as dissonance (not haphazardly, but also, according to the relationship of the second to the primary clang, which is evaluated differently)" (*Hugo Riemann's Theory of Harmony: A Study and History of Music Theory,* Book III, translated and edited by William C. Mickelsen [Lincoln: University of Nebraska Press, 1977], p. 63).

26 The set class 6−22 [012468], an "almost" whole-tone hexachord (along with 6−21 [023468] and 6−34 [024689], Scriabin's "Mystic" chord), engages the phrase ambitus to highlight and make concrete the almost-whole-tone aspect of its abstract structure. In particular, the whole-tone tetrachord 4−21 [0246] controls phrase expansion. Bryan Simms labels only one hexachord as "nearly" whole-tone. He begins with the whole-tone hexachord and allows any one note to be raised or lowered by a half step. This procedure yields a single product, 6−34 [013579]. See his *Music in the Twentieth Century* (New York: Schirmer Books, 1986), on pp. 37–41. My almost-whole-tone label applies to hexachords differently generated. I begin with a whole-tone pentachord, and to that I add any pitch class from its complement. This procedure yields the three hexachords 6−21, 6−22, and 6−34.

27 The rhythmic structure of op. 94a/II is discussed in Chapter 6.

28 I take meter to be initially a result of the interaction of two different, regular patterns. Barlines and notation may, most of the time, accurately indicate the meter perceived, but such barlines and notation are symptoms and not causes of meter. As Rothstein (*Phrase Rhythm,* p. 10), among others, has pointed out, meter is a hierarchical phenomenon, and it may exist on levels higher than those indicated by orthography. I will refer to such higher-level manifestations of meter as hypermeter. (The term "hypermeter" was used at least as early as in Edward T. Cone, *Musical Form and Musical Performance* [New York: W. W. Norton, 1968].) Hypermetric structures reproduce on a higher level the metric structures traditionally indicated by orthograhic and notational means, including metric accentual patterns. As Rothstein, as well as Lerdahl and Jackendoff (*Generative Theory*), point out, phrases—melodic units—may or may not coincide with metric structure. Maury Yeston has discussed how patterns interact to create meter in *The Stratification of Musical Rhythm* (New Haven: Yale University Press, 1977). Lerdahl and Jackendoff discuss meter and grouping ("grouping" is roughly synonymous

with melodic phrase structure). Rothstein, in *Phrase Rhythm,* analyzes metric, tonal, and phrase structures.

29 In this motivic pattern, beginnings of hypermeasures in m. 5 and m. 9 are marked, above all, by a change in texture. M. 5 brings in the dyad C3/E3, and m. 9 brings in the complete triad C3/E3/G3. This textural change, a systematic increase in density, divides the molto perpetuo sixteenths into four-bar units.

30 Arnold Schoenberg, *Style and Idea,* edited by Leonard Stein with translations by Leo Black (University of California Press: Berkeley, 1975), p. 217. One can easily enough understand how a dissonance is emancipated when it is not constrained to resolve in a traditional manner. But is the composer, no longer constrained by tradition, also emancipated? Most likely not: the emancipated dissonance demands that the composer devise strategies for structuring the composition and giving it coherence which do not depend upon traditional tonal relations. Freedom for the dissonance creates new obligations for the composer. In Schoenberg's case the search for structure and coherence in a non-tonal world eventually led to the motivic organization of his so-called atonal music, as well as to twelve-tone serialism.

31 Prokofiev, *Autobiography,* in *Soviet Diary 1927,* p. 255.

32 Ibid., p. 256.

33 Example 2.10 is based on the 1922 Gutheil edition of the *Visions Fugitives* (no. 1629) available from the International Music Company, not the "complete" Muzgiz edition of 1955 (available in a Dover reprint). The 1922 edition presents the pitch-class set 5−21 (67te2) more forcefully in m. 24.

34 The pitch-class set 5−21 is one member of the class of pentachords containing the subset 4−19, and Prokofiev uses this sonority throughout his music. See the Appendix.

35 T6 also describes the root movement of m. 20 to m. 21, where E leads to B♭.

36 Prokofiev, *Autobiography,* in *Soviet Diary 1927,* p. 258.

37 Prokofiev's Piano Sonata no. 7, the slow movement, uses 6−20 in a similar fashion, that is, by parsing it into different pairs of triads. See the discussion in Chapter 4 and the Appendix.

38 Rothstein, in *Phrase Rhythm,* discusses deleting a hypermetric beat under the heading "Successive Downbeats," pp. 58−63.

39 See also Malcolm H. Brown, "Prokofieff's Eighth Piano Sonata," *Tempo* (Autumn 1964): 9−15.

40 The interval spanned in the cadential motion F#−B♭ (ip8) has already been heard over mm. 1−3 in the melody between G4 and E♭5, and E♭5 and B5. The term "structural accent" I borrow from Lerdahl and Jackendoff, *Generative Theory.* It is discussed in their book on p. 17.

41 The urge to take a ritard and a slight pause at the end of m. 9, on beat 4, is virtually irresistible. Listen, for example, to the performance by Emil Gilels (Eurodisc 86323 MK) or Barbara Nissman (Newport Classic CD 60093). Both performances, while very different in many ways, take an unwritten ritard at the end of

m. 9 and lengthen the measure's final quarter note about one-half of a beat, making m. 9, beat 4, sound like a relatively strong beat.

3: Analytical Categories

1 While 4–22 [0247] is not a chromatically enhanced chord, it is clearly related to 4–14 [0237], since it can be heard as a major triad with added major ninth.

2 The index number "n" for inversion expressed as TnI is 2. Thus, because 10 + 4, 11 + 3, and 7 + 7 all equal 2, mod 12, T2I(47t) = (37t).

3 See Harlow Robinson, *Sergei Prokofiev* (New York: Paragon House, 1987), pp. 59, 132. Throughout this study, we shall see numerous instances of Prokofiev, a prolific yet thrifty composer, resurrecting or reworking material, often taken from preexisting compositions.

4 V. Kofi Agawu set forth a similar concept in his article "Stravinsky's *Mass* and Stravinsky Analysis," *Music Theory Spectrum* 11/2 (Fall 1989): 139–163. Agawu appeals to our experience with tonal conventions and asks that we hear these conventions in cadences—for example, even when all the aspects of the cadence are not conventional. In discussing a cadence from Stravinsky's *Mass,* Agawu points to its tonal affiliations and confidently asserts that non-tonal aspects of the cadence can be heard as such without damaging the feeling that a dominant-tonic gesture has taken place: "That one can describe this as a V–I cadence is not much in doubt. The behavior of the instrumental parts, however, challenges without negating this sense of cadence by adding to this relatively simply vocal part numerous apparently extraneous notes, including, significantly, a fifth, G–D, to the final A-major chord" (p. 146).

5 The set 5–21 contains the subset 4–19 twice, 4–19's maximum representation in any pentachord.

6 See Edward T. Cone, "Stravinsky: The Progress of a Method," *Perspectives of New Music* 1 (1962): 18–26; and Joseph Straus, "A Principle of Voice Leading in the Music of Stravinsky," *Music Theory Spectrum* 4 (1982): 106–124.

7 Leonard Meyer develops the concepts of expectation and continuation as basic categories of music perception. See his *Emotion and Meaning in Music* (Chicago: University of Chicago Press, 1956). In "The Dialectic of Good Continuation in Tonal Music," *Music Analysis* 4/1–2 (March–July 1985): 5–13, Richmond Browne considers "good continuation" in the context of psychological investigations of the perception of tonal music. Browne argues against oversimplifying the issue and rejects as too naive the definition of good continuation as "sounds moving in the same direction" (p. 6).

8 Christopher Hasty, "Succession and Continuity in Twentieth-Century Music," *Music Theory Spectrum* 8 (1986): 58–74.

9 Allen Forte discusses nexus sets and pitch-class set complexes in *The Structure of Atonal Music* (New Haven: Yale University Press, 1973), part 2.

10 Sergei Prokofiev, *Autobiography,* in his *Soviet Diary 1927 and Other Writings,* translated and edited by Oleg Prokofiev (Boston: Northeastern University Press, 1992), p. 255.

11 David Lewin, in *Generalized Musical Intervals and Transformations* (New Haven: Yale University Press, 1987), calls such a succession of transformations a "retrograde inversion chain (RICH)." He discusses them on pp. 180–188.

12 The first chord in the right hand is a form of 4–19 [0148], a set class also embedded in example 3.10's 5z37. See the Appendix.

13 The 3–12 [048] also meets the criteria for a structural set; it occurs within the first chord of m. 1, it occurs as the left-hand chord of mm. 21–24, and it guides the large-scale melodic descent over mm. 1–6. However, our focus for now is on the topic of fragmentation.

14 Richard Cohn has investigated this topic under the heading "transpositional combination." See his "Bartok's Octatonic Strategies: A Motivic Approach," *Journal of the American Musicological Society* 44/2: 262–300; and his "Inversional Symmetry and Transpositional Combination in Bartok," *Music Theory Spectrum* 10 (1989): 19–42.

15 On p. 189 of *Generalized Musical Intervals and Transformations*, Lewin discusses this transformation under the heading "FLIPSTART."

16 I follow the symbology and terminology of John Rahn when pitch-class set equivalence is determined according only to transposition or according to transposition and inversion. See John Rahn, *Basic Atonal Theory* (New York: Schirmer Books, 1980), chapter 4.

4: Piano Music

1 Prokofiev, *Autobiography*, in his *Soviet Diary 1927 and Other Writings*, translated and edited by Oleg Prokofiev (Boston: Northeastern University Press, 1992), pp. 246–247.

2 Ibid., p. 248.

3 Opp. 136–138, the last three works in the catalogue, are all incomplete, being either projected but never realized or only partially sketched. See Israel Nestyev, *Prokofiev*, translated by Florence Jonas (Stanford, Calif.: Stanford University Press, 1960), p. 513. Henceforth I refer to this as Nestyev's second biography (1957).

4 The literature on Prokofiev's piano music not cited elsewhere in this book includes Patricia Ruth Ashley, "Prokofiev's Piano Music: Line, Chord, Key," Ph.D. diss., University of Rochester, 1963; Frank Merrick, "Prokofiev's Ninth Piano Sonata," *Musical Times* (1956): 649; and Sonia Klosek Vlahecevic, "Thematic-Tonal Organization in the Late Sonatas of Sergei Prokofiev," Ph.D. diss., Catholic University, 1975.

5 *Prokofiev by Prokofiev*, translated by Guy Daniels (London: MacDonald General Books, 1979), p. 102.

6 Shortly thereafter, in 1953, Prokofiev began rewriting the E-minor Sonatina, op. 54, no. 1 (composed in 1931–1932), with the intention of using it as the basis for his unfinished Piano Sonata no. 10, op. 137. Only a brief fragment of the last piano sonata was completed.

7 Harlow Robinson, *Sergei Prokofiev* (New York: Paragon House, 1987), p. 459.

8 Prokofiev's most famous composition for children, *Peter and the Wolf*, op. 67, was completed less than a month after op. 65 was.

9 For example, in describing a recital given on 28 January 1927, Prokofiev comments: "I start with the Third Sonata. . . . After that, ten of the Visions Fugitives. Both works are well received, if not specially warmly. The Fifth Sonata is greeted altogether with some reserve. . . . My real victory began with the March from the Oranges" (Prokofiev, *Soviet Diary 1927*, p. 39).

10 While Pieter van den Toorn's entire book *The Music of Igor Stravinsky* (New Haven: Yale University Press, 1983) is concerned with octatonic structure in Stravinsky's music, pp. 48–60 provide an introduction to it. Allen Forte, in "Debussy and the Octatonic," *Music Analysis* 10/1–2 (March–July 1991): 125–169, discusses in some detail important aspects of the octatonic collection's subset structure; see pp. 125–132. Richard Taruskin discusses some occurrences of octatonic pitch structure in Russian music in his "Chernomor to Kashchei: Harmonic Sorcery; or, Stravinsky's 'Angle,'" *Journal of the American Musicological Society* 38 (1985): 72–142.

11 See van den Toorn, *Music of Igor Stravinsky*.

12 The listening strategy outlined in Chapter 3 applies here as well. F♯ is at least somewhat unexpected in the opening, though it can be interpreted tonally. It is not until the development section that Prokofiev exploits the tritonal relation first created between F♯ and C, in a sense justifying F♯'s earlier appearance.

13 See, for example, Alban Berg's op. 4/2, a piece rich in these linked inversions.

14 On such linked inversions, or "retrograde inversion chains," see David Lewin, *Generalized Musical Intervals and Transformations* (New Haven: Yale University Press, 1987), pp. 180–188.

15 I cannot resist a brief comparison of Prokofiev and Stravinsky, Prokofiev's senior by nine years. Both composers were notably precocious. Stravinsky produced his Sonata in F♯ minor at age twenty-one, the same age at which Prokofiev composed his Sonata no. 2. But Stravinsky's sonata has romantic roots and lacks the distinctive characteristics that its composer would develop before long. Stravinsky completed the ballets *Firebird* and *Petrushka* before his thirtieth birthday. *Le Sacre du Printemps*, begun before the composer turned thirty, was completed one year later. In Chapters 1 and 2 in particular, I have analyzed Prokofiev's close relation to Romanticism. Stravinsky rejected Romanticism altogether. As Pieter van den Toorn points out, he skipped romantic music and reached back to more distant musical style periods (for example, baroque music) for his influences: "But what may seem peculiar or even unprecedented from an analytical-theoretical or historical perspective is the *non-immediacy* of all these transient 'influences,' the distance that now separates Stravinsky from his past, his 'models.' . . . And there is that curious indifference toward—or ignorance of—the music of his immediate predecessors and contemporaries" (van den Toorn, *Music of Igor Stravinsky*, p. 257).

16 One of the most single-minded developments of this kind of intermovement unity occurs in the Piano Sonata no. 9. In that work Prokofiev resorts to a kind of "fore-imitation" in which each movement quotes a portion of the succeeding one, including the last movement, which wraps around to quote part of the first. The result is a circular form.

17 The three-element stepwise descent of these chords in m. 23 recalls how the neighbor note E of m. 3, analyzed in example 4.4, was embellished by a three-note descent through D♯ to C♯ before resolving to D♯ in m. 4.

18 Prokofiev, *Autobiography,* in *Soviet Diary 1927,* p. 298.

19 Ibid. Prokofiev also singles out the Symphony no. 3 as a work of particularly high quality.

20 In this example, I follow Robert Morris's conception of contour. Contour pitches (cps) are labeled in unit increments from lowest to highest, beginning with 0 and continuing through $n-1$, where n is the number of distinct pitches. Contour inversion is produced by transforming each cp by $(n-1)-x$, where x is the original cp. Thus, I<0312> = <(4−1)−0, (4−1)−3, (4−1)−1, (4−1)−2> = <3021>. See Robert Morris, *Composition with Pitch Classes: A Theory of Compositional Design* (New Haven: Yale University Press, 1987), pp. 26−33.

21 Were one to grant equal status to the F♯ augmented triad which example 4.8's open noteheads assert as the underlying structure and to the F♯-major triad which example 4.8's lower beam asserts as the underlying structure, then the pitch-class set produced is (t126), a form of 4−19 [0148], one of Prokofiev's favorite collections.

22 William Austin, *Music in the 20th Century* (New York: W. W. Norton, 1966), pp. 465−466. Also see D. L. Kinsey, "The Piano Sonatas of Sergei Prokofiev," Ph.D. diss., Columbia Teacher's College, 1959; and Francis Poulenc, "La musique de piano de Prokofieff," in *Musique Russe,* vol. 2, edited by Pierre Souvtchinsky (Paris: Presses Universitaires de France), pp. 269−276.

23 Fragmentation transforms 3−1 into 3−2. We can exhaustively partition 3−1 into the two overlapping subsets 2−1 [01] and 2−2 [02]. These constituent subsets can then be reassembled to form [013] (which can also be exhaustively partitioned into the two overlapping subsets [01] and [02]).

24 Within the E-major tonal focus of the first thematic group, motive v−, by giving E's major and minor chord thirds, suggests another of Prokofiev's favorite sonorities, 4−17, the major/minor chord.

25 We have already heard how prominent G♯ is in mm. 1−4. F♯ in m. 9 also receives special emphasis. The pianist performing this piece is especially aware of the leap between the F♯ at the downbeat of m. 9 and the subsequent D triad with F♯ in the upper voice, since this leap necessitates lifting up the hand completely. Prokofiev further highlights the event by contrasting the inner-voice mezzo forte dynamic with the outer-voice piano marking.

26 The appearance of G♭ in the upbeat to m. 32 is perhaps somewhat weak support for hearing it as a component of D♭ if one considers that the piece began with an analogous upbeat in which D led through D♯ to E; in the context of the opening, D does not weaken the E-major tonal focus which follows. The passage beginning poco più animato is not entirely analogous, however, because it does focus on D♭ major (not A♭ major) in the ways discussed in the text and because G♭ has been a prominent feature of the music for at least the seven measures prior to m. 32.

27 I am hearing along Riemannian lines here. Riemann's three categories—tonic, dominant, and subdominant—subsume all triadic functions. In his theory, substitute chords can be derived by extending the parent chord's tertiary structure into a quarternary one and then deleting a pitch. In the present case, B–D♯–F♯ is transformed into B–D♯–G♯ by adding G♯ above the chordal fifth, F♯, and then deleting the fifth F♯. The chord is spelled enharmonically as C♭–E♭–A♭. See Hugo Riemann, *Harmony Simplified* (London: Augener 1893), pp. 79–80.

28 This transformation of motive *v* still preserves the small equal steps and continuous (decreasing) contour of the original.

29 As is evident from the analysis, the tonal-interpreting harmonies do not encompass all the notes sounding at any given point. The tonal interpreters embedded within the music here help guide our hearing according to familiar chord progressions.

30 The main theme of the third movement revolves around a rhythmically aggressive statement of a B♭ major-minor chord (a form of 4–17 [0347]). One need not look far to discover such structures in Prokofiev's music.

31 The transpositional relation of the forms of 5–21 at m. 13 and m. 1 is identical with the "key" relation established by the tonal interpreters between the two sections: (C triad) = T8(E triad) and, likewise, [5–21(e0347)] = T8 [5–21(3489e)].

32 There are, in fact, six distinct triadic subsets (of the Tn/TnI-type [037]) of 6–20. Exactly three pairings of these triads will produce 6–20. Prokofiev uses the E-major / C-minor and the C-major / A♭-minor pairs but does not use the remaining A♭-major / E-minor pair, at least not in undisguised foreground alternation. See the Appendix.

5: Orchestral Music

1 Nancy Van Norman Baer, comp., *The Art of Enchantment: Diaghilev's Ballets Russes, 1909–1929* (San Francisco: Fine Arts Museums, 1988), includes a color reproduction of the design for *Chout*'s decor on p. 46.

2 See Sergei Prokofiev, *Soviet Diary 1927 and Other Writings,* translated and edited by Oleg Prokofiev (Boston: Northeastern University Press, 1992), pp. 29, 62; and Harlow Robinson, *Sergei Prokofiev* (New York: Paragon House, 1987), p. 271.

3 The specific form of 4–23 is (2479).

4 "It was at this time [1924, in Paris], however, that I first heard a reproach that was to be cast at me more than once subsequently: namely, that I was living off my old compositions. This decided me to write a large symphony 'to be made of iron and steel.' I had already composed the main theme. It was somewhat similar in outline to that of Beethoven's Sonata op. 111" (Prokofiev, *Autobiography* in *Soviet Diary 1927,* p. 275).

5 Harlow Robinson's estimation of the *Prodigal Son* is very high: "*Prodigal Son* is one of the most successful scores of Prokofiev's entire career, and a turning point in his development as a dramatic composer" (Robinson, Prokofiev, pp. 225–226).

6 Malcolm Brown points out that the composition of Symphony no. 5 was at least

partly motivated by Prokofiev's desire to create music in a new style that was accessible but that nevertheless maintained high artistic standards: "The Fifth Symphony consummates, in a sense, the new style Prokofiev had been trying to work out ever since he returned to the U.S.S.R." (Malcolm Brown, "The Symphonies of Sergei Prokofiev," Ph.D. diss. Florida State University, 1967, p. 429). While Prokofiev's desired product may have conformed to party ideology, the government did not pressure Prokofiev as it had following the Decree of 1948.

7 Brown is not entirely positive in his estimation of the "Classical" Symphony. He finds it problematic that Prokofiev's thematic-motivic development was not stylistically authentic. "He [Prokofiev] could approximate the formal gestures. . . . He could appropriate the mannerisms. . . . He could even abstract the essence of classical tonality. . . . But he did not succeed completely in capturing the crux of classicism—its thematic process" (Brown, "Symphonies of Sergei Prokofiev," p. 15.)

8 I cannot help but be struck by the strong resemblance between motive y_2 and the theme which enters at rehearsal B+4 in Tchaikovsky's Symphony no. 6/III.

9 See William Rothstein, *Phrase Rhythm in Tonal Music* (New York: Schirmer Books, 1989), pp. 58–63.

10 This unmediated whole-step progression echoes the movement's opening large-scale tonal motion D–C(–D).

11 See Fred Lerdahl and Ray Jackendoff, *A Generative Theory of Tonal Music* (Cambridge: MIT Press, 1983), pp. 17–18.

12 Heinrich Schenker shows this sort of duality in the "8–7" motions so typically spread out over development sections and in the interruption produced by the development's dominant.

13 Brown also recognizes this feature of the development: "The tonality [at the end of the development] stabilized in C major. The reprise of the fanfare and Theme 1 also takes place in C major. Thus, the juncture between the development and the recapitulation is completely elided in the tonal realm" (Brown, "Symphonies of Sergei Prokofiev," pp. 26–27).

14 Harlow Robinson describes the premiere with Prokofiev conducting, an event which built around the Symphony no. 5 a certain mythology. Of particular interest is the cannon fire, which entered as a sort of anacrusis to the work as a whole. As Robinson reports, "The salvos . . . came from Soviet cannons, paying tribute to the Red Army soldiers who were finally crossing the Vistula on their victory march into Nazi Germany" (Robinson, *Prokofiev*, pp. 431–436).

15 Boris Schwarz, *Music and Musical Life in Soviet Russia, 1917–1981* (Bloomington: Indiana University Press), p. 197.

16 Robinson, *Prokofiev*, p. 436.

17 William Austin also points out E♭'s role, in "Prokofiev's Fifth Symphony," *Music Review* 17 (1956): 205–220.

18 Both [015] and [016] can be arranged as a pair of overlapping dyads, one spanning a perfect fifth and one spanning a half step. In the case of (45t), Lewin's FLIP-START inverts pc5 about pc4 to yield pc3, thus transforming (45t) into (t34); (t34)

is a form of [015]. See David Lewin, *Generalized Musical Intervals and Transformations* (New Haven: Yale University Press, 1987), p. 189.

19 Lewin would call this chain a retrograde inversion chain. See his *Generalized Musical Intervals and Transformations,* pp. 180–188.

20 F, though it anchors the beginning and ending points of a progression dividing the octave equally, is the dominant of Bb and not a key area. Thus, in addition to hearing A within the progression F–A–Db–F, one can hear it as a tonic built on Bb's leading tone. We shall see that the succession of tonal area separated by a half step (T1 or T11) is one expression of chromaticism.

21 In pitch-class terms the three upward transpositions of a fourth can be represented as $(T5)^3 = T3$, the three downward chromatic slips as $(T11)^3 = T9$, and the combination of the two strings of operations as $(T5)^3(T11)^3 = (T3)(T9) = T0$.

22 Gb–to–F also helped to move the development into the recapitulation.

23 Alexander Werth, *Musical Uproar in Moscow* (1949; reprint, Westport, Conn.: Greenwood Press, 1973), p. 24.

24 Ibid., p. 25.

25 Nicolas Slonimsky, *Music Since 1900,* 3rd ed., rev. (New York: Coleman-Ross Co., 1949), p. 685.

26 Ibid., p. 686.

27 That Prokofiev seriously considered the charges contained in the Decree of 1948 is borne out by his letter in response, translated and reprinted in Slonimsky, *Music Since 1900,* pp. 704–706.

28 The cruel situation in which the Decree of 1948 placed Prokofiev, coupled with his already poor health, is offered by Victor Seroff as evidence that the government, as much as anything, was responsible for Prokofiev's death. See Victor Seroff, *Sergei Prokofiev: A Soviet Tragedy* (New York: Taplinger, 1969), pp. 297–306.

29 Malcolm Brown speaks of such startling juxtapositions of tonal areas as instances of "unprepared tonal displacement." See Brown, "Symphonies of Sergei Prokofiev," pp. 486 ff.

30 In the first movement of the Symphony no. 5, mm. 1–11, weak-beat arrivals also helped distract the listener's attention from hypermetric regularity.

31 The String Quartet no. 1, op. 50, relies very heavily on 5–6 motions in its voice leading. The 5–6 motion also resurfaces in the present movement in theme C.

32 This is an instance of alternating triadic flips: fifth flip followed by third flip followed by fifth flip.

33 In the Piano Sonata no. 7, the slow movement, discussed in the previous chapter, Prokofiev also takes considerable time to unwind the pent-up energy of the development in a kind of harmonically static passage which precedes the recapitulation.

6: Chamber Music

1 Beethoven's influence in this instance is not isolated. His last piano sonata, op. 111, provided a model and some inspiration for the composition of the Symphony no. 2, a two-movement work deriving from the form of Beethoven's

sonata, and the Symphony no. 6, a work which shares the opus number 111 with Beethoven's work, as well as its tonic note (if not the same mode of the first movement).

2 Prokofiev, *Autobiography,* in his *Soviet Diary 1927 and Other Writings,* translated and edited by Oleg Prokofiev (Boston: Northeastern University Press, 1992), p. 291.

3 A similar substitution occurs in op. 35/1, when E minor replaces an expected E♭ major at the end of the first subphrase, in m. 3.

4 Prokofiev was very interested in this set class in opus 83/II. See the discussion of the Piano Sonata no. 7/II in Chapter 4.

5 These oscillations are both instances of the third flip.

6 The modal variability of a triad whose major and minor forms may be presented successively, as is the case here, or simultaneously is characteristic of Prokofiev's harmonic vocabulary. The set class produced is 4−17 [0347].

7 See the analysis of the Piano Concerto no. 5/IV in Chapter 7. There, forms of 4−23 harmonize a melody whose points of articulation mark out 8−23.

8 The pitch-class set 7−21 is 8−19's only multiply represented heptachordal subset; it occurs twice. See also the Appendix.

9 Israel Nestyev, *Prokofiev,* translated by Florence Jonas (Stanford, Calif.: Stanford University Press, 1960), p. 140. I refer to this as Nestyev's second biography (1957). See Harlow Robinson, *Sergei Prokofiev* (New York: Paragon House, 1987), pp. 484−486, 427.

10 A similar relation exists between [014] and [015].

7: Concertos

1 Pieter van den Toorn and Arthur Berger would term the referential pitch class the "pitch class of priority." See Arthur Berger, "Problems of Pitch Organization in Stravinsky," *Perspectives of New Music* 1 (1963): 11−42; and Pieter van den Toorn, *The Music of Igor Stravinsky* (New Haven: Yale University Press, 1983). Because of the symmetrical properties of the octatonic collection, a listener's ability to locate a tonic note within it is, in principle, more difficult and more context-dependent than for either 8−23 (with two degrees of symmetry) or 7−35 (also with two degrees of symmetry).

2 Four times is the maximum number of occurrences of any hexachord in 8−23. The 6z25 also occurs four times in 8−23's subset structure.

3 But the connection to m. 11 is even stronger. The violin in m. 6 returns to the opening theme by first running from A5 in m. 6 down to C♯4 in m. 7. If we include C♯ with A and D, then [015] is formed, the same set class featured in example 7.5b.

4 See Harlow Robinson, *Sergei Prokofiev* (New York: Paragon House, 1987), pp. 164−165; Victor Seroff, *Sergei Prokofiev: A Soviet Tragedy* (New York: Taplinger, 1969), pp. 118−119; or Israel Nestyev, *Prokofiev,* translated by Florence Jonas (Stanford, Calif.: Stanford University Press, 1960), pp. 193−194—I refer to this as Nestyev's second biography (1957). The passage in Nestyev offers a complete

translation of Balmont's poem on the Concerto no. 3; Robinson quotes (and translates) the last three lines.

5 Sergei Prokofiev, *Soviet Diary 1927 and Other Writings,* translated and edited by Oleg Prokofiev (Boston: Northeastern University Press, 1992), p. 30.

6 Prokofiev, *Autobiography,* in *Soviet Diary 1927,* p. 271.

7 Sergei Prokofiev, *Sergej Prokofjew: Dokumente, Briefe, Erinnerungen,* compiled, edited, and annotated by S. Schlifstein; translated into German by Felix Loesch (Moscow: Staatlichen Musikverlag, 1961), p. 455; English translation by Harlow Robinson in Robinson, *Prokofiev,* p. 351.

8 The variation form was not a common one for Prokofiev, especially in larger works (though the ballet *Romeo and Juliet* contains variations). Of the symphonies and the remaining concertos, only the Symphony no. 2 features a variation movement. Its second movement of two is a theme and variations, modeled on Beethoven's op. 111.

9 The Symphony no. 6/I and the String Quartet no. 1 (discussed in Chapter 6) both feature minor dominants.

10 The set [0257] makes a notable appearance in variation IV beginning one measure before R72 and extending to the end of R72+2. Taken together, the last beats of these four measures are a form of [0257], and each of these beats initiates a local form of [0257].

11 In laying out example 7.10 I resorted to pitch space to show the inversional relation about C. In the pitch-class space, $T_4 - T_8$ represents the symmetrical positioning of E and A♭ about C; $T_3 - T_9$ represents the symmetrical positioning of E♭ and A about C.

12 $R(x-2)(x)(x) = (x)(x)(x-2)$.

13 Prokofiev, *Autobiography,* in *Soviet Diary 1927,* p. 294.

14 As I discuss in the Appendix, $4-23/8-23$ and $5-35/7-35$ are in the relation Kh. Allen Forte, in *The Structure of Atonal Music* (New Haven: Yale Univerity Press, 1973), discusses this relation on pp. 96–104. Robert Morris discusses it in his *Composition with Pitch Classes: A Theory of Compositional Design* (New Haven: Yale University Press, 1987), pp. 98–103; and David Lewin discusses K and Kh relations on pp. 150–151 of his *Generalized Musical Intervals and Transformations* (New Haven: Yale University Press, 1987).

15 See William Rothstein, *Phrase Rhythm in Tonal Music* (New York: Schirmer Books, 1989), pp. 68–70, for a discussion of prefixes.

16 The specific form of $9-7$ in mm. 30–33 is (e01234679). The other nine-note superset of $8-23$ is $9-9$.

17 The descending chords in this transitional passage are linked together by chromatic stepwise voice leading in the upper parts that plays against a bass descending mostly by thirds and derives from the root progression over mm. 30–32.

18 The $5-6$ motions are also prominent in the String Quartet no. 1, first movement, a piece treated in Chapter 6.

8: Vocal Music

1 Harlow Robinson, *Sergei Prokofiev* (New York: Paragon House, 1987), pp. 330, 337, 369. See also Israel Nestyev, *Prokofiev,* translated by Florence Jonas (Stanford, Calif.: Stanford University Press, 1960), pp. 194–195. I refer to this as Nestyev's second biography (1957).

2 Ibid., p. 123.

3 Israel Nestyev, *Sergei Prokofiev: His Musical Life,* translated by Rose Prokofieva (New York: Alfred A. Knopf, 1946), p. 49. I refer to this as Nestyev's first biography (1946).

4 Prokofiev completed op. 27 in 1916; Nestyev's first and second biographies were published in 1946 and 1957, respectively. By 1921 Akhmatova had begun her long ordeal as a target of the government, for in that year her former husband, the poet Nikolay Gumilyov, was arrested and executed. See *The Complete Poems of Anna Akhmatova,* translated by Judith Hemschemeyer; edited by Roberta Reeder (Boston: Zephyr Press; Edinburgh: Canongate Press, 1983), p. 2.

5 Nestyev, second biography (1957), p. 129.

6 *Complete Poems of Anna Akhmatova,* p. 153. The 1947 Boosey and Hawkes edition of the music (no. 20578) gives the title as "Sunlight Streaming in the Chamber."

7 *Complete Poems of Anna Akhmatova,* p. 153.

8 The stepwise descent through a third over mm. 25–28 also recalls a related progression over mm. 6–8, the difference being that mm. 6–8 traverse a minor third and mm. 25–28 traverse a major third.

9 T6 transforms m. 6 into m. 11 and m. 13. Subsequent discussion will develop the play of C against F♯, as well as the tritone transposition.

10 Following Lerdahl and Jackendoff, I give the B♭ chord the weight of structural accent. See Fred Lerdahl and Ray Jackendoff, *A Generative Theory of Tonal Music* (Cambridge: MIT Press, 1983), p. 17.

11 Rather than gloss over the boundary between m. 7 and m. 8, it seems important from a performing point of view to bring out (in some way) the concealed motivic duplication of a descending major third in mm. 1–7 and in mm. 14–18.

12 The gesture is a modified and embellished form of motive *a,* which here, as in all previous occurrences, leads to B.

13 Prokofiev, *Autobiography,* in his *Soviet Diary 1927 and Other Writings,* translated and edited by Oleg Prokofiev (Boston: Northeastern University Press, 1992), p. 259. The February Revolution also inspired Prokofiev in *Visions Fugitives,* no. 19. He tells us that it "partly reflected my impressions [of the February Revolution]—the feeling of the crowd rather than the inner essence of the Revolution" (p. 258).

14 Robinson, *Prokofiev,* p. 329.

15 Ibid., pp. 329–330.

16 Nestyev, second biography (1957), p. 285.

17 The 6–20 contains six forms of 4–19. The other three can be formed by pairing the D augmented triad with E♭, then G, then B. See also the Appendix.

18 On *The Giant* see *Prokofiev by Prokofiev,* translated by Guy Daniels (London: Mac-Donald General Books, 1979), pp. 17–20.

19 "Prokofiev entertained them [Misia Sert, Nouvel, Diaghilev] with some selections from his recent compositions: *Maddalena,* the Second Piano Sonata and the Second Piano Concerto. *Maddalena* did not interest Diaghilev; it was melodramatic, old-fashioned and worst of all, opera, a form he and his disciples scorned" (Robinson, *Prokofiev,* p. 102; see also pp. 153–154).

Eckart Kröplin also points out Prokofiev's commitment to opera: "The work on *Ala and Lolly,* and even Diaghilev's negative attitude toward opera, did not allow Prokofiev's interest in the genre to abate" (Eckart Kröplin, *Frühe Sowetische Oper: Schostakowitsch, Prokofjew* [Berlin: Henschelverlag Kunst und Gesellschaft, 1985], p. 301).

20 See Malcolm Brown, "Prokofiev's *War and Peace,*" *Musical Quarterly* (July 1977): 297–396.

21 Robinson speculates that the cancellation was "most likely due to the chaos in all areas of cultural life that followed the first ('February') Russian Revolution that occurred less than one month later [than January 28, 1917, the date of the first rehearsal]" (Robinson, *Prokofiev,* p. 121).

22 In his passionate, wordless cry, the General evokes Alexis at the end of act I.

23 This is the same pitch-class set as in the first chord in example 8.11, (9014).

Some Thoughts in Closing

1 Italo Calvino, *Mr. Palomar,* translated by William Weaver (San Diego: Harcourt Brace Jovanovich, 1985), p. 55.

2 Knowledge of this interplay leads us to insights into the music even when the interplay is less pronounced and less "grotesque."

3 This music includes the film scores for *Lieutenant Kizhe* and *Alexander Nevsky; Hail to Stalin,* op. 85; *Flourish, O Mighty Land,* op. 114; *On Guard for Peace,* op. 124; and the opera *Story of a Real Man,* op. 117.

4 Harlow Robinson, *Sergei Prokofiev* (New York: Paragon House, 1987), p. 191.

5 Ibid., p. 211.

6 Ibid., pp. 478–482.

Appendix

1 "Six degrees of symmetry" means that there are a total of six different ways that 6–20 maps into itself under either transposition or inversion. See John Rahn, *Basic Atonal Theory* (New York: Schirmer Books, 1980), pp. 90–94.

2 See Allen Forte, *The Structure of Atonal Music* (New Haven: Yale University Press, 1973), part II, for a discussion of K and Kh relations.

Index

Prokofiev's compositions are listed in alphabetical order under the composer and are generally displayed in italic type.

Calvino, Italo: and *Mr. Palomar*, 206
classical line, 104, 134, 135. *See also* five
 lines
Cohn, Richard, 224n14
complementation, 220n16
Cone, Edward T., 66, 221–222n28,
 223n6
Conquest, Robert, 214n26
constellation: defined, 67
contrapuntal emphasis. *See* shift from
 harmonic to contrapuntal emphasis
craft, 12, 14, 122
Cui, Cesar, 217n50

Dalhaus, Carl, 14
Decree of *1948*, 2, 27, 104, 120–122,
 169, 227–228n6, 229n27, 229n28
descendants, 82, 91, 97, 149; defined, 67
design skill, 47–52
development: Prokofiev's approach to,
 93, 100, 123–124, 128, 131, 137–140,
 141
Diaghilev, Sergei, 9, 26, 100, 196–197,
 233n19
Dostoevsky, Fyodor, 197
Dunsby, Jonathan, 218n66

Eikhenbaum, Boris, 215n28
Eisenstein, Sergei, 158–159
Enlightenment: and Romanticism,
 12–13, 216n42. *See also* Romanticism
Evenings of Contemporary Music, 7–8
exoticism, 219n3

February Revolution, 232n13, 233n21
five lines, 24–26, 26–41, 53–54
five-six motions, 126, 131, 135–136,
 138, 175–176, 229n31, 231n18
Fonvisin, Denis: and Slavophilism and
 Westernism, 15
formalism: and judgments of
 Prokofiev's music, 3, 10–11, 213n20;
 and op. *73*, 194; Russian, 215n28

Forte, Allen, 217–218n61, 221n24,
 225n10; and nexus sets, 67; and
 K/Kh relations, 231n14, 233n2
fragmentation, 67, 71–72, 112–113,
 149, 210, 226n23
Freundlich, Irwin, 88

Gadamer, Hans-Georg, 13–14,
 216n43
genius, 12, 13, 14, 122
Gilbert, Steven E., 221n24
Gilels, Emil, 222–223n41
Glazounov, Alexander, 74
Gliere, Reinhold, 7
Glinka, Mikhail, 15
Goethe, Johann Wolfgang, 12
Gorodinsky, Victor, 9–10
Green, Douglass, 220n20
Greenfeld, Liah, 14–15
grotesque line, 78, 87–88, 233n2. *See also*
 five lines
Gumilyov, Nikolay, 232n4
Gutman, David, 4

Hanson, Lawrence, and Elisabeth
 Hanson, 4
harmonic emphasis. *See* shift from
 harmonic to contrapuntal emphasis
Harris, Dale, 219n5
Hasty, Christopher, 66
Haydn, Josef, 220n22
Hemschemeyer, Judith, 178, 232n4
hypermeter: and compositional matu-
 rity, 54

inversional balance, 22, 56, 60–61,
 62, 79, 99, 147, 183–184, 188,
 219n12

Jackendoff, Ray. *See* Lerdahl, Fred, and
 Ray Jackendoff
Jakobson, Roman, 215n28
James, Vaughn, 215n29

Prokofiev (*continued*)
—*Visions Fugitives,* op. *22,* 28, 46, 75, 232n13; no. 10 and harmonic emphasis, 43–45; analysis of no. *4* of, 77–78
—*War and Peace,* op. *91,* 196, 197, 233n20
Pushkin, Alexander, 177

Rahn, John, 218–219n67, 220n14, 233n1 (Appendix)
Ratner, Leonard, 218n64
Resolution of *1932,* 9, 10
Revolution of *1917,* 1–2
Riasanovsky, Nicholas V., 213n2
Richter, Sviatoslav, 75
Ridenour, Robert, 16, 217n51, 217n53
Riemann, Hugo, 221n25, 227n27
Rimsky-Korsakov, Nikolai, 3, 16–18, 75, 217n60, 219n10
Robinson, Harlow, 217, 227n5, 228n14, 230–231n4, 233n21; as biographer of Prokofiev, 4, 9; and op. *125,* 11, 215n35; and op. *100,* 111; and op. *27,* 178; and op. *73,* 194
Rochberg, George, 217n58
Romanticism, xi, 11–18, 80, 122, 158, 169, 207–208, 216n38, 216n42, 225n15
Rostropovich, Msitslav, 11, 145
Rothstein, William, 220n22, 221–222n28, 222n38, 231n15
Rowell, Lewis, 216n42, 219n3

Saint-Exupéry, Antoine de, 18
St. Petersburg Conservatory, 2, 7–8, 16
Salzer, Felix, 38, 213n4
Schenker, Heinrich, 228n12
Schoenberg, Arnold, 8, 17, 30, 42, 80, 208, 222n30
Schwarz, Boris, 9, 11, 111, 215n35
Scriabin, Alexander: piano sonatas of, 74; "Mystic" chord of, 220n26
Sechter, Simon, 6

Selden, Raman, 215n28
Seroff, Victor, 4, 229n28, 230–231n4
Shebalin, Vissarion, 10, 121
shift from harmonic to contrapuntal emphasis, 42–47, 83
Shklar, Judith, 13, 216n42
Shklovsky, Viktor, 215n28
Shostakovich, Dmitri, 2, 9, 10, 120, 121
Simms, Bryan, 221n26
Slonimsky, Nicolas, 229n25, 229n27
Sneerson, Grigori, 120–121
Socialist Realism, 9–11, 140, 152, 207
Soviet government: as figure of authority, 9–11; and pressure on Prokofiev, 104, 229n28; and Anna Akhmatova, 178
Stalin, Josef: death of, 2
Straus, Joseph, 66, 223n6
Stravinsky, Igor, 208; and Rimsky-Korsakov, 18, 217n60; *Symphonies of Wind Instruments* of, 66; and octatonic pitch structure, 75–76; and neo-classicism, 215n37; and *Mass* of, 223n4; and Prokofiev, 225n15
structural sets: types of, 55–57; containing a triadic subset, 55–56; containing *ics,* 56; containing a small chromatic set, 56; remainders, 57; and tonal interpreters, 67
symmetrical pitch structures: and Prokofiev's piano music, 75–78; in op. *36/2,* 190; and "almost" whole-tone structures, 221n26. *See also* octatonic pitch structure

Taneev, Sergei, 7, 8
Taruskin, Richard, 217–218n61, 225n10
Tchaikovsky, Pieter Ilyich, 15; *Symphony No. 6* of, 228n8
toccata line, 145. *See also* five lines
Todorov, Tzvetan, 215n28
tonal interpreters, 89, 93; defined and illustrated, 61–72

tradition and innovation, 32, 78, 87–88, 104, 121–122, 206; and Nestyev's judgments of Prokofiev's music, 4–8; and the grotesque line, 58; and structural sets, 61

triadic flips, 209, 229n32, 230n3, 230n5; defined and discussed, 57–58; in op. *83,* 89; in op. *111,* 131; in op. *50/I,* 137; in op. *26,* 162; in op. *55,* 173

types, 19, 43, 53, 218n64

van den Toorn, Pieter, 225n10, 225n15, 230n1

Van Norman Baer, Nancy, 219n5, 227n1

Vlahacevic, Sonia Klosek, 224n4

Volkov, Solomon, 214n25

Voltaire, 12

Webern, Anton, 80

Werth, Alexander, 120, 214n26

White, Eric Walter, 217n60

white-key melody, 4, 159, 200, 214n15

Whittall, Arnold, 216n38, 218n66

Wilson, Paul, 217–218n61

wrong notes, 1, 60, 61, 65, 66, 67, 75, 101, 102, 104, 107, 208; described by Jonathan D. Kramer, 5; and surface ornament and underlying structure, 19–20; and Moisson-Franckhauser's analysis of Prokofiev's music, 6; and a listening model, 58–59

Yeston, Maury, 221–222n28

Zhdanov, A. A.: and Soviet musical policy, 9–10; and Slavophilism, 15; and Conference of Musicians of *1948,* 10–11, 120, 169, 216–217n49; and op. *111,* 120–122; as party chief in Leningrad, 215n26; and formalism, 213n28